indian
home cooking

indian
home cooking

a fresh introduction to indian food, with more than 150 recipes

suvir saran and stephanie lyness

clarkson potter/publishers
new york

Published by Clarkson Potter/Publishers, New York, New York
Member of the Crown Publishing Group, a division of Random House, Inc.
www.crownpublishing.com

CLARKSON N. POTTER is a trademark and POTTER and colophon are registered trademarks
of Random House, Inc.

Printed in China

Design by Maggie Hinders

Library of Congress Cataloging-in-Publication Data
Saran, Suvir.
    Indian home cooking : a fresh introduction to Indian food, with more than 150 recipes /
Suvir Saran and Stephanie Lyness ; foreword by Michael Batterberry.
      p.   cm.
1. Cookery, Indic.   I. Lyness, Stephanie.   II. Title.
TX724.5.14S298   2004
641.5954—dc21   2003013653

ISBN 0-609-61101-1

10   9   8   7   6   5   4   3   2   1

First Edition

To my two grandmothers, Dadi (Kamla Bhatnagar) and
Nani (Shanti Bhardwaj), my mother, Sunita Saran, and to all of the women
who have shared their love through food—with deep gratitude. S.S.

contents

foreword

In this tantalizingly redolent book on the simple home cooking of his native India, Suvir Saran writes with the authority and affection of a favorite uncle urged to chronicle the culinary ecstasies and kitchen alchemies accumulated over a long, joyous lifetime.

We ourselves first caught wind of Suvir in the mid-1990s when an Indian travel consultant, patronized by the footloose culinary cognoscenti for her private gastronomic tours of the subcontinent, told us of a young caterer catching fire along New York's food-centric party circuits. His style of cooking, at once fresh and authentic, she suggested would be of particular interest to *Food Arts* magazine subscribers, professionals who are always eager to hear about newly flowering talent with secrets of the world's tastiest cuisines to spill.

Contacting each other by phone, Suvir and I made a date for a quick editorial lunch. While the magazine's offices lie within the Flatiron district's tight mesh of postmodern restaurant thrills, they also abut a Little India enclave known as Curry Hill, a short city stroll as aromatic as any in New Delhi, peppered with unpretentious eating places and intriguingly crammed food shops that draw Indian expats and adventurous American chefs and home cooks from near and far. With all these polyglot choices, where would he like to go?

Happily, Suvir proposed that we explore a new vegetarian regional Indian restaurant right around the corner, its menu posting in the window as indecipherable to me as an atomic physicist's jottings.

Suvir, who has the gift of immediate intimacy, tempered by ancestral decorum, proved to be an ideal table companion, a charming raconteur and, quite clearly, a born teacher with the ability to set the unfamiliar in engaging context. The arrival of each dish provoked from him an informative meander of recognition, definition, and recollection glinting with colorful detail. Suvir appeared especially adept at explaining the simple techniques that create the remarkably complex flavors of Indian cuisine.

And that is precisely what he has done in this, his first collection of recipes. Faced with the tastes, needs, and resources of contemporary American home cooks, Suvir Saran fully understands Escoffier's dictum that "the art of cookery is the constant expression of the present." His Indian recipes are remarkably accessible and modern, and encourage the reader rather than intimidate. Even his recipe for the rice pudding prepared by his childhood cooking mentor, Pantitji, illustrates his practical policy of making respectful adjustments and substitutions, "streamlining," as he puts it, to bring Indian cooking into twenty-first-century American kitchens.

Generosity, spontaneity, warmth, and explosions of flavor are hallmarks of Indian hospitality, and all of these qualities are present in the recipes in *Indian Home Cooking*. All are easy to follow, and most of the ingredients are available at the corner grocery. The more exotic spices, in the Internet age, are available to anyone with a mailing address, and can usually be omitted, as well.

As collaborator, Stephanie Lyness has done a commendable job of bringing much-needed clarity and depth to the often-mysterious world of Indian cooking. Just like the late, great *New York Times* food editor and cookbook author Craig Claiborne, who took scrupulous notes of every phase of Pierre Franey's cooking, Stephanie has gathered Suvir's wealth of tricks and food lore into book form, with remarkable results.

But, as with any lasting contribution to cookbook literature, the ultimate proof of a new work's value indeed lies in the pudding (or *kheer* as the case may be here). *Indian Home Cooking* is perfectly in sync with American food lovers today, who hunger for bolder, more complexly flavored dishes without any fuss. Who could resist Suvir Saran's bugle call to pull up a chair to his soul-reviving Indian table, where "We don't just love the taste of our food, we live for the taste?" Certainly not I.

MICHAEL BATTERBERRY

FOUNDING EDITOR OF *FOOD ARTS* AND *FOOD AND WINE* MAGAZINES

introduction

 I was once asked by a student why my food tasted so different from other Indian food he'd eaten in America. My first response was that there really isn't any one such thing as "Indian food." The food that most Indian restaurants in America serve is northern Indian cuisine, the meat cuisine of the Moguls—Muslim Turks who invaded India in the sixteenth century and built the great Mogul empire. But I, a Hindu and a vegetarian, also teach a lot of meatless Indian cuisine, dishes that I have adapted from the largely vegetarian communities of northern and southern India. Some of these dishes are spiced quite differently from Mogul food and are unfamiliar to many Americans.

But perhaps more important, my food is very definitely Indian *home* cooking. By that I mean, first, that it is the food that we Indians make in our homes, not the food that we eat in restaurants. It is also not the food that is served in most Indian restaurants here in America, which I find to be comparatively heavy and one-dimensional. It is, however, the food that I, as an Indian expatriate living in New York City, working a full schedule and entertaining several times a week, cook in my own home. When I entertain, often last-minute, there are often a dozen or more guests. This lifestyle has given me the knack of finding smart ways to prepare Indian cuisine without compromising its brilliance. With some exceptions it is simple, tasty, satisfying food, not fancy.

I do not pretend to have compiled a collection of "classic" Indian recipes.
There are several excellent examples of such on the market, published by writers to whom I am indebted for doing the hard work of bringing a foreign cuisine to America at a time when even French food was exotic. Those authors have written extensively about our Indian culture, foods, ingredients, and techniques. You can read and cook out of those books to get a taste of classical northern Indian dishes such as *roghan josh,* a lamb stew thickened with ground almonds, or the northern Indian chicken dishes *murgh mussallam* (a whole chicken marinated, then stewed) and chicken *moghlai* (chicken in a rich saffron-flavored sauce). While delicious, many of these dishes require days of marinating and use ingredients that are exotic even to contemporary Indian pantries. This is not the kind of everyday cooking that makes sense for a busy schedule.

Even in India, Indian food has changed dramatically in the last fifty years.
The country has modernized ingredients, recipes, and cooking techniques with extraordinary quickness so that Indian food and culture have moved into the twenty-first century. India is also a country that has learned over thousands of years to adapt successfully to cultural incursions—from the Arabs, Turks, Mongols, British, Dutch, French, and Portuguese, among others. So Indian culture has in all ways quite literally leapt into the modern age. (Look at how quickly computer technology has taken hold there.) Fifty years ago, all middle-class Indian households had servants. They certainly had a cook whose daily job it was to grind spices and make fresh yogurt, to make pickles and chutneys, and to prepare meals in which a number of small dishes were served at the same time.

In India now, as in America, few households retain servants. We live busy lives that afford little time for cooking. Like Americans, we use convenience foods such as frozen vegetables. And we streamline and substitute: we use prepared spice

You really don't need any special equipment to make the food in this book, outside of a spice grinder, a blender, and a food processor. I use an attachment on my Osterizer blender that is perfect for grinding spices, as well as small amounts of wet ingredients such as garlic, herbs, and coconut for the occasional spice paste. I also use a piece of Indian cookware called a *kadai*—a wok-shaped two-handled pot, available in a range of sizes. A *kadai* is particularly useful for deep-frying because its rounded shape allows you to use less oil than needed in a pan with a flat bottom, but a wok or saucepan will work fine, too.

mixtures in lieu of our own, buy tofu instead of making paneer (a fresh Indian cheese), and substitute a mixture of whole wheat and all-purpose flours for the traditional chapati flour. This is *my* generation of Indian cuisine.

While many of the recipes in this book are, in fact, traditional, my approach to Indian food is eclectic and, perhaps more important, pragmatic. I devise recipes on the basis of what tastes good to me—mixing spices from different regions and using American ingredients in place of some traditional Indian ones. I simplify wherever possible and, because twenty-first-century culture seems to require it and it is my preference, I also use substantially less oil than my teachers in India cooked with. Although I eat meat occasionally and cook it quite a lot for friends, I was raised Hindu and a vegetarian. So, although this is by no means a vegetarian cookbook, if you are vegetarian you'll find lots of vegetarian recipes here.

My cooking has been shaped by two main influences. I got my first and most important training in the kitchen of my New Delhi home from a man named Panditji. Panditji was (and still is) the chef of my family's household and one of the best cooks and human beings I know. Like many chefs in India, he is from the Brahman class and was trained as a priest. His family have been chefs to our family for generations.

Indeed, one can't really understand Indian cooking without a sense of just what an important role food plays in Indian spiritual life. Panditji's kitchen was a sacred place, as is the kitchen, traditionally, in most Indian households. It housed our family's temple, set up on shelves behind the cupboard doors. There were images of gods and goddesses, statuary, incense, and other ritual objects. Very early every morning my grandmother, having bathed to purify herself, would go down to the kitchen to perform morning prayers at the temple. Panditji's part in the ritual was to prepare the first food of the day. This was offered to the gods during prayers, then later fed to us kids.

I learned from Panditji to cook the vegetarian cuisine of Delhi. That cuisine is my home ground. It's an exciting cuisine. Delhi is to India what Washington, D.C., is to America—that is, both the political capital and a kind of a separate country within the country. Unlike Washington, however, Delhi is also the food capital of India and in that sense, it is much more like New York City. Delhi has been invaded frequently in its history, and each invasion brought new foods and cooking techniques to influence the existing cuisine. So, like New York, Delhi is a melting pot of cultures, rich in cuisines from foreign influences and all regions of India.

When I was a small child, my family moved to Nagpur, a city in western India. My parents left the servants at home—they wanted us to learn how to take care of ourselves. During those three years, my mother cooked and I got to see how Panditji's more traditional food could be revised and simplified when there was no chef. My mother's food was always delicious, and she didn't spend all day making it. I also fell in love with south Indian cooking in Nagpur, where I had a friend whose mother cooked in that style. I'm still attached to that cuisine, and the recipes in this book reflect that influence, too.

My experience teaching Indian cooking to Americans is another essential influence. Through the classes I've taught, I've found that the best way to teach people to cook Indian food is to demystify it for them—to show them that it's just not all that hard to cook. I do that by starting people off with a simple recipe and then giving them variations so that they can understand how a recipe works and build from there. Very soon, inspired by the recipes that they've learned, my students invent dishes for themselves.

When people don't believe that they can improvise their own Indian food, I tell this story: I had a couple in one of my classes one evening who had taken all of the classes that I offered at New York University. In one of my earlier classes, the man—I'll call him Mark—had learned to cook *poha,* an Indian snack made with pounded, dehydrated rice. That particular evening, Mark, catching sight of a package of the pounded rice on the counter, came up to me and told me that since the time he and his wife, Cindy, had learned the dish, they had made it several times at home. Eventually they had begun to play with it. Using the recipe as a guide, they had preserved the traditional spice mixture but substituted other vegetables for the potato, tomato, and peas. The man was absolutely exuberant: they had just had so much fun experimenting and recreating the dish. "So, you'll teach the class to make *poha* this evening!" I countered, putting him on the spot. (I'm afraid that I'm often not nice.) He could use whatever ingredients he could pull together in the school kitchen. He did a brilliant job, using the spices listed in the recipe but substituting scallions and cauliflower for the tomato and peas.

I've organized this book in the same way that I teach my classes, by starting with straightforward recipes that you can learn to embroider. Most (but not all) of the chapters begin with a simple recipe, followed by one to three variations. So while I believe that the recipes are uncomplicated enough that you can pick up the book and start cooking from anywhere, I also think that you'll be more satisfied if you start at the beginning and cook your way through it. Soups give you an easy first taste of Indian cuisine. Those recipes show you how to play with spices and to make a *tarka,* or tempering oil—a spiced oil that is added to the food just before serving to give a fresh layer of spicing. The dal chapter gives you more experience with spices and tarkas, and shows how to cook onions until they are very brown and flavorful, one of the few techniques there is to learn in Indian cooking, called *bhunao.*

The vegetable chapter is organized in strictly alphabetical order (using the techniques in the preceding chapters) and introduces a method for quick, stir-fried vegetables that you can use to invent your own vegetable dishes. The rice chapter introduces what I think will be brand-new but easy techniques for cooking rice that you can serve as main courses or side dishes. The meat and chicken chapters begin with recipes for basic stews or curries (with variations), followed by recipes from all over India. And so on.

I want you to be able to cook these recipes easily, so wherever possible I've called for common supermarket ingredients, easy to find and familiar to use. For those recipes that specify more exotic ingredients, I've listed substitutions wherever possible and/or made ingredients optional if I thought the dish could possibly be made without them. Occasionally, as with the South Indian soups called *rasams,* there simply is no substitute for the South Indian spices that are critical to the taste of the dish. You can buy those ingredients at Indian or Asian grocery stores, or on the Internet. And eventually, when you find yourself cooking Indian food regularly, you may want to set up a pantry of some Indian ingredients. I hope that you will use this book to experiment as lavishly and with as little fear as possible. You will in that way fill the food, and therefore your guests, with your love and spirit of adventure.

BLACK PEPPER RASAM WITH TAMARIND

PINEAPPLE RASAM WITH TAMARIND

TOMATO RASAM

SHRIMP RASAM

 soups

LEMON RASAM

SPICED TOMATO SOUP WITH VEGETABLES AND INDIAN CHEESE

CARROT AND PEA SOUP

CHILLED YOGURT SOUP WITH CUCUMBER AND MINT

MY MOTHER'S TOMATO SOUP

LEBANESE LENTIL SOUP WITH ORZO AND LEMON

There is a Hindu saying, *atithi deva bhaav,* which means that when a guest walks into your house, God comes with him. This is the essence of Indian hospitality. We treat our guests as if they were gods because we believe that God is in all of us. So, in India, if you have only two chapatis, you give them both to your guests; whatever is left when they have satisfied their hunger is for you.

In most of India, as in America, when you visit someone in his or her home you are offered a drink of some sort. Southern Indian homes do something special. There, guests are welcomed with a choice of steaming hot, fragrant *rasams*: brothy, highly spiced soups that are served in glasses as hot beverages. Their heady fragrance and brilliant tastes inspire the appetite despite the intense heat of southern India, yet they don't weigh our bellies down.

In choosing recipes for this chapter I've wanted to share some soups that are different from what can be found in other Indian cookbooks. I'm particularly fond of rasams because my guests love them, they are quick to make, and they give readers an entirely new way to make soups. So the chapter begins with several—my variations on traditional rasams found across the southern states of India. In addition you'll find a cold yogurt soup, two of my favorite tomato soups, and a refreshingly different lentil soup made with both lentils and orzo and brightened with lemon juice.

RASAMS AND TEMPERING OILS

A rasam is different from a western-style soup. The closest thing in spirit is a consommé—both consommés and rasams are thin soups that taste of the essence of their ingredients. That said, practically speaking, they are quite different: consommés are made with stock while rasams are made with water and are much easier and quicker to make.

There are three parts to a rasam, as you can see by looking at the recipes. There is a ground spice mixture that is traditionally made very, very hot with black pepper or red chiles. Then there is the broth that is made with water, flavored with sweet, sour, pungent, and/or tart ingredients such as lemon, tomato, tamarind, pineapple, fresh ginger, and garlic, as well as with the ground spice mixture. Then often, but not always, the soup is flavored at the end with a combination of whole or ground spices cooked briefly in a little hot oil, called a *tarka* or tempering oil. The tempering oil gives the soup a burst of fresh flavor and adds complexity to the layering of spices. Adding a fresh tempering oil is a good way to give new life to a reheated, day-old soup or any other Indian dish. It's important that the spices in the tempering oil not burn; when I smell that the spices are cooked, I splash in a little water to stop the cooking before adding to the soup. This also helps wash all of the oil and spices out of the pan. Start tarkas with longer-cooking whole spices; add ground spices after, so that they don't burn.

You can buy a traditional blend of southern Indian spices called a rasam powder in Indian grocery stores. Two of the recipes in this chapter call for rasam powder; you can buy it or make your own from the recipe I've given in the Glossary. (If you like, substitute a commercial or homemade rasam powder for any of the spice mixtures in the recipes.) In general, I like to vary the spices rather than use a prepared powder; that way each rasam has a unique taste. But all of the soups will taste just fine with the prepared mixture.

Some rasams use the cooking water from boiled lentils in place of water as the broth. (The cooked lentils can be used to make another dish; I've given some recipes for cooked lentils in the Dal chapter.) Some of these rasams also use black gram beans for flavoring, like an additional spice. You'll need to shop at an Indian grocery store or online for these.

black pepper rasam with tamarind

SERVES 4 TO 6

I remember drinking this rasam as a child at the home of a school friend whose family had recently moved to Delhi from South India. I had tasted rasams before, but in her home I fell in love anew with the wonderfully exotic flavors of South India. I especially like this soup because the black pepper gives the broth such a rich taste and lasting liveliness. The taste of the pepper comes through as a spice—like cumin or coriander—with both flavor and heat.

While this rasam is traditionally made with tamarind as a souring agent, you can use lemon juice instead. Add the lemon at the end; unlike tamarind, lemon loses its souring properties as it cooks.

SPICE MIXTURE

2 teaspoons canola oil
2 teaspoons coriander seeds
1 teaspoon black mustard seeds
1 teaspoon cumin seeds
1 teaspoon black peppercorns
1½ tablespoons yellow split peas
4 whole dried red chiles
⅛ teaspoon asafetida (optional)

BROTH

2 teaspoons tamarind concentrate or the juice of 2 lemons
½ cup warm water (if using tamarind concentrate)
1 tablespoon canola oil
1 teaspoon black mustard seeds
3½ cups water
2 teaspoons salt, or to taste
1 tablespoon fresh lemon juice
¼ cup chopped fresh cilantro

For the spice mixture, combine the oil and all of the spices in a small frying pan or saucepan over medium-high heat. Cover (mustard seeds splatter and pop) and cook until the cumin and *urad dal*, if using, turn a light golden brown and the mixture is fragrant, 1 to 2 minutes. Remove the pan from the heat and let the spice mixture cool to room temperature. Then grind to a powder in a spice grinder. Set this powder aside.

For the broth, if using tamarind, measure the warm water into a small bowl or measuring cup. Add the tamarind concentrate and stir to dissolve. Rinse the measuring spoon and your fingers in the water to dissolve all of the sticky tamarind. Set this tamarind water aside.

Combine the oil and the mustard seeds in a medium saucepan over medium-high heat. Cover and cook until you hear the seeds crackle, 1 to 2 minutes.

Add the tamarind water, if using, the 3½ cups water, the spice mixture, and the salt. Bring to a boil, turn the heat down, and simmer 3 minutes. Stir in the lemon juice if using and cilantro, and serve hot.

pineapple rasam with tamarind

SERVES 4 TO 6

I first tasted a pineapple rasam when I was a child vacationing with my family at a fancy beach resort in Kerala, in the south of India. My grandmother, who was with us, loved pineapple and the chef knew it. I didn't know what to make of this soup then; it wasn't a juice and it wasn't quite a soup. But I remembered it and when I was old enough to appreciate it, I put together this recipe.

Pineapple gives the soup just the right amount of sweetness so that the spices tease the palate in a very pleasant way. The variety of tastes—the sweetness of the pineapple, the tang of the tamarind, and the heat from the spices—sates my senses' every need and delivers every flavor that my taste buds crave.

SPICE MIXTURE
3 whole dried red chiles
1/2 teaspoon cumin seeds
1/4 teaspoon coriander seeds
1/4 teaspoon black peppercorns

BROTH
2 1/2 cups warm water
2 teaspoons tamarind concentrate or the juice of 1 lemon
2 cups pineapple juice
1/4 cup chopped fresh cilantro
2 teaspoons salt, or to taste

TEMPERING OIL
2 teaspoons canola oil
1 1/2 teaspoons black mustard seeds (optional)
3 fresh hot green chiles, stemmed and slit the length of the chile
8 fresh or 12 frozen curry leaves, torn into pieces (optional)
1/4 teaspoon asafetida (optional)
1/4 teaspoon cayenne pepper

1/2 cup chopped fresh pineapple

For the spice mixture, combine all of the spices in a spice grinder and grind to a powder. Set aside.

For the broth, if using tamarind, measure the warm water into a small bowl or measuring cup. Add the tamarind concentrate and stir to dissolve it. Rinse the measuring spoon and your fingers in the water to dissolve all of the sticky tamarind.

Combine this tamarind water, if using, or 2 1/2 cups plain water, the spice mixture, pineapple juice, cilantro, and salt in a medium saucepan. Bring to a boil, then turn the heat down so that the soup barely simmers. Add the lemon juice, if using.

For the tempering oil, heat the oil with the mustard seeds, if using, and the green chiles in a small frying pan or saucepan over medium-high heat, 1 to 2 minutes. (If using mustard seeds, cover—the seeds splatter and pop—and cook until you hear the seeds crackle.) Add the curry leaves, if using, and stir. (Stand back; curry leaves spit as they hit the hot oil.) Add the asafetida, if using, stir, and remove from the heat. Add the cayenne and a drizzle of tap water, and pour immediately into the soup. Stir in the chopped pineapple and serve hot.

tomato rasam

SERVES 4 TO 6

This rasam brings back memories of being a young boy in Nagpur, a small city in the western state of Maharashtra where my family lived for about three years. My dad's boss there was South Indian, and I was introduced to the exotic smells and tastes of southern Indian cooking in his home. Every time we went there for dinner, his wife would meet us with glasses of this rasam. It took only a very short time for me and my family to become enchanted by these wonderful tastes, and soon rasams, *sambhaars* (South Indian-style *dals*), *idlis* (steamed lentil and rice cakes), and *dosas* (lentil and rice crêpes) were as common to my vocabulary as the northern Indian lentil dishes, flatbreads, and spinach that I had grown up on.

2 medium tomatoes, one quartered and one chopped
1 garlic clove
4 cups water
2 teaspoons minced fresh ginger
1/4 cup chopped fresh cilantro
1/2 fresh hot green chile, cut crosswise into 4 pieces
1 teaspoon store-bought curry powder, or 2 teaspoons
    rasam powder (page 251)
1/2 teaspoon ground cumin
1/2 teaspoon ground black pepper
2 teaspoons salt, or to taste

TEMPERING OIL
2 teaspoons canola oil
1/4 teaspoon black mustard seeds
2 whole dried red chiles
4 fresh or 6 to 8 frozen curry leaves,
    torn into pieces (optional)
1 teaspoon unsweetened shredded coconut (optional)

Puree the quartered tomato with the garlic in a blender or food processor. Set aside.

Bring the water to a boil in a medium saucepan. Add the chopped tomato, the ginger, cilantro, and green chile. Turn the heat down and simmer 3 minutes.

Add the tomato–garlic puree, the curry or rasam powder, cumin, black pepper, and salt and simmer 5 minutes.

For the tempering oil, combine the oil and mustard seeds in a small frying pan or saucepan over medium-high heat. Cover (the mustard seeds splatter and pop) and cook until you hear the mustard seeds crackle, 1 to 2 minutes. Add the chiles and cook uncovered, stirring, until they start to brown, about 30 more seconds. Add the curry leaves and coconut, if using, and cook, stirring, until the coconut turns golden brown, about 30 more seconds. Pour immediately into the soup and stir. Serve hot.

shrimp rasam

SERVES 4 TO 6

I developed this recipe for an Indian restaurant in Manhattan. The food there was a fusion of Indian, Asian, and western flavors. They were looking for a way to use the considerable quantity of shrimp shells that they collected every day, peeling shrimp for the shrimp dishes on the menu. This lightly creamed soup with traditional rasam spicing is entirely nontraditional. The shells give the soup a rich seafood flavor while the spices brighten it and give it a very clean aftertaste. When I make this, even I, despite my confirmed vegetarian palate, want to cheat and sit down to a bowl of it.

Some fish stores or supermarkets will sell you shrimp shells. Otherwise, shell the shrimp and use them in Mangalore Fried Shrimp (page 156), or make this rasam into a main-course soup by poaching the shrimp in the soup for about 1 minute (just until opaque) before adding the tempering oil. And if you can get even more shrimp shells, do; the more shells you use, the more flavor the broth will have.

BROTH

1 tablespoon canola oil
1/2 teaspoon whole cloves
1/2 teaspoon black peppercorns
3 bay leaves
1 medium onion, chopped
Shells from 1 1/2 pounds shrimp, rinsed and patted dry
6 cups water
1 medium tomato, chopped
2 teaspoons minced fresh ginger
1/2 fresh, hot green chile, cut crosswise into 4 sections
1 1/2 teaspoons store-bought curry powder,
    or 1 tablespoon rasam powder (page 251)
1/2 teaspoon ground cumin

1/2 teaspoon ground black pepper
2 teaspoons salt, or to taste
1 cup half-and-half

TEMPERING OIL

2 teaspoons canola oil
1/4 teaspoon black mustard seeds
2 whole dried red chiles
4 to 6 fresh or 6 to 8 frozen curry leaves,
    torn into pieces (optional)
1 teaspoon unsweetened shredded coconut (optional)

1/4 cup chopped fresh cilantro

For the broth, combine the oil, cloves, peppercorns, and bay leaves in a medium saucepan over medium-high heat. Cook, stirring, until the cloves begin to pop, 1 to 2 minutes.

Add the onion and cook, stirring, until it softens, about 2 minutes. Add the shrimp shells and cook, stirring, until they turn pink, about 1 minute. Add the water, bring to a boil, turn the heat down, and simmer vigorously for 20 minutes. Strain the cooking liquid and return it to the saucepan.

Add the tomato, ginger, and green chile to the pan and simmer 3 minutes. Stir in the curry or rasam powder, cumin, ground black pepper, salt, and half-and-half. Bring to a boil, reduce the heat, and simmer 5 minutes.

For the tempering oil, combine the oil with the mustard seeds in a small frying pan or saucepan over medium-high heat. Cover (the mustard seeds splatter and pop) and cook until you hear the mustard seeds crackle, 1 to 2 minutes. Then add the chiles and cook uncovered, stirring, until they start to brown, about 15 seconds. Add the curry leaves and coconut, if using, and cook, stirring, until the coconut turns a golden brown, about 15 more seconds. Pour immediately into the soup. Stir in the cilantro and serve hot.

lemon rasam

SERVES 4 TO 6

This is my favorite rasam. The broth is made with water in which legumes (I use yellow split peas) have been cooked, and it has a very light, subtle flavor that I love. I often add a teaspoon of lemon zest to the tempering oil along with the mustard seeds. This is not traditional at all, but it gives another delicious layer of flavor to the broth. Lemons and limes originated in India and neighboring areas, where they have been used for thousands of years to add sour taste to foods. Along with lemons, this soup is soured with tamarind, which, unlike lemons, can cook for a long time without losing its souring properties. You can substitute more lemon juice, but it must be added at the end.

When I was shopping recently, a crate of Meyer lemons caught my eye. I had never seen this type of lemon in America before, but my heart gave a little leap as I realized that this was the lemon we have in India. It is an extraordinary balance of sweet and astringent, with a beautiful aroma. If you can get hold of Meyer lemons, use them in this soup.

Use the cooked split peas in Warm Lentil Salad with Coconut and Tomato (page 35).

SPICE MIXTURE
1 tablespoon coriander seeds
1½ teaspoons black peppercorns
1 teaspoon cumin seeds
½ teaspoon cayenne pepper

BROTH
1 cup yellow split peas
½ teaspoon turmeric
6 cups water
1½ teaspoons tamarind concentrate or the
    juice of 1 lemon
½ cup warm water (if using tamarind)
2 medium tomatoes
2 garlic cloves

1 lemon, cut in half and juiced, juice and
    halves reserved separately
¼ teaspoon asafetida (optional)
4 fresh hot green chiles, stemmed and slit
    the length of the chiles
2 teaspoons salt, or to taste

TEMPERING OIL
2 teaspoons canola oil
2 teaspoons black mustard seeds (optional)
3 whole dried red chiles
4 fresh or 6 to 8 frozen curry leaves, torn into pieces
    (optional)

¼ cup chopped fresh cilantro

For the spice mixture, combine the spices in a spice grinder and grind to a powder. Set aside.

For the broth, combine the split peas, turmeric, and 6 cups water in a medium saucepan. Bring to a boil and skim well. Then turn the heat down and simmer vigorously, partially covered, until the legumes are tender, 35 to 40 minutes. Stir occasionally to keep the legumes from sticking to the bottom of the pot, and skim as you need to.

Meanwhile, if using tamarind, measure the warm water into a small bowl or measuring cup. Add the tamarind concentrate and stir to dissolve it. Rinse the measuring spoon and your fingers in the water to dissolve all of the sticky tamarind. Set this tamarind water aside.

Coarsely chop 1½ of the tomatoes and put them in a food processor or blender with the garlic and process to a puree; set aside.

When the split peas are cooked, strain them over a 4-cup or larger measuring cup and reserve for another use (see headnote). Add water, if necessary, to the cooking broth to make up 4 cups broth and return to the saucepan. Add the juiced lemon halves and bring the broth to a boil. Skim the foam that rises to the top. Then add the tamarind water, if using, the tomato-garlic puree, the spice mixture, the asafetida, if using, green chiles, and salt. Turn the heat down so that the soup simmers vigorously and cook, partially covered, for 10 minutes.

Chop the remaining ½ tomato and add it to the soup. Cook 3 more minutes.

For the tempering oil, combine the oil and the mustard seeds, if using, in a small frying pan or saucepan over medium-high heat. Cover (the mustard seeds splatter and pop) and cook until you hear the mustard seeds crackle, 1 to 2 minutes. Add the chiles and cook uncovered, stirring, until they start to brown. Then add the curry leaves, if using, and stir. (Stand back; curry leaves spit as they hit the hot oil.) Pour immediately into the soup. Stir in the lemon juice and the cilantro and serve immediately.

spiced tomato soup with vegetables and indian cheese

SERVES 4 TO 6

This soup is as young as India itself. I know that sounds odd. But when I say that, I'm thinking of the India that was created just fifty years ago, a union of many states and profoundly influenced by the West. This soup has a western look and taste (my students tell me that it reminds them of the Campbell's tomato soup they grew up on), but the Indian spices make it warm and exotic tasting and bring out the flavor of the tomato in a lovely new way. The fresh Indian cheese *paneer* and abundant mixed vegetables make it a meal in itself.

1/2 recipe paneer cheese (see page 70), cut into cubes

2 tablespoons canola oil

1 medium onion, coarsely chopped

2 bay leaves

1 tablespoon all-purpose flour

3 large tomatoes, chopped

2 cups homemade or store-bought tomato sauce

1 1/2 teaspoons minced garlic

1 1/2 teaspoons minced ginger

1/2 teaspoon cayenne pepper

1/2 teaspoon garam masala (page 250)

1/4 teaspoon turmeric

3 cups water

1 red boiling potato, peeled and cut into small cubes

1 medium carrot, peeled and cut into small cubes

3/4 cup chopped green beans

3/4 cup chopped green cabbage

Salt

1/4 cup chopped fresh cilantro, or a combination
    of fresh cilantro and mint

Heat the oven to 400°F. Put the cheese in a single layer on a baking sheet and bake until lightly browned, about 20 minutes.

Meanwhile, heat the oil in a 3-quart saucepan over medium heat. Add the onion and bay leaves, and cook until softened, about 2 minutes.

Add the flour and cook, stirring, until lightly browned, 1 to 2 minutes. Add the tomatoes, tomato sauce, garlic, ginger, cayenne, garam masala, turmeric, and water. Bring to a boil, turn the heat down, and simmer 10 minutes. Let the soup cool for a few minutes, then puree in a blender or food processor.

Return the soup to the pan. Add the vegetables and simmer, partially covered, until the vegetables are tender, about 10 more minutes. Add salt to taste.

Just before serving, add the cubed cheese and simmer until warmed through. Add the cilantro and mint, if using, and serve hot.

carrot and pea soup

GAAJAR MATAR KA SHORVA

SERVES 4

This smooth soup has a creamy texture that works beautifully with its Indian spices. If you don't have cheesecloth, a tea diffuser can be used to hold the spices.

8 cups vegetable stock or water
1/2 teaspoon crushed black peppercorns
8 green cardamom pods, crushed
4 cloves
1-inch stick cinnamon
2 bay leaves
1 1/2 cups peeled, chopped carrots

1 cup fresh or frozen green peas
1/2 teaspoon cayenne pepper
Juice of 1 lemon
Salt
1/4 cup heavy cream
2 tablespoons chopped fresh cilantro leaves

Heat the stock in a saucepan. Place peppercorns, cardamom, cloves, cinnamon, and bay leaves in a square of cheesecloth and tie the cloth closed. Add to the pot, along with the carrots, peas, cayenne pepper, lemon juice, and salt to taste. Bring to a boil. Reduce heat and simmer until the liquid is reduced by half. Remove from heat and discard the bag of spices.

Let the soup cool slightly, then puree in a food processor or blender until smooth. Force the soup through a strainer into a clean pan. Add the heavy cream and bring the soup to a simmer, skimming if necessary. Ladle into bowls and garnish with chopped cilantro.

chilled yogurt soup with cucumber and mint

SERVES 4 TO 6

This is the perfect starter or light meal for a hot summer day. The yogurt makes the soup taste and feel luxuriously creamy without the heaviness of cream. You may substitute beet for the cucumber (or combine beet and cucumber): boil the beet until tender, grate it finely, and add it instead of or along with the cucumber. The beet will give the soup a lovely rose color. If you'd like a thinner soup, add milk until the consistency is as you like it.

1½ teaspoons cumin seeds
3½ cups plain yogurt
1 medium cucumber, peeled and coarsely grated
3 tablespoons finely chopped fresh mint leaves
1 fresh hot green chile, seeded and finely chopped

¼ teaspoon garam masala (page 250)
1 teaspoon salt, or to taste
⅛ teaspoon freshly ground white pepper
Whole fresh mint leaves, for garnish

Toast the cumin seeds in a dry frying pan or saucepan over medium heat until lightly browned and fragrant, 2 to 3 minutes. Grind to a powder in a spice grinder; set aside.

Combine the yogurt and cucumber in the bowl of a food processor and process until smooth. Scrape the mixture into a bowl. Add the cumin and all of the remaining ingredients except for the whole mint leaves and stir well. Chill the soup until you are ready to serve. Serve in bowls topped with the fresh mint leaves. (You can also sprinkle on some toasted cumin seed powder, if you like.)

my mother's tomato soup

I grew up on this simple tomato soup. Now, many seas away from home, I remember holding a cup of it between my hands during the bitter Delhi winters and being warmed both by its heat and its warm flavors. My mother sometimes made it with milk—you can add 1/2 cup or so of half-and-half to enrich it, if you like. People can never believe that, rich as it tastes, this soup is made with no cream and almost no fat. My mother used to garnish bowls with fried croutons or *amul* cheese (the only western-style cheese available in India until just a few years ago), grated over the top of each bowl just before serving. Baby Gouda is a good substitute for *amul*.

2 tablespoons butter

2 medium onions, coarsely chopped

2 medium carrots, peeled and coarsely chopped

4 garlic cloves

1/4 teaspoon black peppercorns, plus freshly ground black pepper to taste

1 bay leaf

2 teaspoons salt, or to taste

2 1/2 pounds tomatoes, coarsely chopped

1/2 teaspoon sugar

3 cups water

Heat the butter in a 3-quart saucepan over medium heat. Add the onions, carrots, garlic, peppercorns, bay leaf, and salt and cook, stirring, until the onions are wilted, 4 to 5 minutes.

Add the tomatoes, sugar, and water. Bring to a boil, turn the heat down, and simmer, partially covered, until the vegetables are very soft, about 20 minutes.

Remove the bay leaf. Puree the soup in a blender or food processor, or with a hand-held mixer. Return the soup to the pan and simmer 5 minutes or until thickened somewhat. Ladle into bowls and grind a generous amount of black pepper over the top of each. Serve hot.

lebanese lentil soup with orzo and lemon

SERVES 6 TO 8

It was impossible for me to write a soup chapter that didn't include this. It had me hooked the first time I tasted it almost ten years ago at my friend Mary Ann Joulwan's house. Although it's a Lebanese recipe, I've made it so often that my Indian friends now think of it as an Indian soup. Simple to make and rich in flavor, this is my own chicken soup for the soul, even though it's vegetarian!

You can use any lentil in the soup, but I like to use unhulled Indian brown lentils *(sabut masoor dal)* or French green lentils *(lentilles de Puy),* for their texture.

The soup must stand 4 to 6 hours before serving in order to thicken. You can make it a day or two ahead, if you like; the flavors only get better. It also freezes well.

2 cups lentils
12 cups water
1 tablespoon salt, or to taste
1/4 cup extra-virgin olive oil
2 medium red onions, finely minced

1/2 teaspoon ground black pepper
1/4 cup uncooked orzo pasta
Fresh lemon juice
Chopped fresh cilantro or parsley, for garnish
Lemon wedges, for garnish

Combine the lentils, water, and salt in a medium soup pot. Bring to a boil and skim any scum that rises to the surface. Then lower the heat, cover, and simmer very gently while you cook the onions, about 20 minutes.

Meanwhile, heat the olive oil in a frying pan over medium-high heat. Add the onions and cook, stirring often, until they turn a very dark brown color, about 20 minutes. Stir constantly during the last 5 to 10 minutes of cooking to keep the onions from burning.

When the onions are well browned, add 1 cup of the simmering lentil water to the pan with the onions. Stand back; the water will sizzle and steam. Continue cooking, stirring every now and then, until the water has almost totally evaporated, about 5 minutes.

Scrape the onion mixture into the pot with the lentils. Stir in the pepper. Cover and simmer 10 more minutes. Add the orzo, cover, and simmer until the orzo is just tender and the lentils are completely cooked, about 15 minutes. Remove the soup from the heat and let stand 4 to 6 hours before serving.

To serve, reheat the soup and ladle into bowls. Stir 1/2 tablespoon lemon juice into each bowl and finish each with a sprinkle of cilantro or parsley. Serve lemon wedges alongside.

SIMPLE LENTIL DAL WITH CUMIN AND DRIED RED CHILES

SIMPLE LENTIL DAL WITH FRESH GINGER, GREEN CHILES, AND CILANTRO

EMPRESS DAL

SIMPLE LENTIL DAL WITH WHOLE CINNAMON, CARDAMOM, AND CLOVES

*dals

SIMPLE GUJARATI DAL WITH THREE CHILES

YELLOW MUNG BEANS WITH SPINACH AND PANCHPHORAN

WARM LENTIL SALAD WITH COCONUT AND TOMATO

"KWALITYS" CHICKPEAS

SOUR CHICKPEAS WITH GARAM MASALA AND TOASTED CUMIN

SPICY SQUASH, EGGPLANT, AND LENTIL STEW

RED KIDNEY BEANS WITH GINGER, TOMATO, AND CURRY LEAVES

CURRIED BLACK-EYED PEAS

Legumes are the backbone of Indian cuisine. Lentils, peas, beans, and chickpeas are cooked into velvety purees, chunky and fragrant stewlike preparations, and chewy pilaflike dishes.

The most common way to cook Indian-style lentils or beans is in a preparation called a *dal*. A dal is a dish of cooked legumes, using one or more type of lentil or bean, flavored with spices and aromatics. Although they are the most basic food, dals are very savory, tasty, and satisfying.

Dals that are served in Indian restaurants are sometimes thick, heavy, and dull tasting. Don't be daunted—your homemade dal can be much better and fresher-tasting by adding spices and aromatics in layers to punch up the flavor of the legumes, which are essentially bland. You can make the dal as thick or thin as you like by adding more water or by reducing. I like mine thin so I add more water during cooking, or at the end if I notice that the mixture is dry. I usually mash about 1/2 cup of the lentils when the dal is cooked to give it a velvety consistency, with some texture. If you like a thicker and smoother dal, whisk the dal into a puree when the lentils are soft. Restaurants usually make dals with quite a lot of fat; you'll find these recipes to be very light.

I teach my students to make dals for dinner to eat over rice or with a good bread and a vegetable. You can make a large batch and keep it in the refrigerator for several days so that you have a quick meal when you need it. Particularly if you are a vegetarian, a dal is a good dish to know how to make; eating legumes with rice gives the body a complete and inexpensive protein.

Try starting with one of the four very simple recipes that begin this chapter. In these, one variety of lentil is cooked in water until soft, and then seasoned with a *tarka,* or tempering oil, made by cooking a mixture of spices in ghee (clarified butter) or vegetable oil to release the flavor and fragrance of the spice. (If you'd like a buttery flavor in your dal, ghee is best.)

The first recipe in the chapter, Simple Lentil Dal with Cumin and Dried Red Chiles, follows this basic technique. The three successive variations are made exactly the same way but are varied in their flavors by using different tempering oils. Dal recipes later in the chapter are more complex, using a variety of legumes, vegetables, and tempering oils, sometimes more than one in a single dal. But you'll see that, no matter how many steps or ingredients a recipe has, its foundation is the same simple dal; you just add more spices at different times.

I didn't want you to have to run out to an Indian grocery store in order to experiment with dals, so the first several recipes in the chapter are made with ordinary lentils. In the headnotes of those recipes I've made note of the variety of Indian lentils that I like to use. Recipes later in the chapter call for more exotic varieties of Indian lentils and peas, in the hope that you will eventually have access to Indian ingredients. In any event, the lentils and peas in all of these dals are, for the most part, interchangeable.

I've ended this chapter with some recipes for familiar legumes such as chickpeas, kidney beans, and black-eyed peas. These recipes use canned, not dried, beans. Dried beans are indisputably tastier than canned, but I confess that I rarely use anything but the latter since they're *so* much quicker and easier and still completely satisfying.

Bhunao—or cooking onions to brown them and concentrate their flavor—is an important but simple technique that is used over and over in Indian cooking. You'll use the technique to make several of these dal recipes. The recipe instructions will tell you to set a cup of water by the stove as the onions cook, and sprinkle water over the onions, about 1 teaspoon at a time, as they begin to stick to the bottom of the pan. (See Sour Chickpeas with Garam Masala and Toasted Cumin, page 38.) This will keep the onions as well as the spices from burning so that they cook long and evenly, building a wonderful base of flavor.

simple lentil dal with cumin and dried red chiles

SAADI MASOOR DAL

SERVES 4

This simple dal is prepared almost daily in most northern Indian homes. Once you feel comfortable with this recipe, try the three that follow it. All four are based on the same lentil mixture tempered at the end and/or at the beginning with different spices. Taste how each tempering oil gives the lentil a completely different flavor.

I make this dal with pink lentils *(dhuli masoor dal)*, brown lentils that have been hulled (underneath the hull they are pink) so they collapse easily into puree. Pink lentils only take about 15 minutes to cook. You can also use yellow split peas, which cook in 45 minutes.

1 cup lentils, picked over, washed, and drained
1/2 teaspoon turmeric
1 teaspoon salt, or to taste
4 cups water

TEMPERING OIL
2 1/2 tablespoons canola oil
1 1/4 teaspoons cumin seeds
2 whole dried red chiles
1/2 teaspoon cayenne pepper

Juice of 1/2 lime or lemon

Put the lentils into a large saucepan with the turmeric, salt, and water. Bring to a boil and skim well. Turn the heat down and simmer, covered, until the lentils are soft, 20 to 30 minutes. Add more water if necessary. Taste for salt and add more if you need to.

Ladle about 1/2 cup of the lentils into a small bowl and mash them with a spoon. Return the mashed lentils to the pot and give the dal a stir. Then continue cooking at a simmer, uncovered, for 5 minutes to thicken. If you like a thicker dal, use a whisk to break up the lentils into a puree. If you like a thinner dal, add water.

For the tempering oil, heat the oil in a small frying pan or *kadai* over medium-high heat. Add the cumin seeds and cook, stirring, until they turn a light brown color, 1 to 2 minutes. Add the whole chiles and cook, stirring, about 30 more seconds. Remove the pan from the heat, add the cayenne, and sprinkle in a few drops of water to stop the cooking.

Stir half of the tempering oil and all of the lime or lemon juice into the dal and simmer gently, uncovered, for 5 minutes. Transfer the dal to a serving bowl and pour the remaining tempering oil over the top. Serve hot.

simple lentil dal with fresh ginger, green chiles, and cilantro

MASOOR DAL BAGHAAR WAALI

SERVES 4

This tempering oil, with fresh aromatics as well as dried spices, gives the lentils a deeper, more complex flavor than in the previous recipe. I like using small hot Thai chiles for this recipe because they add a lot of flavor as well as heat. (If you can find them, use two.) Even finely chopped bell pepper will work well if you can't find some kind of hot chile. As my grandmother always says, "Add nothing to your grocery list that will cause you angst; your frustrations will pour out into the food for your guests to take away with them."

I make this recipe with pink lentils (*dhuli masoor dal*). Pink lentils cook in about 15 minutes. You can also use yellow split peas, which cook in 45 minutes.

1 cup lentils, picked over, washed, and drained
1/2 teaspoon turmeric
1 teaspoon salt, or to taste
4 cups water

TEMPERING OIL
2 1/2 tablespoons canola oil
1 1/4 teaspoons cumin seeds

2 whole dried red chiles
1 tablespoon minced fresh ginger
1 teaspoon minced garlic
1 fresh hot green chile, minced
1/2 teaspoon cayenne pepper

1/4 cup chopped fresh cilantro
Juice of 1/2 lime or lemon

Put the lentils into a large saucepan with the turmeric, salt, and water. Bring to a boil and skim well. Reduce the heat and simmer, covered, until the lentils are soft, 20 to 30 minutes. Add water during cooking, if necessary. Taste for salt and add more if you need to.

Ladle about 1/2 cup of the lentils into a small bowl and mash them with a spoon. Return the mashed lentils to the pot and give the dal a stir. Then continue cooking at a simmer, uncovered, for 5 minutes to thicken. If you like a thicker dal, use a whisk to break up the lentils into a puree. If you like a thinner dal, add water.

For the tempering oil, heat the oil with the cumin seeds in a small frying pan or *kadai* over medium–high heat. Cook, stirring, until the cumin turns a light brown color, 1 to 2 minutes. Add the dried chiles, ginger, garlic, and green chile and cook, stirring, until the garlic no longer smells raw and turns a golden brown color, about 30 more seconds. Remove the pan from the fire, add the cayenne, and sprinkle in a few drops of water to stop the cooking.

Stir half of the tempering oil, half of the cilantro, and all of the lime or lemon juice into the dal. Simmer very gently, uncovered, for 5 minutes. Transfer the dal to a serving bowl. Pour the remaining tempering oil over the top and sprinkle with the remaining cilantro. Serve hot.

empress dal

MALIKAYE MASOOR

SERVES 4

There is something wonderfully warm and tasty about this dal. It's exceptionally simple to make (there is no tempering oil), yet the flavors are very full. Dried mango powder (you can also use lemon juice) gives it a lovely sourness that balances the meaty taste of the lentils. Of all of the dals I make, this is the one I want when I have a craving for something simple and homey, but still savory. It's no wonder that it's called *malikaye*, meaning "empress"; to me, this is the empress of dals.

This dal is traditionally made with a brown lentil *(sabut masoor dal)* that is exactly the same as the pink lentil *(dhuli masoor dal)* used in the preceding recipes but with the brown hull still attached. The hull gives the lentil a terrific meaty texture; French green lentils *(lentilles de Puy)* are an excellent substitution.

3 tablespoons canola oil

2 teaspoons cumin seeds

3 whole dried red chiles

1/2 teaspoon turmeric

1 small garlic clove, minced, or 1/8 teaspoon asafetida

1 cup lentils, picked over, washed and drained

1/4 teaspoon cayenne pepper

1 tablespoon dried mango powder *(amchur),*
     or the juice of 1 lemon

4 cups water

1 teaspoon salt, or to taste

Combine the oil, cumin, red chiles, and turmeric in a large saucepan over medium–high heat. Cook, stirring, 1 to 2 minutes. Add the garlic or asafetida, lentils, cayenne, and mango powder, if using, and cook, stirring, 1 minute.

Add the water, bring to a boil, and skim well. Reduce the heat and simmer, covered, until the lentils are soft, 20 to 30 minutes. Add more water during cooking, if necessary. Taste for salt and add more if you need to.

Ladle about 1/2 cup of the lentils into a small bowl and mash them with a spoon. Return the mashed lentils to the pot and give the dal a stir. Then continue cooking at a simmer, uncovered, for 5 minutes to thicken. If you like a thicker dal, use a whisk to break up the lentils into a puree. If you like a thinner dal, add more water. Stir in the lemon juice, if using. Serve hot.

simple lentil dal with whole cinnamon, cardamom, and cloves

MASOOR DAL KHADE MASALE WAALI

SERVES 4

A final variation on a simple dal recipe, this one will make you fall in love with dals: the mashed garlic, cloves, and cinnamon give the lentils a lovely, warm aftertaste and a heavenly fragrance. In this recipe, whole spices are cooked in oil to infuse it with their flavor before the lentils are added, and the dal is finished with a fresh tempering oil, as well.

I make this recipe with pink lentils *(dhuli masoor dal)*, which take only about 15 minutes to cook. You can also use yellow split peas, which cook in 45 minutes.

1 1/2 tablespoons canola oil
A 1-inch piece cinnamon stick
1 teaspoon cumin seeds
3 whole cloves
4 green cardamom pods
1 cup lentils, picked over, washed, and drained
1/2 teaspoon turmeric
4 cups cold water
1 teaspoon salt, or to taste

TEMPERING OIL
1 tablespoon canola oil
1 medium onion, finely chopped
3 garlic cloves, mashed to a paste (about 1/2 tablespoon)
1 tablespoon minced fresh ginger
1 fresh hot green chile, minced

1/4 cup chopped fresh cilantro
Juice of 1/2 lemon or lime

Heat the oil with the cinnamon stick in a large saucepan or *kadai* over medium-high heat. Cook, stirring, until the cinnamon unfurls, 1 to 2 minutes.

Add the cumin, cloves, and cardamom and cook, stirring, until the cumin turns a golden brown color, about 1 more minute. Add the lentils, turmeric, water, and salt. Bring to a boil and skim well. Turn down the heat and simmer, covered, until the lentils are soft, 20 to 30 minutes. Add more water during cooking, if necessary. Taste for salt and add more if you need to.

Ladle about 1/2 cup of the lentils into a small bowl and mash them with a spoon. Return the mashed lentils to the pot and give the dal a stir. Continue cooking at a simmer, uncovered, for 5 minutes to thicken. If you like a thicker dal, use a whisk to break up the lentils into a puree. If you like a thinner dal, add water. Remove the cinnamon stick.

For the tempering oil, heat the oil in a small saucepan or *kadai* over medium-high heat. Add the onion and cook until it just begins to brown around the edges, 4 to 5 minutes. Add the garlic paste, ginger, and minced chile and cook just to mellow the raw taste of the garlic, 10 to 15 seconds.

Stir half of the tempering oil into the dal along with half of the cilantro and all of the lemon or lime juice. Simmer very gently for 5 minutes. Transfer the dal to a serving bowl, pour the remaining tempering oil over the top, and sprinkle with the remaining cilantro. Serve hot.

simple gujarati dal with three chiles

MASOOR DAL TEEN MIRCHON WAALI

SERVES 4

In most of India, three red chiles would be considered a sign of sorrow, but in Gujarat (in western India), where one might eat a dal like this one, the number 3 is considered an auspicious garnish. It's also a delicious one, adding a gentle heat and plenty of flavor to the dal.

I make this recipe with pink lentils *(dhuli masoor dal)*, which take about 15 minutes to cook. You can also use yellow split peas, which cook in 45 minutes.

1 cup lentils, picked over, washed, and drained
1/2 teaspoon turmeric
1 teaspoon salt, or to taste
4 cups water

TEMPERING OIL
2 1/2 tablespoons canola oil
1 teaspoon black mustard seeds (optional)
1/2 teaspoon cumin seeds

3 whole dried red chiles
1 fresh hot green chile, minced
8 fresh or 12 frozen curry leaves,
     torn into pieces (optional)
1 small garlic clove, minced
1/2 teaspoon cayenne pepper

3 heaping tablespoons chopped fresh cilantro
Juice of 1/2 lime or lemon

Put the lentils into a large saucepan with the turmeric, salt, and water. Bring to a boil and skim well. Turn the heat down and simmer, covered, until the lentils are soft, 20 to 30 minutes. Add more water during cooking, if necessary. When the lentils are cooked, taste for salt and add more if you need to.

Ladle about 1/2 cup of the lentils into a small bowl and mash them with a spoon. Return the mashed lentils to the pot and give the dal a stir. Then continue cooking at a simmer, uncovered, for 5 minutes to thicken. If you like a thicker dal, use a whisk to break up the lentils into a puree. If you like a thinner dal, add more water.

For the tempering oil, if using mustard seeds, heat the oil with the mustard seeds in a small frying pan or *kadai* over medium-high heat. Cover (the mustard seeds pop and splatter) and cook until you hear the mustard seeds crackle, 1 to 2 minutes. Add the cumin seeds, cover, and cook, stirring once or twice, until golden, about 30 more seconds. (Or heat the oil with the cumin over medium-high heat and cook, stirring, until golden, 1 to 2 minutes.) Add the dried red chiles, green chile, curry leaves, if using, and garlic and cook, stirring, 30 more seconds. (Stand back if using curry leaves; they spit when they hit the oil.) Remove the pan from the fire and add the cayenne and a few drops of water to stop the cooking.

Stir half of the tempering oil, half of the cilantro, and all of the lime or lemon juice into the dal. Simmer very gently for 5 minutes. Transfer to a serving bowl. Pour the remaining tempering oil over the top and sprinkle with the rest of the cilantro. Serve hot.

yellow mung beans with spinach and panchphoran

MUGER DAL

SERVES 4

Panchphoran is an aromatic combination of spices that the Bengalis in eastern India use; it is a mixture of fennel, fenugreek and cumin seeds, nigella seeds *(kalaunji),* and a spice called *radhuni.* The spinach gives the dal a rich, creamy texture when, in truth, it is light in oil and uses no butter or cream. Mango powder adds a pleasant sour flavor that we Indians love without overwhelming the delicate flavors of the lentils and spinach; you can use lemon juice as well. In Bengal, cooks would make this with mustard oil, but I like it just as well cooked with canola or ghee.

You may use yellow split peas or lentils in place of mung beans.

1 tablespoon canola oil

1 cup split yellow mung beans *(moong dal),* picked over, washed, and drained, yellow split peas, or lentils

1/2 teaspoon turmeric

4 cups water

1 bay leaf

1 1/2 teaspoons salt, or to taste

2 cups firmly packed stemmed fresh spinach, finely chopped

1/2 teaspoon cayenne pepper

TEMPERING OIL

2 tablespoons canola oil or ghee

2 teaspoons *panchphoran* (Bengali five-spice mix); or mixture of 1 teaspoon cumin seeds, 1/2 teaspoon coriander seeds, and 1/2 teaspoon fennel seeds

3 whole dried red chiles

1/2 fresh hot green chile, minced

Juice of 1 lemon, or 1/2 teaspoon dried mango powder *(amchur)*

Heat the oil in a large saucepan over medium-high heat. Add the mung beans or split peas and turmeric and cook, stirring, 1 to 2 minutes. Add the water, bay leaf, and salt. Bring to a boil and skim well. Then reduce the heat and simmer, partially covered, until the beans are tender, about 20 minutes.

Add the chopped spinach and cayenne and cook, partially covered, 15 minutes longer. Taste for salt and add some if you need to.

For the tempering oil, heat the oil with the *panchphoran,* or the cumin, dried chiles and fresh chiles in a small frying pan or *kadai* over medium heat. Cook, stirring, until the cumin turns golden brown, 1 to 2 minutes. Take the pan off the heat and stir in the lemon juice or mango powder.

Pour the tempering oil into the saucepan with the dal and stir. Transfer to a serving bowl and serve hot.

warm lentil salad with coconut and tomato

DAL KEE SALAAD

SERVES 4

In this recipe, I play the role of a well-trained French home cook or, for that matter, any savvy home cook. I use the leftover cooked split peas from one of the rasams in the Soup chapter (page 16) to make a quick South Indian inspired snack or lunch dish that will delight you and anyone else you're cooking for. You can make it spicier, tangier, or more herbal by adding more chiles, lemon juice, or cilantro. Myself, I never seem to make this dish the same way twice. I'm always playing with the seasonings and I suggest that you do, too. Change them to suit your mood and whatever taste you're hungry for. The idea is to enliven the relatively bland flavor of the lentil with acidity, heat, and spice.

2½ tablespoons canola oil

1 tablespoon black mustard seeds (optional)

1 teaspoon yellow split peas

1 teaspoon cumin seeds

2 whole dried red chiles

8 fresh or 12 frozen curry leaves, torn into pieces (optional)

⅛ teaspoon asafetida (optional)

1 fresh hot green chile, cut crosswise into thin slices

1 red onion, sliced

1½ teaspoons salt, or to taste

2 tablespoons unsweetened shredded coconut (optional)

1 small tomato, chopped

1 cup split peas or lentils simmered in water to cover until tender, and drained

Juice of ½ lemon

¼ cup chopped fresh cilantro

Combine the oil, the mustard seeds, if using, and yellow split peas in a large, heavy-bottomed saucepan or casserole over medium-high heat. Cook, stirring, until the mustard seeds crackle and/or the dal begins to color, 1 to 2 minutes. (Cover the pan if using mustard seeds; they pop and splatter.)

Add the *urad dal,* if using, and the cumin and cook, stirring, until the cumin turns golden brown, about 1 minute.

Add the dried chiles, and the curry leaves and asafetida, if using, and cook, stirring, about 1 more minute. (Stand back if using curry leaves; they spit when they hit the oil.)

Add the fresh chile, onion, and salt and cook until the onion softens, 2 to 3 minutes. Add the coconut, if using, and cook, stirring, until it turns golden brown, about 2 more minutes. Add the tomato and cook, stirring, 1 minute.

Add the cooked lentils, lemon juice, and cilantro and stir until the lentils are warmed through. Taste for salt. Spoon the salad into a serving bowl and serve warm or at room temperature.

"kwalitys" chickpeas

CHOLAS

SERVES 4 TO 6

The taste of these chickpeas invariably takes me back to my childhood. My brothers, sister, and I took the bus home from school every day. Every now and then we'd get off the bus to find my mother waiting in the car to take us out to lunch. Our favorite lunch place was the Bengali Sweet Center, where they served these *Kwalitys* chickpeas made famous by the restaurant of that name. With Bhaturas (page 192), they were the best treat we could imagine after a long day at school.

The dried mango powder and the pomegranate powder (both souring agents) are essential to reproduce the taste of this dish as it was made at Kwalitys; they contribute a sourness that is altogether different from that of limes or lemons. But if you don't have those powders, go ahead and make it without; it will still be very good, if not exactly "Kwalitys" authentic. Chickpeas like these are served with chilled, sliced red onions and pickles.

3 tablespoons canola oil

1 teaspoon cumin seeds

1/4 teaspoon black peppercorns

4 whole cloves

4 green cardamom pods

3 whole dried red chiles

A 1 1/2-inch piece fresh ginger, minced

4 fresh or 6 frozen curry leaves, torn into pieces
    (optional)

2 red onions, finely chopped

3 fresh hot green chiles, slit the length of the chile

1 1/2 teaspoons salt, or to taste

2 teaspoons dried mango powder *(amchur)*,
    or the juice of 1 lemon

2 teaspoons pomegranate powder *(anaardaana)*,
    or the juice of 1 lemon

2 teaspoons toasted ground cumin (see sidebar,
    page 39)

1/2 teaspoon turmeric

1 teaspoon garam masala (page 250)

1/2 teaspoon cayenne pepper

1/2 teaspoon ground black pepper

1 1/2 cups water

3 (19-ounce) cans chickpeas, drained and rinsed

Combine the oil, cumin seeds, peppercorns, cloves, cardamom, and red chiles in a large saucepan over medium-high heat. Cook, stirring, until the cumin begins to brown, 1 to 2 minutes.

Add the ginger and curry leaves, if using, and cook, stirring, about 30 seconds. (Stand back if using curry leaves; they spit when they hit the oil.) Add the onions, green chiles, and salt and cook, stirring often, until the onions turn a uniformly dark brown color, about 20 minutes. Keep a cup of water beside the stove as the onions cook. As the onions begin to stick to the bottom of the pan, add water, about 1 teaspoon at a time, and stir and scrape the bottom of the pan with the spoon to pull up the browned bits and keep the onions and spices from burning. Do this as often as necessary (five or six times) until the onions are well browned.

When the onions are cooked, add the mango and pomegranate powders, if using, as well as the ground toasted cumin, turmeric, and 1/2 teaspoon of the garam masala; cook, stirring, about 30 seconds.

Stir in the cayenne and black peppers. Immediately add the water and all but about 1/2 cup of the chickpeas. Mash the rest of the chickpeas to a puree with the back of a fork and add them to the pan along with the remaining 1/2 teaspoon garam masala. Bring to a simmer, stirring, and cook gently, partially covered, for 15 minutes. Stir in the lemon juice, if using. Taste for salt and serve hot.

sour chickpeas with garam masala and toasted cumin

KHATTE CHANNA

SERVES 4

If you love sour foods, and we do in India, this recipe is a wonderful excuse for indulging that passion. As in the "Kwalitys" chickpeas on page 36, pomegranate and mango powders give the dish a tangy sourness; the tamarind used here adds even more. The ketchup adds a sweet undertone that balances these sour tastes and makes for a delicate sweet-and-sour flavor. I love this with plain steamed rice or with pooris (pages 193 and 198). Traditionally, this dish would have been found exclusively in the north of India, but in the last decade or so, chickpeas have become common across most of the country.

1 1/2 teaspoons tamarind concentrate or
    the juice of 2 lemons
1/2 cup warm water (if using tamarind concentrate)
1/4 cup canola oil
1 teaspoon cumin seeds
8 fresh or 12 frozen curry leaves, torn into pieces
    (optional)
2 cups minced red onion
2 1/2 teaspoons salt, or to taste
1 tablespoon minced fresh ginger
1/2 teaspoon turmeric
3 teaspoons dried mango powder (*amchur;* optional)
2 teaspoons pomegranate seed powder
    (*anaardaana;* optional)

1/2 teaspoon cayenne pepper
2 medium tomatoes, quartered and pureed in a food
    processor or blender
2 (19-ounce) cans chickpeas, drained and rinsed
1 1/4 teaspoons garam masala (page 250)
1 1/4 teaspoons ground toasted cumin (see sidebar,
    page 39)
1 tablespoon ketchup
1 medium red onion, peeled and thinly sliced, for
    garnish
2 fresh hot green chiles, seeded and minced, for garnish
2 tablespoons chopped fresh cilantro, for garnish

If using the tamarind, measure the warm water into a small bowl or measuring cup. Add the tamarind concentrate and stir to dissolve it. Rinse the measuring spoon and your fingers in the water to dissolve all of the sticky tamarind. Set the tamarind water aside. (If using the lemon juice, do not add it until the end of the cooking time.)

Heat the oil with the cumin seeds and curry leaves, if using, in a large, heavy-bottomed frying pan over medium-high heat. Cook, stirring, until the cumin begins to brown, about 30 seconds. (Stand back if using curry leaves; they spit in hot oil.)

Add the minced onion and salt, and cook until the onion turns a uniformly golden brown color, 10 to 15 minutes. Keep a cup of water beside the stove as the onion cooks. As the onion begins to stick, add water, about 1 teaspoon at a time, and scrape the bottom of the pan with the spoon to pull up the browned bits and keep the spices from burning. Do this as often as necessary (five or six times) until the onion is well browned.

Add the ginger and cook, stirring, 1 to 2 minutes. Add the turmeric and cook, stirring, 1 more minute. Add the mango and pomegranate seed powders, if using, and the cayenne and cook, stirring, for about 15 seconds. Add the tomato puree and the tamarind water, if using. Bring to a simmer, turn the heat down to low, and simmer 15 minutes.

Add all but about $1/2$ cup of the chickpeas to the pan along with the garam masala, ground toasted cumin, and ketchup. Mash the remaining chickpeas to a puree with the back of a fork and add it to the pan, too. Bring to a boil, reduce the heat, and simmer gently, partially covered, 10 more minutes. Stir once or twice during cooking. Stir in the lemon juice, if using.

Taste for salt and then spoon the chickpeas into a serving dish. Garnish with the sliced onion, minced chiles, and chopped cilantro, and serve hot.

Ground toasted cumin is used in this recipe as well as in the "Kwalitys" Chickpeas on page 36, and a number of other recipes in this book, so it makes sense to toast and grind a few tablespoons at a time to have on hand. Toast the cumin in a dry frying pan over medium heat, stirring, until fragrant and lightly browned, 2 to 3 minutes. Grind to a powder and store in an airtight container.

spicy squash, eggplant, and lentil stew

DHAANSAAK

SERVES 6 TO 8

This is my adaptation of a famous Parsi dish. At first, the lovely spices in the stew taste subtle and familiar. Then, as you keep eating they expand on your palate so that you get their full flavor and warmth. What I call the back heat—that is, the heat of the spices rather than the chiles—of this dish makes it hotter than any of the other recipes in this chapter. But it's the kind of heat that invites you to keep on eating and eating.

This recipe is a perfect one-pot meal. You can change the vegetables according to your taste and to what's in the market. You can also change the proportion in which you use them. You can make the dish with 1 3/4 cups lentils or split peas alone, but a combination of the two gives the dish a greater complexity of flavor.

I particularly like this recipe for fall; it lends itself to fall vegetables and the colors are wonderful fall hues. Serve this with Plain Basmati Rice (page 91) to make the kind of hearty weekend lunch one would eat at the Bombay Gymkhana or any of the elite clubs in Bombay, or for a festive dinner party.

1 cup yellow split peas, picked over, washed, and
    drained

3/4 cup lentils, picked over, washed, and drained

6 1/2 cups water

2 garlic cloves, minced

1 tablespoon minced fresh ginger

2 teaspoons garam masala (page 250)

1 teaspoon turmeric

1 teaspoon cayenne pepper

1/4 teaspoon ground cloves

2 bay leaves

1 to 2 fresh hot green chiles, minced

2 1/2 teaspoons salt, or to taste

3/4 pound tomatoes, chopped

3 cups skinned and seeded butternut squash chunks
    (1-inch), about 1 small squash

5 cups eggplant chunks (1-inch) with skin
    (about 1 medium)

1 medium red onion, cut into 1-inch pieces

1 cup fresh or frozen corn kernels

12 fresh spinach leaves, stemmed, washed, and torn
    into bite-size pieces

TEMPERING OIL

1/4 cup canola oil

1 teaspoon black mustard seeds (optional)

1 small red onion, finely chopped

1 teaspoon ground cumin

1 garlic clove, minced

1/4 cup chopped fresh cilantro

Juice of 1/2 lemon

Put the split peas and lentils in a large soup pot along with 4 1/2 cups of the water. Bring to a boil and skim well. Then add the garlic, ginger, garam masala, turmeric, cayenne, cloves, bay leaves, chiles, and salt. Turn the heat down and simmer, covered, until the legumes are tender but not falling apart, about 20 minutes. Stir every now and then to prevent the dal from sticking to the bottom of the pot.

Add the tomatoes, squash, eggplant, onion, corn, spinach, and the remaining 2 cups of water. Return the stew to a boil, turn the heat down, and simmer, covered, until the vegetables are tender but still hold their shape, about 15 minutes. Take the stew off the heat.

For the tempering oil, heat the oil with the mustard seeds, if using, in a medium frying pan or *kadai* over medium-high heat. Cover and cook until you hear the mustard seeds crackle, 1 to 2 minutes. (Or heat the oil in the same pan over medium-high heat.) Add the chopped onion and the cumin and cook, stirring, until the onion is well browned around the edges, about 5 minutes. Turn the heat down to medium, add the garlic, and cook a few seconds. Now add the cilantro and stir. Add the lemon juice, remove from the heat, and scrape the tempering oil into the stew.

Stir dal well and taste for salt. If the stew is a bit thick (it should have a lightly thickened, velvety consistency), add ¼ to ½ cup water. Spoon into a serving bowl and serve hot.

red kidney beans with ginger, tomato, and curry leaves

RAJMA

SERVES 4 TO 6

Rajma chaawal (kidney beans and rice) is Sunday lunch food for many people in Punjab and Delhi. While the exact seasoning of the kidney beans will be slightly different from one home to the next, this recipe is pretty representative of what most home cooks are making in those areas. Growing up, we used to eat these beans quite simply with basmati rice, a plate of chilled sliced red onion seasoned with lemon juice, and homemade yogurt.

5 tablespoons canola oil

1 teaspoon cumin seeds

1/2 teaspoon whole cloves

1/4 teaspoon black peppercorns

A 1-inch piece cinnamon stick

4 whole dried red chiles

8 green cardamom pods

3 bay leaves

8 fresh or 12 frozen curry leaves, torn into pieces (optional)

A 2-inch piece fresh ginger, peeled and minced

1/8 teaspoon asafetida (optional)

2 medium red onions, finely chopped

2 teaspoons salt, or to taste

3 garlic cloves, minced

1 tablespoon ground coriander

1 teaspoon ground cumin

1/2 teaspoon turmeric

1 fresh hot green chile, slit the length of the chile

1/2 teaspoon cayenne pepper

2 medium tomatoes, quartered and pureed in a food processor or blender

1 (8-ounce) can tomato puree

1 teaspoon garam masala (page 250)

3 (19-ounce) cans red kidney beans, drained and rinsed

1 1/2 cups water

Combine the oil, cumin seeds, cloves, peppercorns, cinnamon stick, chiles, cardamom, and bay leaves in a large saucepan over medium-high heat. Cook, stirring, until the cinnamon unfurls, 1 to 2 minutes.

Add the curry leaves, if using, and ginger and cook, stirring, 1 minute. (Stand back if using curry leaves; they spit when they hit the hot oil.) Add the asafetida, if using, and stir. Then add the onions and salt and cook, stirring often, until the onions are a uniformly dark brown color, 20 to 25 minutes. Keep a cup of water by the stove as the onions cook. As the onions begin to stick, add water, about 1 teaspoon at a time, and stir and scrape the bottom of the pan with the spoon to pull up the browned bits and keep the onions and spices from burning. Do this as often as necessary (five or six times) until the onions are well browned.

Add the garlic and cook until the raw smell disappears, about 30 seconds. Add the coriander, ground cumin, turmeric, and green chile and cook 30 seconds. Stir in the cayenne. Immediately add the fresh and canned tomato purees. Bring to a boil, reduce the heat, and simmer, uncovered, 10 minutes to reduce.

Stir in the garam masala, then the beans and water. Bring to a simmer and cook gently, partially covered, 10 minutes. Taste for salt. Remove the bay leaves. Spoon into a serving bowl and serve hot.

curried black-eyed peas

LOBIA

SERVES 4 TO 6

I have very fond memories of this dish. My mother's mother used to make it for my family often. She moved to the United States when I was still in school, but she left her home in charge of her cook, Chotu, a Nepalese man. I often stayed with him since the house was close to my school. Chotu made a version of this dish from his own culture: he called it *rongee*. Fifteen years later the flavor of my grandmother's recipe still lingers in my mind and on my palate. I can never make it without thinking of her and Chotu.

I often eat this on New Year's Eve—an Indian twist on the tradition of the American South, where black-eyed peas are served at on New Year's Day celebrations.

¼ cup canola oil

4 whole cloves

¼ teaspoon black peppercorns

6 green cardamom pods

A 1-inch piece cinnamon stick

3 whole dried red chiles

½ teaspoon cumin seeds

2 bay leaves

A 1½-inch piece fresh ginger, peeled and minced

1 large red onion, finely chopped

2 teaspoons salt, or to taste

2 garlic cloves, mashed in a mortar and pestle
  with ⅛ teaspoon cumin seeds

1 tablespoon ground coriander

1 teaspoon ground cumin

½ teaspoon turmeric

½ teaspoon cayenne pepper

3 medium tomatoes, quartered and pureed
  in a food processor or blender

¼ cup plain yogurt

½ teaspoon garam masala (page 250)

3 (15½-ounce) cans black-eyed peas, drained and rinsed

1 cup water

Combine the oil with the cloves, peppercorns, cardamom, cinnamon, chiles, cumin seeds, and bay leaves in a large saucepan over medium-high heat. Cook, stirring, until the cinnamon unfurls, 1 to 2 minutes.

Add the ginger and cook 1 minute. Add the onions and salt, and cook, stirring, until the onions turn a uniform golden brown color, about 15 minutes. Keep a measuring cup of water by the stove. As the onions begin to stick to the bottom of the pan and burn, add water, about 1 teaspoon at a time, and scrape the pan with a wooden spoon to pull up the browned bits and keep the onions and spices from burning. Do this as often as necessary (five or six times) until the onions are well browned.

When the onions are cooked, add the garlic and cook, stirring, 1 to 2 minutes. Add the coriander, ground cumin, and turmeric and cook until the raw smell of the spices disappears, about 30 seconds. Add the cayenne and then immediately the pureed tomato. Bring to a boil, reduce the heat, and simmer, uncovered, until a film of oil pools on the surface of the sauce, about 5 minutes.

Meanwhile, in a measuring cup or bowl, whisk or stir the yogurt until smooth. Stir about 2 tablespoons of the hot sauce into the yogurt to temper it. When the tomato sauce has cooked 5 minutes, stir in the tempered yogurt, the garam masala, black-eyed peas, and water. Turn the heat to medium and heat until a bubble or two just breaks the surface, 5 to 7 minutes. (Do not boil or the yogurt in the sauce will curdle.) Taste for salt. Serve hot.

STIR-FRIED GREEN BEANS WITH COCONUT

STIR-FRIED GREEN BEANS WITH CUMIN

STIR-FRIED CABBAGE WITH SOUTH INDIAN SPICES

STIR-FRIED CARROTS WITH CUMIN AND LIME

CAULIFLOWER HYDERABAD STYLE

CAULIFLOWER IN A PIQUANT TOMATO SAUCE

PARTY CAULIFLOWER

*vegetables

STIR-FRIED CAULIFLOWER AND POTATO WITH CRUNCHY BENGALI SPICES

CAULIFLOWER SAUTÉED WITH GREEN PEPPERS, TOMATO, AND YOGURT

MY SISTER'S FAVORITE CORN CURRY

CORN BRAISED GUJARATI STYLE

SMOKED SPICED EGGPLANT

CHILLED SMOKY EGGPLANT WITH YOGURT AND CILANTRO

STIR-FRIED MUSHROOMS WITH ONIONS AND TOMATOES

MUSHROOMS IN A CORIANDER-SCENTED WHITE SAUCE

CRISP WHOLE OKRA WITH FENNEL AND CORIANDER

STIR-FRIED OKRA WITH TOMATOES, ONIONS, AND NORTHERN SPICES

SPICY PEAS SAUTÉED WITH GINGER

SWEET GREEN PEAS AND FRESH INDIAN CHEESE IN A FRAGRANT
  TOMATO SAUCE

STUFFED BELL PEPPERS

PLANTAINS IN CURRY

STIR-FRIED SWEET PEPPERS

POTATOES BRAISED IN A FRAGRANT YOGURT SAUCE

CRISPY POTATOES WITH CUMIN

WHOLE SPICED BABY POTATOES

INDIAN CHEESE IN AN HERBED GREEN SAUCE

SPINACH WITH POTATOES

SWEET-AND-SOUR BUTTERNUT SQUASH WITH GINGER AND CHILES

STIR-FRIED MIXED SUMMER SQUASH

CRISP YAM AND GREEN PEAS

VEGETABLE JHALFRAZIE

If legumes are the backbone of Indian cuisine, then vegetables are its heart. Over 50 percent of Indian households are vegetarian for religious or cultural reasons, and still others eschew meat out of economic necessity. Even nonvegetarian households eat far more vegetables than meat, which they may eat only three or four times a week. It's not surprising that the art of cooking vegetables has reached its zenith in Indian culture, and I think that India has some of the best vegetarian cuisine in the world.

In this book I can only begin to introduce you to Indian vegetarian cuisine. You'll find a few classical Mogul dishes such as Indian Cheese in an Herbed Green Sauce, Plantains in Curry, Chilled Smoky Eggplant with Yogurt and Cilantro, Potatoes Braised in a Fragrant Yogurt Sauce, and Party Cauliflower. I've given several South Indian recipes, many of them stir-fries, because South Indian vegetarian cuisine is one of my favorites. And then there are a few recipes such as the Cauliflower Hyderabad Style that are the result of the magical marriage of Mogul and local cuisines, which has given birth to some of the best food I know.

The remainder of the recipes are interpretations of traditional dishes from regions of India through which I have traveled, eating voraciously, as well as some recipes of my own. These are stir-fries such as the Stir-Fried Green Beans with Coconut, Stir-Fried Cabbage with South

Indian Spices, and Stir-Fried Carrots with Cumin and Lime. They follow a recognizable pattern that, once you learn it, will give you the freedom to invent your own Indian-flavored stir-fried vegetables. They use one pan and they're so quick and easy to make that you can enjoy them any night of the week.

VEGETABLE STIR-FRIES

Most of the vegetable stir-fries in this book follow this simple pattern:

1. Put a few tablespoons of canola oil in a large wok, *kadai,* or frying pan along with a combination of longer-cooking spices that may include a dal or two. (Mustard seeds, *channa dal,* fenugreek seeds, cinnamon stick, cardamom seeds, whole cloves, peppercorns, and bay leaves are good candidates.)

2. Heat the spice mixture over medium-high heat, stirring constantly so that the spices cook evenly, until the spices have released their scent and flavor into the oil. (A wide, rigid spatula is a good tool for stirring.)

3. Add chopped fresh ginger and fresh chiles, if you're using either, and a second tier of quicker-cooking spices such as *urad dal,* cumin seeds, coriander seeds, whole dried red chiles, or curry leaves. Cook, stirring constantly, until the fresh spices soften and the dried spices are fragrant.

4. Add the vegetable, either raw or parboiled, and salt (for some vegetables, salt may be added at the end) and cook, stirring often if not constantly, until the vegetable is browned and cooked through. Sometimes the pan is covered to hasten the cooking; the vegetable will brown despite the cover.

5. Add yogurt or tomato, or even water, if desired; all of the liquid will eventually be cooked out. Stir the mixture several times during the cooking in order to keep the spices from burning and also to check on the progress of the cooking: if the food looks like it's going to brown too much before it's cooked through, turn the heat down. If the food isn't browning at all, turn the heat up. If there is moisture in the pan once the vegetables are cooked, uncover and cook until the liquid evaporates.

6. Sometimes, ground spices—cayenne, garam masala, rasam or sambhaar powders, and coconut, to name a few—are added at the end of cooking, since they burn quickly if exposed to high heat (water is often added along with it for added protection) and because their scent and flavor are so subtle that more than a little heat will mute them or turn them bitter.

7. Sprinkle the dish with lemon or lime juice and fresh chopped cilantro before serving.

I use whole spices instead of ground because it's simpler, the spices don't need to be freshly ground, and I like biting into them: at first bite, the individual flavors break in waves in your mouth, then the flavors and aromas marry with the food in lovely ways. You can pick out the spices at the end of cooking, too, or remove them as you eat.

stir-fried green beans with coconut

BEAN PORIYAL

SERVES 4

Everyone I cook most often for seems to love coconut; I've realized finally that it's a very easy way to keep them all happy. What I like about this particular dish is that the coconut adds flavor without excessive richness. Serve this as a side dish to a more formal meal or with lentils and rice for a simple dinner at home.

3 tablespoons canola oil

2 teaspoons yellow split peas

1 tablespoon black mustard seeds (optional)

1 teaspoon hulled black gram beans (*urad dal;* optional)

3 whole dried red chiles

8 fresh or 12 frozen curry leaves, torn into pieces (optional)

1 teaspoon cumin seeds

$1/8$ teaspoon asafetida (optional)

$1/2$ cup unsweetened shredded coconut

$3/4$ pound green beans, both ends trimmed, beans cut on an angle into 1-inch pieces

1 teaspoon salt, or to taste

$1/2$ teaspoon saambhar powder or rasam powder (page 251) (optional)

1 cup water

Combine the oil, yellow split peas, and mustard seeds, if using, in a large wok, *kadai,* or frying pan over medium-high heat. Cook, stirring, until the split peas turn golden brown, 1 to 2 minutes. (Cover if using mustard seeds—they pop and splatter—and cook until you hear them crackle.)

Add the *urad dal,* chiles, curry leaves, if using, and cumin and cook uncovered, stirring, 1 more minute. (Stand back if using curry leaves; they spit when they hit the oil.)

Add the asafetida, if using, and $1/4$ cup of the coconut and cook, stirring, 30 seconds. Add the beans and salt and cook, stirring, 5 minutes.

Add the remaining $1/4$ cup coconut, the saambhar or rasam powder, if using, and the water. Bring to a simmer, cover, and cook until the beans are tender, about 10 minutes.

Uncover and cook, stirring often, until all of the water has evaporated, about 5 more minutes. Taste for salt and serve hot.

stir-fried green beans with cumin

GWAR KI PHALI

My father loves this dish and requests if often, served with a plain dal, like the Simple Lentil Dal with Cumin and Dried Red Chiles on page 27 and a raita. I find that I have similar cravings now that I live in New York. This is easy to make and satisfying, and friends love it, so I end up making it often.

1 pound green beans, both ends trimmed

2 tablespoons canola oil

1 teaspoon cumin seeds

1/2 teaspoon carom seeds (*ajawain;* optional)

1/8 teaspoon asafetida (optional)

A 2-inch piece fresh ginger, peeled and finely grated

3/4 teaspoon salt, or to taste

1 tablespoon fresh lime or lemon juice

1/8 teaspoon cayenne pepper (optional)

Bring a large saucepan of water to a boil. Add the beans, return the water to a boil, and cook 2 minutes. Then drain the beans, cool under cold running water, and drain again.

Combine the oil, cumin, and carom and asafetida, if using, in a large wok, *kadai,* or frying pan over medium heat. Cook, stirring, 1 minute. Add the ginger and cook, stirring, 1 minute.

Add the beans and stir to coat with the oil and spices. Sprinkle with the salt and stir. Cover, turn the heat down very low, and cook, stirring three or four times, until the beans are tender and lightly browned, 10 to 15 minutes.

Add the lime or lemon juice and sprinkle with the cayenne, if using. Stir well and taste for salt. Serve hot.

stir-fried cabbage with south indian spices

PATTA GOBI

SERVES 4

It happens often in my household that I'll be putting the finishing touches on a dinner for friends and suddenly I'll realize that, through casual phone calls throughout the day, the guest list has grown beyond the amount of food I've planned. At that point I head out to the corner market for a head of cabbage (which they always carry) and cook this South Indian stir-fry. I like my cabbage crisp, not mushy, so I cook it very briefly. I use a mixture of red and green for color, but you can use either. Served with rice and dal, it makes a complete meal.

3 tablespoons canola oil

1 tablespoon yellow split peas

1 tablespoon black mustard seeds (optional)

1 teaspoon cumin seeds

3 whole dried red chiles

1/2 fresh hot green chile, minced, with seeds

1/8 teaspoon asafetida (optional)

12 fresh or 15 frozen curry leaves, torn into pieces (optional)

2 tablespoons unsweetened shredded coconut (optional)

1/2 small head green cabbage, cored and finely chopped (about 4 cups)

1/2 small head red cabbage, cored and finely chopped (about 4 cups)

1/2 teaspoon salt, or to taste

Juice of 1/2 lime

Combine the oil, yellow split peas, and mustard seeds, if using, in a large wok, *kadai*, or frying pan over medium-high heat. Cook for 1 to 2 minutes. (Cover the pan if using mustard seeds—they pop and splatter—and cook until you hear them crackle.)

Add the cumin; red and green chiles; *urad dal*, asafetida, curry leaves; and coconut, if using, and cook uncovered, stirring, until the cumin and/or the legumes turn golden brown, 2 to 3 minutes. (Stand back if using curry leaves; they spit when they hit the oil.)

Add the cabbages and cook, stirring, until warmed through and barely wilted, 3 to 5 minutes. Stir in the salt. Transfer to a serving dish and squeeze the lime over. Serve hot or cold.

stir-fried carrots with cumin and lime

GAAJAR KEE SABZI

SERVES 4 TO 6

I am not especially fond of carrots, but I really do love them in this dish. Perhaps because they are grated they seem to absorb the flavors of the spices better. Their sweetness is accentuated by the taste of the cumin and the sour lime. Serve this warm, as a vegetable side dish, or chill it and serve it as a salad.

2½ tablespoons canola oil

2 teaspoons black mustard seeds (optional)

A 1-inch piece fresh ginger, peeled and cut into a fine julienne

½ fresh hot green chile, minced

3 whole dried red chiles

1 teaspoon cumin seeds

8 fresh or 12 frozen curry leaves, torn into pieces (optional)

1½ pounds carrots, peeled and grated on the large holes of a grater

¾ teaspoon salt, or to taste

Juice of ½ lime or lemon

Combine the oil and mustard seeds, if using, in a large wok, *kadai,* or frying pan over medium-high heat. Cover (the mustard seeds pop and splatter) and cook until you hear the mustard seeds crackle, 1 to 2 minutes. (Or heat just the oil in the same pan.)

Add the ginger, fresh and dried chiles, cumin, and curry leaves, if using, and cook uncovered, stirring, until the ginger crisps a little, about 1½ minutes. (Stand back if using curry leaves; they spit when they hit the oil.)

Add the carrots and cook, stirring, until warmed through, 3 to 4 minutes. Stir in the salt and the lime or lemon juice. Taste for salt and serve hot or cold.

cauliflower hyderabad style

HARE MASAALE KEE GOBHI

SERVES 4 TO 6

With its delicate balance of herbs and spices, this cauliflower dish is a magnificent journey into the aromatic world of spices. Hyderabad is one of the fortunate cities of India that has been home to a successful marriage of Mogul and local cultures, creating a brilliant new cuisine rich in the tastes of both. This lovely celadon green sauce celebrates the distinctive tastes of both the south and the Mogul north: mustard seeds, coconut, and curry leaves from the south meet the haunting flavors of cinnamon, cloves, cardamom, and cumin that are a hallmark of Mogul cooking. It is perfect eaten with rice, Simple Gujarati Dal with Three Chiles (page 30), and yogurt.

ONION-COCONUT PASTE

1 large red onion, quartered
¼ cup unsweetened shredded coconut, blanched almonds, or cashews
2 green cardamom pods
2 tablespoons water

GREEN PASTE

¼ cup firmly packed stemmed fresh mint leaves
¼ cup firmly packed stemmed fresh cilantro leaves
1 fresh hot green chile, stemmed
1 tablespoon water

¼ cup canola oil
Two 1-inch pieces cinnamon stick
4 green cardamom pods
4 whole cloves

½ teaspoon cumin seeds
½ teaspoon black mustard seeds (optional)
10 fresh or 15 frozen curry leaves, torn into pieces (optional)
¼ teaspoon nigella seeds (*kalaunji*; optional)
Salt
A 1½-inch piece fresh ginger, peeled and finely chopped
2 medium garlic cloves, minced
1 large head cauliflower (about 3 pounds), cored and cut into medium florets
2 cups coconut milk
1 teaspoon ground cumin
¼ teaspoon cayenne pepper
¼ teaspoon garam masala (page 250)
1 tablespoon chopped fresh cilantro

For the onion-coconut paste, combine all of the ingredients in a blender or food processor and process to a paste. Set aside.

For the green paste, combine all of the ingredients in a small blender or food processor and process to a paste. Set aside.

Combine the oil, cinnamon, cardamom, cloves, cumin seeds, mustard seeds, curry leaves, and nigella, if using, in a large frying pan or heavy-bottomed soup pot over medium-high heat. Cover if using mustard seeds (they splatter and pop) and cook, stirring occasionally, until the cinnamon stick unfurls, 1 to 2 minutes.

Add the onion-coconut paste and 1 teaspoon salt and cook uncovered, stirring, until the mixture dries out a bit and puffs, and the oil begins to separate from the mixture, 5 to 7 minutes.

Add the ginger and garlic and cook, stirring, 3 minutes. Add the cauliflower and stir to coat with the onion mixture. Then cook, uncovered, until the cauliflower is half-tender, stirring three or four times during the cooking, about 5 minutes.

Add 1 cup of the coconut milk, the ground cumin, cayenne, and the green paste and stir well. Cook 5 minutes, uncovered, stirring once or twice.

Add the remaining coconut milk and the garam masala and stir well. Bring to a simmer, cover, and cook until the cauliflower is tender, about 5 minutes. Then uncover and simmer about 3 more minutes to thicken the sauce. Taste for salt. Sprinkle with the cilantro and serve hot.

cauliflower in a piquant tomato sauce

GOBI JHALFREZIE

SERVES 4

Abha Aunty, one of my mother's closest friends in Delhi, used to make this simple cauliflower stir-fry for special occasions when I was a child. It's slightly unusual, in that the sauce is seasoned with vinegar and is a thinner consistency than most Indian tomato sauces. Cauliflower, cumin, and a handful of julienned ginger are lightly browned to concentrate their flavor. Chopped tomatoes add moisture and a bit of sweetness. This is best made at the peak of summer when tomatoes are very ripe and flavorful, but in the winter you can substitute an 8-ounce can of tomato sauce; the final cooking, to reduce the sauce, won't be necessary.

1/4 cup canola oil

3 whole dried red chiles

1 1/2 teaspoons cumin seeds

A 2-inch piece fresh ginger, peeled and cut into julienne

1 small head cauliflower (about 2 pounds), cored and cut into medium florets

1 teaspoon salt, or to taste

1 teaspoon ground black pepper

2 medium tomatoes, chopped

1 tablespoon white vinegar

2 tablespoons chopped fresh cilantro

Combine the oil, dried red chiles, and cumin in a large wok, *kadai,* or frying pan over medium-high heat. Cook, stirring, until the cumin begins to brown, about 1 minute.

Add the ginger and cook, stirring, 30 seconds. Add the cauliflower and cook, stirring, until it begins to brown, 2 to 3 minutes.

Add the salt and black pepper and mix well. Then turn the heat down to medium. Cover and cook, until the cauliflower is almost tender, 7 to 8 minutes. (Stir the cauliflower three or four times and check the cooking: if it browns too fast or the spices begin to burn, turn the heat down. If the cauliflower doesn't brown, turn the heat up a bit.)

Add the tomatoes and vinegar and stir well. Cover and continue cooking, stirring every now and then, until the cauliflower is tender, 2 to 3 more minutes. Then uncover, raise the heat, and boil to thicken the sauce, about 2 more minutes. Taste for salt, sprinkle with cilantro, and serve hot.

party cauliflower

GOBHI MASALAM

SERVES 4 TO 6

Panditji used to make this dish for my mother's very fancy annual dinner parties when I was a child. I loved those parties: the table would be lavishly set with our best china, silverware, and linens and we all feasted on a vast array of exquisite foods complemented by Panditji's best pickles. I make this now for special occasions because it never fails to impress.

For this Mogul dish, a whole head of cauliflower is first steamed until almost tender (Panditji taught me to add a little milk to the water to keep the cauliflower white), then deep-fried to enhance its flavor, then finally glazed with a spiced tomato sauce. Because the dish takes some time to make and it reheats well, I always make it in advance and heat it in the oven just before serving.

2 tablespoons milk

¹/₈ teaspoon garam masala (page 250)

1 large head cauliflower, trimmed completely of leaves, stem trimmed flat

TOMATO SAUCE

3 medium red onions

2 medium garlic cloves

A 1¹/₂-inch piece fresh ginger, peeled and sliced

3 tablespoons canola oil

A 1-inch piece cinnamon stick

5 whole cloves

3 bay leaves

1 teaspoon salt, or to taste

1 tablespoon ground coriander

¹/₂ teaspoon ground cumin

¹/₄ teaspoon turmeric

¹/₄ teaspoon cayenne pepper

1 (28-ounce) can tomatoes in puree, pureed in a food processor or blender

¹/₂ teaspoon garam masala

Canola oil, for deep-frying

Bring about 1 inch of water to a boil in a saucepan large enough to hold the cauliflower. Add the milk and garam masala. Put the cauliflower in the pan, stem end down. Cover and steam until the stem is just beginning to soften when you insert a skewer into the head, about 7 minutes. Drain well.

For the tomato sauce, combine the onions, garlic, and ginger in a food processor and process to finely chop. Set aside.

Combine the oil, cinnamon, cloves, and bay leaves in a large wok, *kadai,* or frying pan over medium-high heat. Cook, stirring, until the cinnamon unfurls, 1 to 2 minutes. Add the pureed onion mixture and the salt and cook, stirring often, until the onions begin to brown around the edges, about 10 minutes. Add the coriander, cumin, turmeric, and cayenne and cook, stirring, 1 minute. Add about 1 tablespoon of water and cook, stirring, until the onions begin to stick to the pan, about 1 more minute. Add the pureed tomatoes and stir to combine. Add the garam masala and cook, stirring often, 5 minutes. Taste for salt and set the sauce aside.

To fry the cauliflower, heat 1¹/₂ to 2 inches of oil in a medium wok, *kadai,* or large saucepan over medium-high heat to 360°F to 375°F. (To gauge the temperature of the oil without using a thermometer, drop a piece of bread about 1-inch square into the hot oil over medium heat, turning often; when the oil is hot enough the bread will begin to brown almost immediately and turn an even, golden brown color—like a crouton—in about

30 seconds.) Holding the cauliflower by the stem, lower it gently into the pot of oil. The oil will come about halfway up the head. Cook until the top of the head is nicely browned, about 1 minute. Turn the head carefully with a slotted spoon and cook until the other side is browned, 2 to 3 more minutes. Drain on a paper towel−lined plate. Then carefully set the head, stem side down, into an ovenproof serving dish and ladle the tomato sauce over to completely cover.

When you are ready to eat, preheat the oven to 300°F. Bake the cauliflower until warmed through, about 15 minutes. Cut into wedges and serve hot.

stir-fried cauliflower and potato with crunchy bengali spices

GOBHI ALOO KEE SABZI

SERVES 4

This is one way that I make cauliflower when I'm cooking for intimate parties at home. I've combined spices that are commonly used in Bengali cooking (nigella, cumin, and mustard seeds) and added cayenne and fresh ginger. The Bengali spices add a little zing to the warmer cayenne and ginger. The nigella adds crunch. Although this will go well with almost any combination of Indian foods, it's particularly good with Sweet Green Peas and Fresh Indian Cheese in a Fragrant Tomato Sauce (page 70) and raita, served with Chapatis (page 190) or toasted pita bread.

3 tablespoons canola oil

1 teaspoon nigella seeds (*kalaunji;* optional)

1 teaspoon cumin seeds

Rounded ¼ teaspoon coriander seeds

A 2-inch piece fresh ginger, peeled and chopped

1½ pounds red boiling potatoes, peeled, halved, and sliced lengthwise about ½ inch thick

1 small to medium head cauliflower, cored and cut into medium florets

⅛ teaspoon ground cumin

⅛ teaspoon cayenne pepper

1 fresh hot green chile, chopped

1 teaspoon salt, or to taste

2 tablespoons chopped fresh cilantro

Combine the oil, nigella, if using, cumin, and coriander seeds in a large wok, *kadai,* or frying pan over medium-high heat. Cook, stirring, until the cumin turns golden brown, 2 to 3 minutes.

Add the ginger and cook, stirring, 1 minute. Add the potatoes and stir well to coat with the spices. Then cover and cook until the potatoes have browned some and have begun to soften and stick to the bottom of the pan, 8 to 10 minutes. Stir three or four times during this time and check the cooking. If the potatoes brown too quickly, turn the heat down. If they aren't browning at all, raise the heat.

Add the cauliflower, ground cumin, cayenne, and fresh chile and stir to coat the cauliflower with the spices. Then cover and cook, stirring and scraping the bottom of the pan three or four times during cooking, until the potatoes are well browned, about 10 minutes.

Sprinkle the vegetables with salt, cover, and continue cooking until the cauliflower is nicely browned and the vegetables are tender, 5 to 10 more minutes. Stir the vegetables every 3 to 4 minutes and check the cooking; if they begin to stick badly and burn, add a teaspoon of water and scrape with a spatula to loosen the spices and crispy bits from the bottom of the pan. Sprinkle with the chopped cilantro and serve hot.

cauliflower sautéed with green peppers, tomato, and yogurt

GOBI TAKA TAK

SERVES 4 TO 6

In India, there are restaurants that feature large, circular griddles on which the chefs prepare a variety of dishes called *taka tak*. "Taka taka" is the noise that you hear as the chefs chop and cook the food on the metal griddle, a style of cooking that originated with Indian street vendors. In this recipe, I chop the cauliflower into very small pieces to mimic the results of *taka tak* without the clamor.

2/3 cup canola oil

1 medium head cauliflower, cored and cut into small florets

1/2 teaspoon cumin seeds

1 small or 1/2 large onion, cut into 1/2-inch dice

1 teaspoon salt, or to taste

A 2-inch piece fresh ginger, peeled and minced

2 garlic cloves, minced

1/2 fresh hot green chile, chopped, with seeds

2 teaspoons ground cumin

2 teaspoons garam masala (page 250)

1/2 teaspoon cayenne pepper

1/2 cup plain yogurt

1 green bell pepper, stemmed, seeded, and finely chopped

1 medium tomato, finely chopped

1 tablespoon chopped fresh cilantro

A 1 1/2-inch piece fresh ginger, peeled and cut into julienne, for garnish

Heat the oil in a large wok, *kadai,* or frying pan over medium–high heat. Add the cauliflower and cook, stirring often, until lightly browned, about 10 minutes. Remove with a slotted spoon and drain on paper towels.

Add the cumin seeds to the oil that remains in the pan and cook, stirring, for 1 minute. Add the onion and salt and cook, stirring, until the onion turns brown around the edges, about 5 minutes.

Add the minced ginger, garlic, and green chile and cook, stirring, for 1 minute. Add the ground cumin, garam masala, cayenne, and yogurt and cook, stirring, 2 minutes.

Add the bell pepper, tomato, and cooked cauliflower and cook, stirring, 5 more minutes. Taste for salt. Transfer to a serving dish and sprinkle with the cilantro and julienned ginger. Serve hot.

my sister's favorite corn curry

MAKAYEE NOO CURRY

SERVES 4

My older sister lives in Dallas. Every time I go to see her, she and my brother-in-law make a big fuss about the visit. They invite a lot of their friends and acquaintances to come meet me; this means many dinners at their home. And since my sister has bragged for months about my cooking prowess, I am now called upon to prove it. I invented this dish for one of those occasions. It was inspired by memories of eating similar Gujarati-style corn curries in Bombay while I was in art school there.

GREEN PASTE

1 fresh hot green chile, stemmed and cut in half

½ teaspoon cumin seeds

A 2-inch piece fresh ginger, peeled and cut into large chunks

12 fresh or 16 frozen curry leaves, torn into pieces (optional)

¼ cup fresh cilantro sprigs (with tender stems only)

2 tablespoons water

1 cup milk

1 cup half-and-half

3 tablespoons canola oil

1½ teaspoons cumin seeds

1 teaspoon black mustard seeds (optional)

3 whole dried red chiles

¼ teaspoon turmeric

6 fresh or 10 frozen curry leaves, torn into pieces (optional)

⅛ teaspoon asafetida (optional)

1 tablespoon all-purpose flour

¾ teaspoon salt, or to taste

4 cups fresh corn kernels (cut from about 6 ears) or frozen corn

For the green paste, combine all of the ingredients in a small food processor and process to a paste. Set aside.

Combine the milk and half-and-half in a 2-cup measure or small bowl.

Combine the oil, cumin, and mustard seeds, if using, in a large saucepan over medium-high heat. Cover if using mustard seeds (they pop and splatter) and cook until the cumin turns golden brown or you hear the mustard seeds crackle, 1 to 2 minutes.

Add the chiles, turmeric, and curry leaves and asafetida, if using, and stir. (Stand back if using curry leaves; they spit when they hit the oil.) Immediately add the green paste and turn the heat down to low. Then cook, stirring, 1 minute.

Add the flour and cook, stirring, 1 more minute, scraping the bottom of the pan to keep the flour from sticking. Gradually add the milk mixture, about 1 tablespoon at a time at first, to make a smooth paste. Start to add the milk more quickly, adding the final cup all at once. Stir in the salt and the corn, and bring to a boil. Reduce the heat and simmer, uncovered, until the corn is tender, about 4 minutes. Taste for salt and serve hot.

corn braised gujarati style

MAKAI NU CURRY

SERVES 6 TO 8

This recipe of corn cooked on the cob in a chile-spiked sweet-and-sour broth is inspired by a dish I ate often at my friend Nakul's house in Bombay, where I went to college. His family sort of adopted me because I spent more time at his home than I did at school or in my own room at the YMCA. The corn is traditionally served hot but it tastes good at room temperature too, and as the corn cools it absorbs the spicy broth to become even tastier.

1 cup warm water (if using tamarind)

2 teaspoons tamarind concentrate or
    juice of 1 lemon

3 tablespoons canola oil

1 tablespoon yellow split peas

1/2 teaspoon cumin seeds

1/2 teaspoon coriander seeds

1 branch fresh or frozen curry leaves (optional)

3 tablespoons unsweetened shredded coconut or
    ground almonds

1 1/2 teaspoons ground coriander

1/4 teaspoon turmeric

1/4 cup loosely packed brown sugar

3/4 teaspoon cayenne pepper

1/2 teaspoon garam masala (page 250)

2 teaspoons salt, or to taste

4 fresh ears corn, husked, broken into thirds, and
    washed

4 cups water

1 tablespoon chopped fresh cilantro

If using tamarind, measure the warm water into a small bowl or measuring cup. Add the tamarind concentrate and stir to dissolve it. Rinse the measuring spoon and your fingers in the water to dissolve all of the sticky tamarind. Set this tamarind water aside.

Combine the oil, yellow split peas, cumin, and coriander seeds in a heavy-bottomed soup pot over medium-high heat. Cook, stirring, until the cumin turns golden brown, about 1 minute.

Add the curry leaves, if using, and turn the heat down to low. (Stand back if using curry leaves; they spit when they hit the oil.) Cook, stirring, for 30 seconds.

Add the coconut or ground almonds, ground coriander, and turmeric and cook, stirring, another 30 seconds. Add the tamarind water, if using, or 1 cup water, and bring to a boil. Add the brown sugar, cayenne, garam masala, and salt. Then add the corn and water. Return the liquid to a simmer, cover, and cook 20 minutes.

Remove the corn to a bowl with a slotted spoon. Bring the broth to a boil and boil 5 minutes to reduce. (It will still be quite liquid.) Then return the corn to the pot, turn the heat down, and simmer, uncovered, 5 more minutes. Add the lemon juice, if using, and taste for salt.

Transfer the corn to a serving bowl. Pour the broth over and sprinkle with the cilantro. Serve hot.

smoked spiced eggplant

BAINGAN KAA BHARTAA

SERVES 4 TO 6

This silky-textured spicy and smoky eggplant dish is served in homes across most of northern India. You may know it from Indian restaurant menus in America. I like this particular recipe because it's flavorful and fresh tasting, and not at all oily. Hindus, myself included, don't traditionally like eggplant because its texture is so reminiscent of meat, but prepared this way (and in the recipe that follows), I love it, and most vegetarians I know do, too. Serve this as a vegetable side dish with any Indian meal or grilled meat, poultry, or fish.

1 large eggplant

3 tablespoons canola oil

A 1-inch piece fresh ginger, peeled and finely chopped

1 large red onion, finely chopped

1 teaspoon salt, or to taste

2 garlic cloves, ground to a paste in a mortar and pestle

1 tablespoon unsweetened shredded coconut (optional)

1 tablespoon ground coriander

½ teaspoon ground cumin

½ teaspoon garam masala (page 250)

¼ teaspoon cayenne pepper

2 ripe medium tomatoes, chopped

½ fresh hot green chile, chopped

2 tablespoons chopped fresh cilantro

Juice of ½ lemon

Roast the eggplant directly on the burner of a gas stove over medium heat, turning often, until the skin is completely blackened and the flesh is soft, about 10 minutes. Or, roast the eggplant on a cookie sheet in a 500°F. oven until the skin is blackened, about 20 minutes. Let stand until cool enough to handle, then pull off the skin with your fingers, rinsing your hands under running water as you work. (Don't worry if you can't get all of the charred skin off.) Cut off and discard the stem. Then put the eggplant in a bowl and mash it to a puree with a potato masher.

Heat the oil in a large frying pan, wok, or *kadai* over medium-high heat. Add the ginger and cook, stirring, 30 seconds. Add the onion and salt and cook, stirring often, until the onion begins to brown around the edges, about 10 minutes.

Add the garlic and cook, stirring, until the raw smell disappears, about 30 seconds. Add the coconut, if using, and cook, stirring, 1 minute. Add the coriander, cumin, garam masala, and cayenne and cook, stirring, 1 minute. Now add about 1 tablespoon of water and cook, stirring, until the onion begins to stick, about 1 more minute.

Add the tomatoes and give the mixture a stir. Add the mashed eggplant and cook, stirring often, 5 minutes.

Stir in the fresh chile and 1 tablespoon of the cilantro. Stir in the lemon juice and taste for salt. Spoon into a serving bowl, sprinkle with the remaining tablespoon of cilantro, and serve hot.

chilled smoky eggplant with yogurt and cilantro

DAHI WAALA BHARTAA

Bhartaa literally means "mush" and this eggplant "mushed" with yogurt tastes like an Indian *baba ghanoush*. I serve it as a vegetable side dish, but you might like to try it in place of a raita: it's similarly cool, creamy, and soothing when you eat it with spicy foods. The technique of charring the eggplant gives the dish a nutty flavor that is in lovely contrast to the fresh, acidic taste of the yogurt. This recipe comes from the Mathur families of my Kayastha community.

1 large eggplant

3 tablespoons canola oil

1 medium red onion, chopped, but not too fine

1 teaspoon salt, or to taste

2 cups plain yogurt

A 1-inch piece fresh ginger, peeled and minced

1/2 fresh hot green chile, chopped

2 tablespoons fresh chopped cilantro

1/4 teaspoon garam masala (page 250)

Roast the eggplant directly on the burner of a gas stove over medium heat, turning often, until the skin is completely blackened and the flesh is softened, about 10 minutes. Or, roast the eggplant on a cookie sheet in the oven at 500˚F. until blackened, about 20 minutes. Either way, when cooked, let stand until cool enough to handle. Then pull off the skin with your fingers, rinsing your hands under running water as you work. (Don't worry if you can't get all of the charred skin off.) Cut off and discard the stem. Then put the eggplant in a bowl and mash to a puree with a potato masher.

Heat the oil over medium–high heat in a large frying pan, wok, or *kadai*. Add the onion and salt and cook until the onion is translucent, about 5 minutes.

Add the mashed eggplant and cook, stirring often, until dry, about 10 minutes. Take the pan off the heat and let the eggplant cool for about 5 minutes.

Whisk the yogurt until smooth in a large bowl. Add the eggplant and all of the remaining ingredients and stir well. Chill until cold. Taste for salt and serve cold.

stir-fried mushrooms with onions and tomatoes

KARAHI MUSHROOMS

SERVES 4

Mushrooms are a popular vegetable in northern Indian cuisine, but vegetarian households throughout the country shun them. Don't ask me why; I've asked a hundred times, and the most meaningful answer I've gotten to date is that their texture is too close to that of meat. I like mushrooms a great deal and cook them often—especially in this spicy curry. This recipe is also wonderful served on top of toast as I first tasted it at the Srinagar Club, in the city formerly called Kashmir. I often add dried fenugreek leaves to this curry; their slight bitterness adds a lovely depth of flavor to the sauce. If you'd like to try it, add fenugreek along with the coriander and cayenne.

1/4 cup canola oil

1 teaspoon cumin seeds

1/4 teaspoon carom seeds (*ajawain;* optional)

3 whole dried red chiles

A 2-inch piece fresh ginger, peeled and grated on the large holes of a grater

1 large red onion, cut into 1/2-inch dice

1 fresh hot green chile, cut crosswise into 4 pieces

1 teaspoon salt

2 garlic cloves, minced

1 tablespoon ground coriander

1/4 teaspoon cayenne pepper

1 pound white mushrooms, trimmed and halved or quartered, depending on size

1 large tomato, cut into 1/2-inch dice

1 (8-ounce) can plain tomato sauce

1/4 cup plus 1 tablespoon chopped fresh cilantro

Heat the oil with the cumin, carom seeds, if using, and red chiles in a large wok, *kadai,* or frying pan over medium-high heat. Cook, stirring, until the cumin turns light brown, 1 to 2 minutes.

Add the ginger and cook, stirring, 30 seconds. Add the onion, green chile, and 1/2 teaspoon of the salt and cook, stirring often, until the onion is wilted and beginning to brown around the edges, about 5 minutes.

Turn the heat down to low. Add the garlic, coriander, and cayenne and cook, stirring, 1 minute. Add the mushrooms and turn the heat back up to medium-high. Cook, stirring every now and then, until the mushrooms are mostly cooked through, about 5 minutes.

Now stir in the tomato, tomato sauce, and 1/4 cup of cilantro. Adjust the heat so that the sauce simmers and cook, stirring often, until the sauce thickens around the mushrooms, about 5 more minutes. Taste for salt. Transfer to a serving dish and sprinkle with the remaining tablespoon of cilantro. Serve hot.

mushrooms in a coriander-scented white sauce

KHUMBH DOODHIYA

SERVES 4

I love the dense, meaty texture of mushrooms; as a vegetarian, I don't get to eat many foods with such a satisfying chew. This recipe has a lovely, woodsy mushroom fragrance in a lightly spiced, buttery, creamy sauce. It's excellent with pooris (pages 193 and 198) and a raita.

½ cup (1 stick) unsalted butter

1 medium onion, finely chopped

1 teaspoon salt, or to taste

1 large garlic clove, mashed to a paste in a mortar and
    pestle, or minced

2 teaspoons ground coriander

1½ teaspoons ground cumin

1 tablespoon all-purpose flour

1 cup milk (skim, low-fat, or whole)

1 pound white mushrooms, trimmed and halved or
    quartered, depending on size

¼ teaspoon garam masala (page 250)

1 teaspoon ground white pepper

Heat the butter in a heavy-bottomed saucepan over medium heat. Add the onion and salt and cook, stirring often, until the onion is translucent, about 3 minutes.

Add the garlic and cook, stirring, 1 minute. Add the coriander and cumin and cook, stirring, 1 minute.

Remove the pan from the heat and stir in the flour. Then replace the pan over medium heat and cook, stirring, 2 more minutes. Gradually pour in the milk, stirring constantly to prevent lumps. Then add the mushrooms, give them a stir, and simmer very gently for 5 minutes. Stir often while the mushrooms cook, scraping the bottom and into the corners of the pan to keep the sauce from burning.

Stir in the garam masala and continue to cook at a bare simmer until the mushrooms are tender but still have some bite, 3 to 5 more minutes. Stir in the white pepper and taste for salt. Serve hot.

crisp whole okra with fennel and coriander

SABUT BHINDI

SERVES 4

This is a recipe that one would find, with slight variation, in most vegetarian households throughout northern India. Our dear friend Mansingh, a talented designer who works long hours in retail, often comes by late on summer evenings to help me trim and cook 3 to 5 pounds of okra for a late-night meal. My partner, Chuck, buys beautiful okra at the greenmarket near our house, where he is the one man among the many southern ladies who purchase it. They look at him askance, he says, because he's buying such a quantity. He always makes a point of telling them that's he's buying them to cook Indian style.

Friends who have previously hated okra will forget that they ever have once they taste this recipe—they'll even be clamoring for more.

1 pound small okra
2 tablespoons coriander seeds
4 teaspoons fennel seeds
1 teaspoon salt, or to taste

⅛ teaspoon cayenne pepper
⅓ cup canola oil
⅛ teaspoon asafetida (optional)

Wash and drain the okra. Cut off the stems and the pointed ends. Slit each okra along its entire length without cutting all the way through to the other side. Put the okra into a bowl.

Put the coriander and fennel seeds in a spice grinder and grind to a powder. Add to the bowl with the okra. Add the salt and cayenne, and stir to coat the okra with the spices. (Make sure that some of the spices coat the split insides of the okra.)

Combine the oil and the asafetida, if using, in a large wok, *kadai,* or heavy-bottomed frying pan over medium-low heat. Cook, stirring, until fragrant, about 1 minute.

Turn the heat down to low, add the okra, and stir well to coat with the oil and spices. Then arrange the okra in a single layer in the pan, cover, and cook over low heat until the okra is tender and the pan is dry, about 15 minutes. Stir the okra every 3 to 4 minutes, rearranging it in a single layer each time.

Now uncover and cook, stirring two or three times, until the okra browns lightly, about 5 more minutes. Serve hot.

stir-fried okra with tomatoes, onions, and northern spices

SERVES 4

This is how I make okra when I'm cooking it for myself or my family, and I don't want to spend a lot of time or energy. I very often make it in advance, then reheat it in a 300°F. oven for 15 to 20 minutes, keeping a watchful eye on it so that it doesn't burn. Reheating dries it out a bit, concentrating the flavors and making the okra taste even better. It lasts two or three days in the refrigerator, but I doubt if you will have any left over.

1/3 cup canola oil

1 teaspoon cumin seeds

A 2-inch piece fresh ginger, peeled and minced

1 medium red onion, halved and thinly sliced

1 tablespoon ground coriander

1/2 teaspoon ground cumin

1/2 teaspoon turmeric

1/8 teaspoon cayenne pepper

1 pound okra, trimmed of both stem and pointed ends, and cut crosswise into 1/2-inch pieces

1 teaspoon salt, or to taste

2 medium tomatoes, cut into medium dice

1/2 fresh hot green chile, minced

1 tablespoon fresh lemon juice

2 tablespoons chopped fresh cilantro

Combine the oil and cumin seeds in a large wok, *kadai,* or frying pan over medium-high heat. Cook, stirring, until fragrant, 1 to 2 minutes.

Add the ginger and cook, stirring, 30 seconds. Add the onion, turn the heat to medium-high, and cook until wilted, about 3 minutes.

Add the coriander, ground cumin, turmeric, and cayenne; turn the heat down to medium and cook, stirring, for 30 seconds. Add the okra and stir to coat with the spices. Then cover and cook until the okra browns lightly, about 5 minutes. Stir once or twice during this time and check the cooking; if the spices begin to burn, turn the heat down. If the okra doesn't brown at all, turn the heat up a bit.

Give the okra a stir. Add the salt, tomatoes, and green chile and stir well, scraping the bottom of the pan to make sure that nothing is sticking. Then turn the heat down to low, cover, and cook 5 more minutes.

Uncover and cook over high heat, stirring every now and then, until the okra is tender and the liquid has reduced, about 5 more minutes. Stir in the lemon juice and cilantro and taste for salt. Serve hot.

spicy peas sautéed with ginger

MATAR KEE CHAAT

SERVES 4

My father's cousin, Sunita Bua, used to make these peas for me and my family when we'd visit her during the winter months. She knew my father loved them, and as we always dropped by unannounced, she needed a dish that cooked quickly, as these do. We'd eat the peas as a snack, on top of toast, with a dab of mint chutney. You may also serve the peas as a side dish, of course; I particularly like them with a chicken curry. I also use the peas to rim the edge of Party Cauliflower (page 56) for a contrasting color.

Any leftover peas I use in a frittata: put the peas in an ovenproof frying pan seasoned with olive oil, pour over eggs whisked with salt and pepper, and cook, covered, over low heat for about 5 minutes or until the base is just set and the top still liquid. Uncover and finish in a 450°F. oven until the eggs are set and puffy, about 10 minutes.

1 tablespoon plus 2 teaspoons cumin seeds

3 tablespoons canola oil

3 whole dried red chiles

A 4-inch piece fresh ginger, peeled and grated

1 fresh hot green chile, cut crosswise into 5 pieces

1/8 teaspoon asafetida (optional)

2 (10-ounce) packages frozen petite peas, unthawed

1/2 teaspoon cayenne pepper

1 1/2 teaspoons salt, or to taste

1 bunch fresh cilantro, finely chopped

Juice of 1 lime

Lemon wedges, for serving

Put 1 tablespoon of the cumin seeds in a heavy frying pan and toast over medium heat, stirring often, until lightly browned and fragrant, 2 to 3 minutes. Transfer to a spice grinder and grind to a powder. Set aside.

Combine the oil, remaining 2 teaspoons cumin seeds, and the red chiles in a large wok, *kadai,* or frying pan over medium-high heat. Cook, stirring, until the cumin turns golden brown, about 1 minute. Add the ginger, green chile, and asafetida, if using, and cook, stirring, 1 minute.

Add the peas, cayenne, salt, and half of the cilantro. Cover and cook until the peas are tender, about 10 minutes. Stir three or four times and check the cooking; if the spices begin to burn, turn the heat down. Stir in the lime and toasted cumin.

Taste for salt. Transfer to a serving dish and sprinkle with the remaining cilantro. Serve hot, with lemon wedges.

sweet green peas and fresh indian cheese in a fragrant tomato sauce

MATAR PANEER

SERVES 6

You may be familiar with saag paneer (page 80), a standard in Indian restaurants in America. This dish is made with peas instead of spinach and the cubes of paneer (fresh Indian cheese) are cooked with the peas and a thin tomato sauce which has a beautifully light, silky texture (it's almost thin enough to be a soup). Because of the way the spices are cooked into the dish, it has an elegant and complex flavor. Serve with rice and Stir-Fried Cauliflower and Potato with Crunchy Bengali Spices (page 58).

Paneer is traditionally made by bringing whole milk to a boil and curdling it with lemon juice, vinegar, or yogurt. Then the whey is drained off and the curds are wrapped in cheesecloth and weighted to compress the cheese into a firm cake. I've simplified this process by starting with ricotta cheese instead of milk and then baking it to firm it into cheese.

PANEER

1 pound whole-milk ricotta cheese

1/2 to 1 tablespoon canola oil

SAUCE

3 small garlic cloves

1 1/8 teaspoons cumin seeds

1/4 cup canola oil

A 1 1/2-inch piece cinnamon stick

6 green or 3 black cardamom pods

5 whole cloves

12 to 15 black peppercorns

4 whole dried red chiles

1/2 teaspoon coriander seeds

1 bay leaf

1 1/2 medium red onions, chopped

2 teaspoons salt, or to taste

A 2-inch piece fresh ginger, peeled and minced

1 1/2 teaspoons ground coriander

1 teaspoon ground cumin

1/2 teaspoon turmeric

1/4 teaspoon cayenne pepper

1 pound tomatoes (about 3 medium), very finely chopped

2 tablespoons plain yogurt

1 pound frozen petite peas, unthawed

1/8 teaspoon garam masala (page 250)

2 tablespoons chopped fresh cilantro

For the paneer, preheat the oven to 450°F. Spread the ricotta evenly in a 9 x 5-inch bread pan and bake until the cheese is lightly browned on top and firm but not dry, about 40 minutes. Let cool (it will firm as it cools), then cut the paneer into 1- to 1 1/2-inch squares. Reserve half and refrigerate or freeze the rest for another use.

Heat 1/2 tablespoon of the oil in a large nonstick pan over medium-high heat. Add as many squares of paneer as will comfortably fit and brown the squares on all sides. Drain the cheese on paper towels. Continue this way to brown all of the paneer, adding 1/2 tablespoon more oil as needed. Set the paneer aside.

For the sauce, combine the garlic and 1/8 teaspoon of the cumin seeds in a mortar and pestle or an electric spice grinder and grind to a paste.

Put the oil, cinnamon, cardamom, cloves, and peppercorns in a large, deep pot over medium-high heat. Cook, stirring, until the cinnamon stick unfurls, 1 to 2 minutes. Add the chiles, the remaining 1 teaspoon of the cumin seeds, the coriander seeds, and bay leaf and cook, stirring, until the seeds turn golden brown, about 1 minute.

Add the onions and salt and cook, stirring often, until the onions turn a uniform golden brown, 10 to 12 minutes. Keep a cup of water beside of the stove as the onions cook. As the onions begin to stick, add water, about 1 teaspoon at a time, and scrape the bottom of the pan with the spoon to pull up the browned bits and keep the spices from burning. Do this as often as necessary (five or six times) until the onions are well browned.

Add the ginger and cook, stirring, 3 to 4 minutes, adding water as needed to keep the onions and spices from sticking. Stir 1 teaspoon of water into the garlic paste. When the ginger has cooked, add this garlic paste to the pot and cook until the water has evaporated, 1 to 2 minutes.

Add the ground coriander, cumin, turmeric, cayenne, and about 1 tablespoon water and cook until the mixture begins to dry out and stick to the bottom of the pan, about 1 minute. Add the tomatoes and cook until they begin to dissolve, 3 to 4 minutes. Then turn down the heat and cook until the tomatoes have completely melted into the sauce and the oil is starting to pool around the onions, 2 to 3 more minutes.

Whisk the yogurt until smooth in a small bowl. Stir in a spoonful of the hot sauce to temper the yogurt and then return the mixture to the pot. Add 2 cups of water and the peas. Cover, bring to a simmer, and cook until the peas have thawed, 4 to 5 minutes.

Fold in the paneer and sprinkle the garam masala and 1 tablespoon cilantro over the top. Cover and simmer very gently until the peas are softened and the cheese is warmed through, 3 to 5 more minutes. Taste for salt. Transfer to a serving bowl and sprinkle with the remaining cilantro. Serve hot.

stuffed bell peppers

BHARWAAN MIRCHEE

SERVES 4

The connection between food and visual arts has always fascinated me. These spiced potato–stuffed peppers in particular caught my attention as a very young boy because they were the first food that looked as good to me as they tasted. They showed me how easily food could become art. You can increase both the heat and the flavor of this dish by stirring some of the bell pepper seeds into the potato stuffing, as I often do: the seeds give it a spicy, sweet heat that is unique to bell peppers. Or, if you'd like to reduce the spice, use the flesh of the green chile but not its seeds.

1 1/2 pounds red boiling potatoes

4 small bell peppers (red, yellow, and/or orange peppers)

1 teaspoon coriander seeds

1 teaspoon cumin seeds

1/4 teaspoon cayenne pepper

1/2 fresh hot green chile, minced

2 tablespoons chopped fresh cilantro

1 tablespoon chopped fresh mint

Juice of 1 lime or lemon

1 teaspoon salt

1/4 teaspoon freshly ground black pepper

1 large egg whisked with a pinch each of salt and cayenne pepper

2 tablespoons canola oil

Put the potatoes in a saucepan with cold water to cover and boil until very tender, 30 to 40 minutes. Drain.

Meanwhile, cut around the stems of the peppers, removing about a 2-inch round from the top of each. Pull out and discard these tops. Scrape out the ribs and the seeds with a small knife. Set the peppers aside.

Toast the coriander and cumin seeds in a dry skillet over medium-high heat, stirring constantly, until fragrant, 1 to 2 minutes. Coarsely grind in a mortar and pestle or spice grinder.

When the potatoes are cooked, peel and mash them in a large bowl. Add the ground toasted coriander-cumin mixture, the cayenne, green chile, cilantro, mint, lime or lemon juice, salt, and black pepper, and stir to blend. Taste for salt, then spoon the mixture into the peppers.

Preheat the oven to 400°F. Heat the oil in a large ovenproof frying pan over medium heat. When the pan is hot, dip the peppers, cut sides down, into the egg to coat the potato stuffing. Put the peppers egg side down in the pan and cook until the egg has browned and formed a crust, about 3 minutes. Then turn the peppers right side up and put the pan in the oven. Bake until the peppers are tender, about 30 minutes. Serve hot.

plantains in curry

SERVES 8

A curry is an excellent way to prepare plantains. The mild-tasting plantains are first fried, to give them a thin, light crust, then simmered in a yogurt sauce spiced with cinnamon, cumin, cloves, and cardamom that moistens the starchy vegetable while it infuses it with subtle spice.

Some Caribbean cuisines make a similar dish because Indians from the subcontinent, brought to the islands by the British, also brought their green banana curries. The plantains in America are somewhat drier, so I pound them a bit after boiling and before I fry them to help them absorb the sauce. Serve this with an Indian bread or rice and Spicy Peas Sautéed with Ginger (page 69).

4 green (unripe) plantains, unpeeled

1/3 cup canola oil, plus extra for deep-frying

1 large white or red onion, pureed in a food processor

1 teaspoon salt, or to taste

A 2-inch piece fresh ginger, peeled and grated

3 small garlic cloves, minced

A 1-inch piece cinnamon stick

3 whole cloves

1/4 teaspoon black peppercorns

1/4 teaspoon cumin seeds

6 green cardamom pods

1/8 teaspoon ground cardamom

1 teaspoon ground coriander

2 cups plain yogurt, whisked until smooth

1 1/4 cups water

1/2 teaspoon garam masala (page 250)

2 tablespoons finely chopped fresh cilantro

Bring a large pot of water to a boil. Add the unpeeled plantains and simmer 15 minutes. Drain and set aside until cool enough to handle, then peel. Cut each plantain in half crosswise and then cut each half in half again lengthwise.

Heat 1 1/2 to 2 inches of oil in a medium wok, *kadai,* or large saucepan over medium heat to 360°F. (To gauge the temperature of the oil without using a thermometer, drop a piece of bread about 1-inch square into the hot oil over medium heat, turning often; when the oil has reached 360°F., the bread will turn an even, golden-brown color—like a crouton—in about 30 seconds.) Gently slide as many of the plantain quarters as will comfortably fit into the oil and fry, turning every now and then with a slotted spoon until golden brown and crisp all over, 3 to 4 minutes. Drain on paper towels. Repeat to fry all of the plantains. Set aside.

Heat the 1/3 cup oil in a large, heavy-bottomed saucepan over medium-high heat. Add the pureed onion and the salt, and cook, stirring, until the onion is golden brown, about 15 minutes. Keep a cup of water beside the stove while the onion cooks. As the onion begins to stick to the bottom of the pan, add water, about 1 teaspoon at a time, and scrape the pan with the spoon to pull up the browned bits and keep the onion from burning. Do this as often as necessary (five or six times) until the onion is well browned.

Add the ginger and garlic, and cook, stirring, until the raw smell of the garlic disappears, about 1 minute. Sprinkle with about 1 tablespoon water during the cooking and scrape the bottom of the pan to keep the aromatics from sticking.

Add the cinnamon stick, cloves, peppercorns, cumin, whole and ground cardamom, and ground coriander and cook, stirring, 2 minutes. Turn the heat down to low. Stir in the yogurt, adding the first cup ¼ cup at a time, and then the second cup all at once, until blended. Stir in the water and garam masala. Bring to a simmer and simmer gently over low heat for 10 minutes.

Add the fried plantains to the sauce and simmer very gently 5 more minutes. The plantains will absorb some of the sauce and thicken it. Taste for salt. Then carefully transfer the plantains to a serving platter with a slotted spoon and spoon the sauce over. Sprinkle with the chopped cilantro and serve hot.

stir-fried sweet peppers

SIMLA MIRCHI

SERVES 4 TO 6

This is a delectable and very savory dish: the sweetness of the red onion and pepper is beautifully balanced by the heat and spice of the Indian pickle oil. Since I make most of my own pickles, including oil-cured pickles, I always have plenty of some kind of pickle or oil on hand. Use oil from the Green Chile Pickle (page 204) or the tomato chutney, or just buy a pickle (such as mango pickle) from an Indian grocer. Serve with toasted pita bread and plain yogurt.

¼ cup pickle oil from any type of oil-cured Indian pickle, including spices (about half the volume of oil should be spices)

2 tablespoons canola oil

1 teaspoon nigella seeds (*kalaunji;* optional)

1 teaspoon cumin seeds

½ teaspoon green cardamom pods

¼ teaspoon fennel seeds

2 medium red onions, halved through the core end, each half cut in half crosswise and then sliced ½ inch thick (to make short, thick slices)

1 teaspoon salt, or to taste

2 each green, yellow, and red bell peppers, stemmed, seeded, and cut into ½-inch strips

2 medium tomatoes, halved and very thinly sliced

Combine the pickle and canola oils, nigella, if using, cumin, cardamom, and fennel seeds in a large wok, *kadai*, or frying pan over medium–high heat and cook, stirring, until fragrant, 1 to 2 minutes.

Add the onions and salt, and cook, stirring, until the onions are wilted and lightly browned, about 5 minutes.

Add the peppers and cook, stirring, for 3 minutes. Then reduce the heat to low, cover, and cook 10 minutes, stirring three separate times during the cooking. Check the peppers and spices as they cook—if they begin to burn, turn the heat down.

Now add the tomatoes, turn the heat to medium, and cook, covered, for 5 minutes. Turn the heat to high, uncover the pan, and cook, stirring often, until the liquid evaporates, about 5 more minutes. Taste for salt and serve hot.

potatoes braised in a fragrant yogurt sauce

DAM ALOO

SERVES 4 TO 6

A lot of recipes for this potato dish have been published; it's one of the most celebrated in Indian vegetarian cuisine. I have friends from Kashmir and Lucknow, two places that claim ownership of *dam aloo,* who both swear that my recipe is the same as their grandmothers'.

This is even tastier a day or two after it is prepared, so it's a natural for entertaining. Make it ahead of time and refrigerate it, then bring it to room temperature before reheating. For a simple meal, it goes perfectly with rice or warm toasted pita bread. For a more elaborate meal, try it with Smoked Spiced Eggplant (page 63) and a dal.

I make this with the tiniest potatoes I can find, 1 to 2 inches wide, because the dish is pretty that way. But you can use larger potatoes just as well; cut them into 1- to 2-inch pieces.

SPICE POWDER

¼ teaspoon black peppercorns

8 whole cloves

8 green cardamom pods

1 tablespoon coriander seeds

1 teaspoon cumin seeds

3 medium red onions

A 2-inch piece fresh ginger, peeled and cut crosswise into 4 pieces

3 garlic cloves

2 pounds very small (1- to 2-inch-wide) red boiling potatoes, peeled; or larger potatoes, peeled and cut into chunks

Salt

½ cup canola oil, plus extra for deep-frying

A ½-inch piece cinnamon stick

4 green cardamom pods

2 bay leaves

½ teaspoon turmeric

½ teaspoon cayenne pepper

1½ cups plain yogurt

1 cup water

¼ cup chopped fresh cilantro

For the spice powder, combine the ingredients in a small frying pan and toast over medium heat, stirring constantly, until the cumin is a nice golden color, 2 to 3 minutes. Let cool and then grind to a fine powder in a spice grinder. Set aside.

Thinly slice one of the onions and set aside. Coarsely chop the other two onions and put them in a blender or food processor along with the ginger and garlic. Process to a puree, adding 1 to 2 tablespoons water as needed. Set aside.

Put the potatoes in a bowl and add cold water to cover. Add 1 to 2 teaspoons salt; the water should taste lightly salted. Soak the potatoes in this salty water for 15 minutes. Drain and pat dry with paper towels, then arrange on a wide plate.

Heat 1 to 1½ inches of oil in a medium *kadai* or large saucepan over medium heat to about 360°F. (To gauge the temperature of the oil without using a thermometer, drop a piece of bread about 1-inch square into the hot oil over medium heat, turning often; when the oil has reached 360°F., the bread will turn an even, golden-brown color—like a crouton—in about 30 seconds.) Turn the heat down to medium-low and carefully slide about half of the potatoes into the oil. Cook, stirring every now and then, until golden brown all over, about 10 minutes. Remove from the oil with a slotted spoon and drain on a plate lined with paper towels. Repeat to cook and drain the remaining potatoes. Then use a fork to poke the potatoes all over with holes. (This will help them to absorb the sauce.)

While the potatoes are frying, heat the 1/2 cup of oil, the cinnamon stick, cardamom, and bay leaves in a large heavy-bottomed pot over medium-high heat. Cook, stirring, until the cinnamon stick unfurls, 1 to 2 minutes.

Add the reserved pureed onion mixture, the sliced onion, and 1 teaspoon salt and cook, stirring often, until the onion is dry and golden brown and the oil begins to separate out of the mixture, about 30 minutes. The onion will bubble and splatter as it begins to cook, so stand back from the pan. Keep a cup of water next to the stove. As the onion begins to stick to the bottom of the pan, sprinkle a little of the water, about 1 teaspoon at a time, over the onion and scrape the pan with the spoon to pull up the browned bits and keep the onion from burning.

Add the reserved spice powder, the turmeric, and cayenne and cook, stirring, for another minute or two.

Continue to add water as necessary, about a teaspoon at a time, to keep the spices from sticking. Turn the heat down to low.

Whisk the yogurt in a small bowl until smooth. Spoon a few tablespoons of the sauce into the yogurt to temper it and whisk to combine. Now whisk the yogurt into the sauce, 1/2 cup at a time, to make a thick sauce. Add 3/4 teaspoon of salt, the potatoes, and the water and mix well. Cover and simmer very gently until the potatoes are tender, about 30 minutes. Give the potatoes a stir about 5 minutes into the cooking but then keep the pot closed, and just shake it every 5 to 10 minutes to keep the potatoes from sticking. Taste for salt. Transfer to a serving dish and sprinkle with the cilantro. Serve hot.

crispy potatoes with cumin

ZEERA ALOO

SERVES 4

Zeera aloo is one of the most popular potato dishes in the cuisine of northern India. It's simple, tasty, and goes with practically everything. When my friend Rozanne Gold published this recipe in her book *Healthy 1,2,3,* she amended it to use grapeseed instead of canola oil because it has a higher smoking point and browns even better than canola. I've retained her change, but if you can't find grapeseed, canola oil will work well enough. If you like spicy food, add ¹/₂ teaspoon of cayenne at the very end.

1¹/₂ **pounds red boiling potatoes, scrubbed but not peeled**

3 tablespoons grapeseed or canola oil

2 teaspoons cumin seeds

³/₄ **teaspoon salt, or to taste**

¹/₂ **teaspoon ground black pepper**

¹/₂ **teaspoon cayenne pepper (optional)**

Put the potatoes in a pot with cold water to cover. Bring to a boil, turn the heat down, and simmer, covered, until tender, about 30 minutes. Drain, let cool, and refrigerate until very cold. Then peel and cut the potatoes into 1-inch cubes.

Heat the oil with the cumin in a large wok or nonstick frying pan over medium-high heat and cook, stirring, until fragrant, 1 to 2 minutes.

Add the potatoes and cook, stirring often, until a crisp, golden brown crust forms, 10 to 15 minutes.

Stir in the salt, black pepper, and cayenne, if using. Taste for salt and serve hot.

whole spiced baby potatoes

SABUT ALOO

SERVES 4

Panditji used to make this in the spring with the first tiny new potatoes. He would choose the smallest potatoes, with no blemishes, and cook them with their tender peels on. When I can find that quality of spring baby potatoes at our greenmarket, I do the same because I love to eat the peel, but I do peel grocery-store potatoes that are not so fine. These are particularly good with an omelet or scrambled eggs, for brunch, with pooris (pages 193 and 198).

3 tablespoons canola oil

1¼ teaspoons cumin seeds

3 whole dried red chiles

1 pound smallest possible baby potatoes, washed
(larger potatoes peeled and cut into chunks)

1½ teaspoons ground coriander

1 teaspoon ground fennel seed

½ teaspoon turmeric

½ teaspoon garam masala (page 250)

1 teaspoon salt, or to taste

⅛ teaspoon cayenne pepper

½ lemon or lime

Combine the oil, cumin, and red chiles in a large wok, *kadai,* or frying pan over medium–high heat. Cook, stirring, until the cumin browns lightly, 1 to 2 minutes. Add the potatoes and cook, stirring, 3 to 4 minutes.

Add the coriander, fennel, turmeric, garam masala, and salt and stir to coat the potatoes with the spices. Turn the heat down to low, cover, and cook until the potatoes are tender, about 15 minutes. Stir often, very gently, to keep the potatoes from sticking, adding a few tablespoons water if they do begin to stick. (If the spices begin to burn, turn the heat down.)

Sprinkle with the cayenne and squeeze the lemon or lime juice over. Stir and taste for salt. Serve hot.

indian cheese in an herbed green sauce

SAAG PANEER

SERVES 4

Saag paneer is a northern dish that originated in the states of Kashmir and Punjab. These days, cooks throughout India make it. I like to make it with spinach. You might try other tender, fresh greens such as mustard, beet, or collard greens, in combination with spinach. Frozen spinach works just fine, too.

The tempering oil is traditional but not necessary. *Saag paneer* is traditionally eaten with chapatis and plain rice, but I sometimes just toast pita bread to serve with it.

PANEER

1 pound whole-milk ricotta cheese

$^1/_2$ to 1 tablespoon canola oil

A 1-pound bag fresh spinach, stemmed and washed,
    or 1 pound frozen spinach, unthawed

1 tablespoon ghee, butter, or canola oil

3 whole dried red chiles

$^3/_4$ teaspoon cumin seeds

7 green cardamom pods

7 whole cloves

$^3/_4$ teaspoon fennel seeds

$^1/_8$ teaspoon asafetida (optional)

1 tablespoon finely chopped fresh ginger

$^1/_2$ teaspoon salt, or to taste

TEMPERING OIL (OPTIONAL)

1 tablespoon ghee or canola oil

$^1/_2$ teaspoon cumin seeds

$^1/_4$ teaspoon fennel seeds

1 whole dried red chile

$^1/_8$ teaspoon asafetida (optional)

$^1/_8$ teaspoon cayenne pepper

For the paneer, preheat the oven to 450°F. Spread the ricotta evenly in a 9 × 5-inch loaf pan. Bake until the cheese is lightly browned on top and firm but not dry, about 40 minutes. Let cool (the cheese will firm as it cools), then cut into 1- to 1$^1/_2$-inch squares. Reserve half and refrigerate or freeze the rest for another use.

Heat $^1/_2$ tablespoon of the oil in a large nonstick pan over medium-high heat. Add as many squares of paneer as will comfortably fit and brown the squares on all sides. Drain the cheese on paper towels. Continue this way to brown all of the paneer, adding $^1/_2$ tablespoon more oil as needed. Set the paneer aside.

Bring about 2 inches of water to a boil in a large pot. Add the spinach, cover, and steam, stirring every now and then, until fresh spinach is wilted or frozen spinach is thawed, about 5 minutes. Drain, reserving the cooking water, and puree in a blender or food processor, adding a few tablespoons of the cooking water if necessary for pureeing.

Heat the ghee, butter, or oil with the red chiles, cumin, cardamom, cloves, and fennel seeds in a large wok, *kadai*, or frying pan over medium-high heat. Cook, stirring, until the cumin turns a golden brown color, 1 to 2 minutes. Stir in the asafetida, if using. Then add the ginger and cook, stirring, 30 seconds. Add the fenugreek leaves, if using, and cook, stirring, 15 seconds. Add the spinach puree and the salt. Cook, uncovered, over medium heat, 5 minutes.

Gently place the paneer squares on top of the greens. Cover and cook gently 5 more minutes. Halfway through the cooking, use a large spatula to gently turn the paneer in the spinach. (Careful, the paneer will break easily.) Taste the greens for salt.

For the tempering oil (if using), heat the ghee or oil with the cumin, fennel seeds, and red chile in a small frying pan or *kadai* over medium-high heat. Cook, stirring, until the seeds turn a golden brown color, 1 to 2 minutes. Add the asafetida, if using, and cayenne and pour immediately into the spinach mixture. Give it a stir and serve hot.

spinach with potatoes

PAALAK WALLAE ALOO

SERVES 4

This is a version of *saag paneer* (see page 80) made with potatoes instead of paneer. Unlike the traditional recipe, I do not puree the spinach, but leave it just chopped for a rougher, chewier texture. You'll taste many of the same spices as in the original recipe, but I've added garam masala—for its subtle heat—and whole coriander seeds that, along with the fennel, explode in layers of flavor when you bite into them. I cook this recipe when I'm homesick and craving a simple home-cooked Indian meal. Serve with warm toasted pita bread or Parathas (page 194), or with your favorite dal and plain steamed rice.

1 pound fresh spinach, stemmed, washed, and chopped

3 tablespoons canola oil

1 teaspoon cumin seeds

1 teaspoon fennel seeds

2 bay leaves

3 whole dried red chiles

1 medium red onion, thinly sliced

1/2 fresh hot green chile, minced

1 pound red boiling potatoes, peeled and cut into 1/2- to 3/4-inch cubes

2 garlic cloves, minced

2 teaspoons ground coriander

1 teaspoon ground cumin

1/4 teaspoon ground ginger

1 teaspoon salt, or to taste

1/2 teaspoon garam masala (page 250)

Bring about 2 inches of water to a boil in a large pot. Add the spinach, stir well, cover, and steam, stirring every now and then, until wilted, about 5 minutes. Drain and set aside.

Combine the oil, cumin, fennel seeds, bay leaves, and chiles in the same pot over medium-high heat. Cook, stirring, until the cumin darkens slightly, 1 to 2 minutes.

Add the onion and green chile and cook, stirring, about 30 seconds. Add the potatoes and garlic, and cook, stirring and scraping the bottom of the pan, until the potatoes are translucent around the edges, about 5 minutes.

Add the coriander, cumin, and ginger, and stir well to coat the potatoes with the oil and spices. Cover and cook 15 minutes, stirring every 5 minutes, scraping the bottom of the pan to keep the spices from sticking. Add the wilted spinach and the salt, stir well, and cook until the potatoes are tender, about 5 more minutes.

Stir in the garam masala and cook 1 minute. Taste for salt and serve hot.

sweet-and-sour butternut squash with ginger and chiles

KADDU KEE SABZI

SERVES 4 TO 6

In my grandmother's home in Delhi, guests would arrive begging to eat Panditji's preparation of this very simple and humble vegetable. His recipe, reproduced here, was fabled to be deliciously addictive, as you will soon discover. *Kaddu* is the Hindi word for the oblong Indian pumpkin. In America, I use butternut squash instead: it comes close enough in flavor and makes it unnecessary to go hunting for the real thing in Asian markets. The end result is a dish that is authentic in taste and just as beautifully orange. Try it with a traditional Thanksgiving meal.

A 2- to 2 1/4-pound butternut squash

3 tablespoons canola oil

A 1-inch piece fresh ginger, peeled and minced

1 fresh hot green chile, chopped

1/4 teaspoon fenugreek seeds (optional)

1/4 teaspoon cayenne pepper

1/8 teaspoon asafetida (optional)

1 1/2 teaspoons salt, or to taste

1 1/2 teaspoons sugar

Juice of 1/2 lemon or lime, or 2 teaspoons dried mango powder *(amchur)*

Cut the squash in half lengthwise. Peel it with a vegetable peeler or a paring knife and scrape out the seeds. Cut the two halves lengthwise into 1/2-inch-thick strips. Then cut the strips crosswise into 1 1/2-inch pieces.

Heat the oil in a large wok, *kadai,* or frying pan over medium-high heat. Add the ginger and cook, stirring, 1 minute. Add the fresh chile, fenugreek, if using, cayenne, and asafetida, if using, and cook, stirring, 30 seconds.

Add the squash and stir to coat with the oil. Stir in the salt and sugar. Turn the heat down to medium. Cover and cook until the squash is tender, about 25 minutes. Uncover and stir the squash every 5 minutes and check on the cooking; if the spices begin to burn, turn the heat down. If the squash doesn't brown at all, turn the heat up slightly.

Stir in the lemon or lime juice, or dried mango powder. Mash the squash with a spoon to break up some of the pieces. Taste for salt and serve hot.

stir-fried mixed summer squash

SQUASH PORIYAL

SERVES 6

Even in the dead of winter, cooking this dish brings summer into my home. It makes my spirits rise just to look at the green and yellow of the squash. And then as I taste it, I find myself in the bright light of a cool summer morning in India, before the air gets heavy and humid. Coconut and curry leaves lend a deep and satisfying flavor to the otherwise mild squash, and the mustard seeds give it crunch and a nutty taste.

3 tablespoons canola oil

1 tablespoon black mustard seeds

1 teaspoon cumin seeds

1/4 teaspoon turmeric

3 whole dried red chiles

1/2 fresh hot green chile, chopped

12 fresh or 16 frozen curry leaves, torn into pieces

1/8 teaspoon asafetida (optional)

1/4 cup shredded unsweetened coconut (optional)

2 1/2 pounds zucchini and yellow squash, trimmed, halved lengthwise, and then cut crosswise into 1/3-inch-thick slices

1/2 teaspoon salt, or to taste

Combine the oil and mustard seeds in a large wok, *kadai,* or frying pan over medium-high heat. Cover (the mustard seeds pop and splatter) and cook until you hear the mustard seeds crackle, 1 to 2 minutes.

Add the cumin seeds, turmeric, dried and fresh chiles, and curry leaves, and the asafetida and coconut if using. (Stand back; the curry leaves spit when they hit the oil.) Turn the heat down to low and cook uncovered, stirring, until the coconut begins to turn golden brown, about 1 minute.

Add the squash and turn the heat back up to medium-high. Stir to coat the squash with the spices. Then cook, stirring often, for 5 minutes.

Add the salt and cook, stirring, until the squash is tender but still has some bite, 3 to 4 minutes longer. Taste for salt and serve hot.

crisp yam and green peas

MATAR ZIMIKAND

SERVES 4 TO 6

This is North Indian, and particularly Delhi, cuisine. Our Indian *zimikand* are much bigger than American yams and not at all sweet, but I've used yams often in this recipe to replace *zimikand* and they taste perfect. If you want to try the real thing, you can buy *zimikand* in Indian grocery stores as well as in some Caribbean stores.

1 large yam (about 1 pound), washed and cut crosswise
    into 3 pieces
1/4 cup canola oil, plus extra for deep-frying
1/2 teaspoon cumin seeds
2 teaspoons ground coriander
1/2 teaspoon turmeric
1/4 teaspoon ground cumin
1/8 teaspoon cayenne pepper
2 medium tomatoes, pureed in a blender or food
    processor

1 1/2 teaspoons salt, or to taste
1 (10-ounce) package frozen petite peas, unthawed
1 cup water
1 cup plain yogurt
Juice of 1/2 lemon or lime, or 1/4 teaspoon dried mango
    powder *(amchur)*
1/4 teaspoon garam masala (page 250)
1 tablespoon chopped fresh cilantro

Put the yam in a saucepan with cold water to cover and simmer until almost tender, about 25 minutes. Drain and let stand until cool enough to handle. Then skin and cut the yam into 1-inch cubes.

Heat 1 1/2 to 2 inches of oil in a large saucepan or medium *kadai* over medium heat to 360°F. (To gauge the temperature of the oil without using a thermometer, drop a piece of bread about 1-inch square into the hot oil over medium heat, turning often; when the oil reaches 360°F., the bread should begin to brown almost immediately—like a crouton—and turn golden brown in about 30 seconds.) Turn the heat down to medium-low and carefully slide about half of the yam cubes into the oil. Cook, stirring every now and then with a slotted spoon, until they develop a crisp brown crust, about 10 minutes. Remove with a spoon and drain on paper towels; set aside.

Combine the 1/4 cup oil and cumin seeds in a large saucepan over medium-high heat. Cook, stirring, until the cumin begins to brown, 1 to 2 minutes. Add the coriander, turmeric, and ground cumin and cook, stirring, for another minute. Add the cayenne and then immediately pour in the tomato puree. Stir in the salt, bring to a simmer, and cook until the oil forms a glaze on the surface of the sauce, about 5 minutes.

Add the fried yam, the peas, and water and swirl the pan to mix. (The yams are very fragile and will break if stirred.) Simmer until the peas and yam are completely tender, about 10 minutes.

Whisk the yogurt until smooth in a medium bowl. Spoon a few tablespoons of the tomato sauce into the yogurt and stir well to temper the yogurt. Stir in the mango powder, if using, and the garam masala. Then pour into the sauce and swirl to mix well. Cover and cook over low heat 5 more minutes. Add the lemon or lime juice, if using, taste for salt, and transfer to a serving bowl. Sprinkle with chopped cilantro and serve hot.

vegetable jhalfrazie

SERVES 6 TO 8

My mother's friend Abha Aunty (in India, close women friends are often affectionately referred to as "aunty," intimate men friends as "uncle"), who was famous for making dishes that were somewhat exotic for northern Indian cuisine, often served this simple vegetable stew at her home. The ketchup adds a sweet taste that is not often found in northern cuisine, complemented by the cinnamon, cloves, and cumin of the garam masala. You can use any vegetable that you like in this dish, but it's critical that the tomatoes be very ripe.

3 tablespoons canola oil

A 2-inch piece fresh ginger, peeled and minced

2 large onions, coarsely chopped

2 teaspoons salt, or to taste

1½ tablespoons ground coriander

1 pound carrots, peeled and sliced ⅛ inch thick

¾ pound green beans, trimmed at both ends and cut into 1-inch lengths

1 fresh green hot chile, sliced about ⅛ inch thick

½ teaspoon garam masala (page 250)

½ teaspoon cayenne pepper

¼ cup ketchup

2 very ripe tomatoes, cut into medium dice

10 ounces frozen petite peas, unthawed

1 cup water

1 tablespoon chopped fresh cilantro

Heat the oil in a large wok, *kadai,* or frying pan over medium-high heat. Add the ginger and cook, stirring, 30 seconds.

Add the onions and 1 teaspoon of the salt and cook, stirring, until the onions begin to brown around the edges, about 5 minutes. Add the coriander and cook, stirring, 1 minute. Add the carrots, green beans, and fresh chile and cook, stirring often, 15 minutes.

Stir in the garam masala, cayenne, ketchup, tomatoes, peas, the rest of the salt, and the water. Bring to a simmer, cover, and cook over medium heat until the vegetables are tender, about 5 minutes. Taste for salt and serve hot, sprinkled with the cilantro.

PLAIN BASMATI RICE

CUMIN-SCENTED RICE PILAF

LEMON RICE

CHICKEN RICE PILAF

RICE PILAF WITH PEAS, POTATOES, AND WHOLE GARAM MASALA

SWEET SAFFRON PILAF WITH NUTS AND CURRANTS

RICE PILAF WITH "STANDING SPICES"

CHICKEN BIRIYANI WITH CREAM AND GARAM MASALA

COCONUT-MINT RICE

TOMATO RICE

LAMB BIRIYANI WITH ORANGE AND WHOLE GARAM MASALA

SWEET PEPPER BIRIYANI WITH CUMIN AND FENNEL SEEDS

MY GRAND-UNCLE'S KHITCHEREE

It is impossible to overestimate the importance of rice to Indian culture and spiritual traditions. In my Hindu tradition, rice represents Brahma, the creator of all life. For Buddhists, rice is associated with the Buddha, who is said to have broken his final fast with a porridge of rice and milk. Hindus still use such a porridge ritually to celebrate the weaning of a small child from his mother's milk. During the ceremony, the priest writes the word *aum* with the porridge on the baby's tongue to signify the eternal life energy that exists everywhere.

The Indian rice dish best known to Americans is probably biriyani, an elaborate Mogul dish of rice layered with meat and/or chicken. I often cook biriyanis for parties because they can be made in advance and feed a lot of people. But for everyday meals at home, I prefer to cook simpler rice dishes such as plain boiled rice, pilafs, or rice stir-fries.

South Indian–style rice stir-fries are made with cooked, cooled rice fried in oil that has been infused with various spices and aromatic ingredients. (Warm, freshly cooked rice won't work for these—the grains will break during frying and the rice will get mushy.) These dishes are wonderfully savory and relatively quick to make: you can cook the rice, cool it in the refrigerator, and put together any one of the recipes in just about 1 hour. You might also cook a vegetable if you're feeling energetic but poached or scrambled eggs and/or yogurt are really all you need to complete the meal. These stir-fried rices all follow a basic pattern with different spices and flavorings, so feel free to experiment and invent your own.

These stir-fries rely on the tastes of unusual ingredients—black mustard seeds, curry leaves, unsweetened coconut, and tamarind—to give them their authentic South Indian flavor. I didn't want readers to have to shop far afield in order to try these stir-fries, so I tested them with common supermarket foods only, making all the exotic ingredients optional. Cooked this way, the stir-fries are perfectly delicious, if somewhat different tasting from the versions you'd find in India.

A pilaf, or *pulao,* is another home-cooked northern rice dish that is relatively quick to make. For a pilaf, the rice is traditionally soaked in water and then drained. (Soaking helps the rice expand to long, thin grains that don't break during cooking, but I sometimes skip this step.) The drained rice is sautéed in oil with spices, onion, and perhaps a vegetable; sautéing keeps the grains separate and accentuates the flavor and scent of the rice. Water is added and the rice is cooked either entirely on top of the stove, or on the stove first and then in the oven. Baking helps form *khurchan,* the crispy browned rice on the bottom of the casserole that Indians love so much. I like to use the same water for soaking and cooking the rice so that I know that the rice absorbs exactly the right amount of water.

And finally, there are the biriyanis (from the Persian word *birinj,* meaning "rice"), elaborate Mogul preparations made by layering meat or poultry stews with parcooked rice. The whole thing is sealed and baked so that the juices from the meat or poultry infuse the rice with its flavor. Unlike a pilaf or a stir-fry, in which the ingredients are cooked into and infused into the rice, a biriyani is usually cooked in layers of rice and stew so that we taste contrasting layers of color, flavor, and fragrance. Biriyanis are traditionally restaurant food, made at home only for celebratory occasions and particularly in households where there is a kitchen staff to do the work. When you bake a biriyani, don't be too curious: if you open the casserole while the biriyani is in the oven, the steam will be lost and the rice won't cook properly.

Most Indian rice recipes tell you to pick over the rice, then rinse and drain it. You may or may not need to do this, depending on where you're buying your rice. (At the Indian store where I shop, the rice is immaculate and I never even rinse it.) But take a look at your rice before cooking: if there are bits of hull and/or stones in it, pick it over carefully and rinse in a colander before cooking. Basmati rice is sold now in many supermarkets. I recommend buying Indian basmati over the American-grown Texmati rice. True basmati has better flavor, is less starchy, and retains its texture better.

plain basmati rice

OBLE CHAWAAL

SERVES 4 TO 6

This is the way I make rice for most everyday meals at home. It's not quite as elegant-tasting as rice pilaf, but it's the simplest way I know to cook rice and absolutely foolproof. In my home in Delhi, Panditji used to make rice this way when my maternal grandmother, who had diabetes, came to visit from the United States. Boiling rice this way in a large quantity of water reduces the starch (good for a diabetic), while keeping the grains perfectly separate.

10 cups water

2 cups basmati rice

Bring the water to a boil over high heat in a large saucepan. Add the rice and stir gently so that it doesn't stick to the bottom of the pan. Return to a boil, turn the heat down so that the water simmers vigorously, and cook, partially covered, 8 minutes.

Drain the rice, return to the pan, and let stand, covered, until ready to serve.

cumin-scented rice pilaf

SERVES 4 TO 6

This is a streamlined pilaf in which the rice is not soaked before cooking. The grains may not be quite as long and supple as when the rice is soaked, but the nonsoaking method is so much quicker that I make pilaf this way for everyday cooking. For an easy plain pilaf, just omit the cumin.

1 tablespoon canola oil
1/2 teaspoon cumin seeds
2 cups basmati rice

4 cups water
1 teaspoon salt

Combine the oil and cumin in a medium saucepan over medium-high heat and cook, stirring, until the cumin is fragrant, 1 to 2 minutes.

Add the rice and cook, stirring, until the rice gives off a mild, toasted fragrance, about 1 minute.

Add the water and salt, and bring to a boil. Turn the heat down, and simmer vigorously, covered, until the rice is tender and the water has been entirely absorbed, about 10 minutes. Let stand, covered, for 5 minutes to finish cooking.

lemon rice

This is a citrusy, nutty South Indian rice dish. I don't like a lot of lemon in it; I use just enough to barely scent the rice. You can add more if you like by squeezing lemon wedges over the rice on your plate. I sometimes do the same with a lime.

The legumes are used here as a spice; they are sautéed in oil, not simmered in water until tender. This leaves them crunchy, which I like, but this is not traditional. My grandmother always soaked the dal in water to cover for about 10 minutes to soften, then drained them before cooking. Some people like a softer texture; you may want to soak the dal as well.

1 recipe (about 7 cups) cooked Plain Basmati Rice (page 91), drained, spread out on a baking sheet, and cooled to room temperature

3 tablespoons canola oil

2 teaspoons black mustard seeds (optional)

1 tablespoon yellow split peas

¹/₂ cup roasted cashews, chopped

6 whole dried red chiles

1 teaspoon cumin seeds

³/₄ teaspoon turmeric

12 fresh or 16 frozen curry leaves, torn into pieces (optional)

2 teaspoons hulled black gram beans (*urad dal*; optional)

¹/₈ teaspoon asafetida (optional)

1 large red onion, halved through the root end, each half cut in half again crosswise and then sliced ¹/₄ inch thick (to make short, thick slices)

¹/₂ cup chopped scallions (use the white part and about 2 inches of the green)

1¹/₂ teaspoons salt, or to taste

¹/₄ cup water

Juice of 1 lemon

Lemon or lime wedges, for serving

When the rice is cool, combine the oil, mustard seeds, if using, yellow split peas, and cashews in a large frying pan, wok, or *kadai* over medium-high heat. Cook, stirring, 1 to 2 minutes. (If using mustard seeds, cover the pan to avoid splattering and cook until you hear the seeds crackle and pop).

Add the red chiles, cumin seeds, turmeric, curry leaves, *urad dal,* and asafetida, if using, and cook, stirring, until the cashews and *urad dal* turn a uniformly golden color, 1 to 1¹/₂ minutes. (Stand back if using curry leaves; they spit when they hit the oil.)

Add the onion, scallions, and salt and cook, stirring, until the onion is softened, 4 to 5 minutes. (If the onion begins to burn, turn the heat down.)

Add the cooled rice and stir gently (careful not to break the grains) until the rice is uniformly yellow. Then drizzle the water all around the rim of the pan and stir again, gently, scraping the bottom to loosen the spices that stick. Add the lemon juice and cook, uncovered, until the rice is warmed through, about 2 more minutes. Stir gently once or twice during cooking, scraping the bottom of the pan to keep the spices from sticking. Taste for lemon and salt, and serve hot with lemon or lime wedges, if you like.

chicken rice pilaf

MURGH PULAO

SERVES 6 TO 8

Indians rarely cook a chicken biriyani at home—biriyanis are restaurant food. Home cooks would be more likely to make something like this chicken and rice pilaf because it's much quicker to put together with less drama; the rice isn't cooked separately. I make this northern-style pilaf when I need to feed a bunch of hungry friends quickly.

1 large red onion, quartered

4 garlic cloves, peeled

A 2½-inch piece fresh ginger, peeled and cut crosswise into thirds

1 fresh hot green chile, stemmed and cut crosswise into thirds

⅓ cup canola oil

1 tablespoon ground coriander

1 teaspoon turmeric

¾ teaspoon ground black pepper

½ teaspoon cayenne pepper

½ teaspoon garam masala (page 250)

1 cup plain yogurt, whisked until smooth

3 pounds boneless, skinless chicken breasts, cut crosswise into thirds

3½ cups water

2 cups basmati rice

2 teaspoons salt

Juice of 1 lime

Combine the onion, garlic, ginger, and green chile in the food processor and puree; set aside.

Heat the oil in a large ovenproof casserole (preferably one with a lid) over medium-high heat. Add the pureed onion mixture and cook, stirring, until it turns a tan color, about 15 minutes. Keep a cup of water beside the stove as the onion cooks. As the onion begins to stick, add water, about 1 teaspoon at a time, and scrape the bottom of the pan with the spoon to pull up the browned bits and keep the onion from burning.

Add the coriander, turmeric, black and cayenne peppers, and garam masala and cook, stirring, 1 minute. Add 3 tablespoons of the yogurt and cook, stirring, until the liquid evaporates and the oil begins to separate out of the mixture, 45 seconds to 1 minute. Repeat this process, adding about 3 tablespoons at a time and cooking until the liquid evaporates, until you've used up all of the yogurt.

Now add the chicken and cook, stirring, until the chicken turns opaque, about 3 minutes. Add ½ cup of the water, turn the heat down to medium, cover, and simmer 5 minutes. Add the rice, salt, remaining 3 cups water, and the lime juice, and stir gently to combine all of the ingredients without breaking the rice. Bring to a boil, turn the heat down to medium, then cover and simmer vigorously 5 minutes.

Meanwhile, preheat the oven to 350°F.

Cover the casserole tightly with aluminum foil and then the lid, if there is one. Bake 20 minutes. Remove from the oven and let stand 10 minutes at room temperature. Serve hot.

rice pilaf with peas, potatoes, and whole garam masala

TAHIREE

SERVES 6 TO 8

I inherited this dish from my father's side of the family, who came from the state of Uttar Pradesh in the north of India. (Garam masala is a typically North Indian spicing.) Panditji used to make it for our family when we needed a break from rich foods: it is both refreshingly clean-tasting and savory because there is very little oil in it and the spices nonetheless add great flavor. Growing up, we ate this with a simple Mint and Onion Raita made with a chopped tomato (page 180), lots of papadum, and Spicy Mango Chutney (page 214). Now I put out some yogurt and tomato chutney with the rice, and that's it.

I also make this with cauliflower in place of potato, or even with both—use the smallest head of cauliflower you can find and cut it into medium florets.

2 cups basmati rice
4 1/2 cups cold water
3 tablespoons canola oil
A 1-inch piece cinnamon stick
3 whole dried red chiles
4 green cardamom pods
1 teaspoon cumin seeds
8 whole cloves
10 black peppercorns
2 medium red boiling potatoes (about 3/4 pound), peeled and cut into 1/2-inch squares

3/4 teaspoon turmeric
1 fresh hot green chile, stemmed and cut in half lengthwise (optional)
1 (10-ounce) package frozen peas, unthawed
1/4 teaspoon cayenne pepper
3/4 teaspoon garam masala (page 250)
1 1/2 teaspoons salt
1/4 cup chopped fresh cilantro

Combine the rice and water in a bowl and soak for 20 minutes. Drain the rice and reserve the water separately. Preheat the oven to 350°F.

Combine the oil, cinnamon stick, red chiles, cardamom, cumin, cloves, and peppercorns in a large ovenproof casserole over medium-high heat. Cook, stirring, until the cinnamon unfurls, 1 to 2 minutes.

Add the potatoes and cook, stirring, until the edges are translucent, 3 to 4 minutes. Add the turmeric and green chile, and cook, stirring, 30 seconds. Add the peas and cayenne, and cook, stirring, for another minute. Add the drained rice and cook, stirring, about 1 minute.

Add the garam masala, salt, and reserved soaking water, and bring to a boil. Give the rice a stir. Then turn the heat down and simmer vigorously, covered, until the water is entirely absorbed and the rice is cooked through, about 10 minutes. Five minutes into the cooking, stir gently (so as not to break the rice) to distribute the potatoes and peas evenly throughout.

Put the casserole in the oven and bake 10 minutes. Then remove from the oven and let rest 5 minutes at room temperature. Sprinkle with cilantro and serve hot.

sweet saffron pilaf with nuts and currants

ZARDA PULAO

SERVES 4 TO 6

The Mogul emperor Akbar, who ruled India from 1556 to 1605, wrote about this very old and famous rice dish in his memoirs. For Indians, however, this seductive dish has been so widespread for so long that we mostly take it for granted. With its lovely, sweet saffron flavor, it can be served alongside savory dishes or on its own as a snack or dessert. Some Indian households make this with yellow food coloring to give the rice an all-over yellow color, but I just use saffron; I like the way the spice colors the rice unevenly, so that some grains are yellow while others remain white.

1¼ cups basmati rice

2½ cups water

¼ teaspoon saffron threads

1 tablespoon milk or cream

¼ cup ghee or canola oil

A 2-inch piece cinnamon stick

10 green cardamom pods, pounded in a mortar and pestle to break open the shells

A 1-inch piece fresh ginger, peeled and grated

¼ cup dried currants

¼ cup chopped blanched almonds

¼ cup shelled pistachios, chopped

²/₃ cup sugar

Combine the rice and water in a medium bowl and soak 20 minutes. Drain and reserve the water. Set the rice and water aside separately.

Meanwhile, toast the saffron in a small frying pan over medium heat, stirring and pulling the pan off the heat occasionally to keep the saffron from burning, until the saffron darkens to a maroon color and is fragrant, 15 to 20 seconds. Crush to a coarse powder in a mortar and pestle, or in a bowl with the back of a spoon. Stir in the milk or cream, and set aside.

Combine the ghee or oil, cinnamon stick, cardamom, and ginger in a medium heavy-bottomed casserole over medium-high heat. Cook, stirring, until the cinnamon unfurls, 1 to 2 minutes.

Add the currants and nuts and cook, stirring, 1 minute. Add the drained rice and cook, stirring, 1 minute. Add the reserved water, turn down the heat, cover, and simmer very gently over low heat for 15 minutes.

Now uncover and sprinkle the rice evenly with the sugar. Drizzle the saffron mixture over the top. Put the pan over very low heat, cover, and continue cooking 5 more minutes. Serve hot.

rice pilaf with "standing spices"

KHADE MASALE KE CHAAWAL

SERVES 6 TO 8

My maternal grandmother, Nani, whose family is from the Punjab in northern India, used to make this rather special rice pilaf whenever we and any of her other grandchildren came to visit. It is a common Punjabi party dish. *Khade masale,* which literally means "standing spices," refers to the whole spices that are cooked into the rice to flavor it. (I imagine "standing" refers to the fact that the whole spices can be seen from "head" to "toe.") In India, we wouldn't remove the spices from the finished dish. People bite right into them: they enjoy the heat. If you don't want that much heat, wrap the spices in a square of cheesecloth as my father's mother did. Sauté the spice bundle in the oil in step 5, as usual, but cook for 1 1/2 minutes rather than 1 minute. Or, just pick the spices out after the rice is cooked.

When I was a child, the crisp fried-onion garnish was my favorite treat. Whenever I smelled the onions cooking, I'd run to Panditji who, generous man that he was, always gave me a taste. (That said, the rice can also stand on its own without the onions.)

2 cups basmati rice

4 1/2 cups cold water

2 medium red onions

1/4 cup canola oil, plus about 1 cup for deep-frying

1 teaspoon cumin seeds

8 green cardamom pods

A 2 1/2- to 3-inch piece cinnamon stick, broken in half

1/4 teaspoon whole cloves

1/4 teaspoon black peppercorns

1/4 teaspoon coriander seeds

3 bay leaves

3 whole dried red chiles

2 garlic cloves, minced

1 teaspoon salt

Combine the rice and water in a bowl and soak for 20 minutes. Drain the rice and reserve the water separately.

Mince 1 onion and reserve.

For the fried-onion garnish, thinly slice the second onion. Heat the 1 cup oil in a small (about 6-inch), heavy-bottomed saucepan over medium heat to 360°F. The oil should come about 1/2 inch up the side of the pan. If necessary, add more oil. (To gauge the temperature of the oil without using a thermometer, drop a piece of bread about 1-inch square into the hot oil over medium heat, turning often; when the oil reaches 360°F, the bread should begin to brown almost immediately and turn golden brown all over—like a crouton— in about 30 seconds.) Add the sliced onion and deep-fry, stirring often, until the onion turns dark brown, 15 to 20 minutes. Drain on paper towels and then let stand until cool and crisp. Set aside. Discard the oil.

Preheat the oven to 350°F.

Combine the 1/4 cup oil, the cumin, cardamom, cinnamon stick, cloves, peppercorns, coriander, bay leaves, and chiles in a large ovenproof casserole over medium-high heat. Cook, stirring, until the cinnamon unfurls, 1 to 2 minutes.

Add the reserved minced onion and cook, stirring, until wilted, about 5 minutes. If the caramelized sugars from the onion begin to collect on the bottom of the pan, add water, about a tablespoon at a time, and stir, scraping the bottom of the pan to pick up the browned bits.

Add the garlic and cook, stirring, 30 seconds. Add the drained rice and cook, stirring, 1 minute. Add the reserved soaking water and salt, and bring to a boil, stirring occasionally to keep the rice from sticking to the bottom of the pan. Then turn the heat down and simmer vigorously, covered, until the water is entirely absorbed and the rice cooked through, about 10 minutes.

Put the casserole in the oven and bake 10 minutes. Then remove from the oven and let rest 5 minutes. Sprinkle with the fried onions and serve hot.

variation

To make a more colorful, substantial pilaf, add 1 cup of fresh or frozen peas or 2 peeled, grated carrots to the onion mixture when you add the drained rice. Continue to cook as usual.

chicken biriyani with cream and garam masala

MURGH BIRIYANI

SERVES 6 TO 8

Like the chicken kurma with which this biriyani is made, this is a Mogul recipe, exceptionally refined in taste, fragrance, and appearance. In India, we would make this with a "sour" yogurt—that is, a yogurt that is a few days old. (Yogurt is made every day in an Indian kitchen; some of it is eaten fresh and some is aged to make it more sour.) The chicken may be used immediately in the biriyani; the flavors will have a chance to meld while baking.

10 cups water
2 cups basmati rice

1 recipe Braised Chicken in White Sauce with Garam Masala (page 116); see below

Bring the water to a boil in a large saucepan. Add the rice and stir gently so that it doesn't stick to the bottom of the pan. Return to a boil, turn the heat down, and simmer vigorously, partially covered, 6 minutes. Drain, return the rice to the pan, and set aside until ready to use.

Make the chicken, and simmer, stirring occasionally, for 2 minutes after adding the cream; it's ready now to be used immediately.

Preheat the oven to 350°F.

Layer one-third of the cooked rice over the bottom of a large ovenproof casserole, preferably one with a lid. Layer half of the chicken on top and smooth with a spoon. Add another third of the rice and then the rest of the chicken. Top with the remaining rice. Cover tightly with foil and then with the lid, if there is one. Bake 30 minutes.

Remove casserole from the oven and let stand 10 minutes. Transfer to a serving platter and serve hot.

coconut-mint rice

SERVES 4 TO 6

Coconut Rice is another traditional South Indian recipe to which I've added fresh mint, buttermilk, and lime juice: the mint gives the rice a fresh, light taste and the buttermilk and lime cut the sweetness of the coconut.

For a softer texture, soak the split peas in water to cover for 10 minutes, then drain before adding to the dish.

1 recipe (about 7 cups) Plain Basmati Rice (page 91)

CHUTNEY
1 bunch mint sprigs, thick stems trimmed
    (2 loosely packed cups)
1 cup buttermilk
2-inch piece fresh ginger, peeled and cut into
    2 or 3 pieces
3 whole, dried red chiles
1/2 cup unsweetened shredded coconut
1/4 teaspoon black peppercorns
6 fresh or 10 frozen curry leaves, torn into pieces

2 tablespoons unsweetened shredded coconut
3 tablespoons canola oil
1 tablespoon black mustard seeds
1 tablespoon yellow split peas
1/2 cup unsalted, dry roasted peanuts
1 teaspoon cumin seeds
12 fresh or 16 frozen curry leaves, torn into pieces
1 tablespoon all-purpose flour
1/2 cup buttermilk
1 1/2 teaspoons salt, or to taste
Juice of 1/2 lime

Cook the rice, drain it, and spread it out on a baking sheet to cool to room temperature.

For the chutney, combine all of the ingredients in a blender or food processor and grind to a puree. Set aside.

Toast the coconut in a small frying pan over medium heat, stirring, until it begins to turn a yellowish-brown color, 1 to 2 minutes. (Do not burn.)

When the rice is cool, combine the oil, mustard seeds, yellow split peas and peanuts in a large frying pan, wok, or *kadai* over medium-high heat. Cook, stirring, until the mustard seeds crackle, 1 to 2 minutes.

Add the cumin and curry leaves and cook, stirring, until the peanuts turn a nice golden color, about 1 1/2 minutes.

Turn the heat down to low. Add the flour and cook, stirring, for 30 seconds.

Stir in the chutney, buttermilk, and salt and bring to a simmer.

Add the rice and stir gently to blend all of the ingredients. Cook uncovered, stirring every now and then, until the rice is hot, about 2 to 3 minutes.

Stir in the toasted coconut and the lime juice. Taste for salt and serve hot.

tomato rice

SERVES 4 TO 6

This is my version of another traditional South Indian rice dish. I use a small can of tomato paste in place of some of the fresh tomato that is traditional, partly for ease, but also because the paste guarantees a rich red color and good flavor even in the midst of winter. I eat this with scrambled eggs seasoned with chopped cilantro and scallions, and a raita.

1 recipe (about 7 cups) Plain Basmati Rice (page 91)

3 tablespoons canola oil

2 teaspoons black mustard seeds

6 whole cloves

6 whole, dried red chiles

12 fresh or 16 frozen curry leaves, torn into pieces

1 teaspoon cumin seeds

1 large red onion, coarsely chopped (1/2-inch dice)

1 1/2 teaspoons salt, or to taste

2 large tomatoes, chopped, or 1 pound cherry tomatoes

1 (6-ounce) can tomato paste

1 teaspoon sambhaar powder or rasam
   (page 251; optional)

1/4 cup water

Cook the rice, drain it and spread it out on a baking sheet to cool to room temperature.

When the rice is cool, combine the oil, mustard seeds, and cloves in a large frying pan, wok or *kadai* over medium-high heat. Cook, stirring, until the mustard seeds crackle, 1 to 2 minutes.

Add the red chiles, curry leaves and cumin and cook, stirring, for 1 to 1 1/2 minutes more.

Add the onion and salt and cook, stirring, until the onion is soft, about 3 minutes.

Add the tomatoes, tomato paste and spice powder, if using, and cook, stirring often, 5 minutes.

Add the cooked, cooled rice and stir gently to blend all of the ingredients. Drizzle the water all around the rim of the pan and stir again, gently, scraping the bottom to loosen the spices that stick. Then continue cooking, uncovered, until the rice is warmed through, about 2 more minutes. Stir once or twice during cooking, scraping the bottom of the pan to keep the spices from sticking. Taste for salt and serve hot.

lamb biriyani with orange and whole garam masala

KEENU WAALEE BIRYAANI

SERVES 8 TO 10

Unlike the chicken biriyani on page 100, also flavored with garam masala, this lamb biriyani uses no cream but is fragrant with citrus instead. Orange brightens the taste of the lamb and goes beautifully with the garam masala, julienned ginger, and fennel. It's best made with ghee or butter.

This biriyani is traditionally served as part of a celebration of fertility, prosperity, or good fortune. It's flavored with a special citrus fruit grown in India called a *keenu* that is bright orange and perfectly round. Any type of orange that you can find here, however, including blood oranges, will work fine. It's especially authentic to make this with lamb on the bone if you don't mind picking the bones out of your food, because the bone adds great flavor. So I've called for slices of lamb shank along with boneless, cubed leg. If you can't get shank, however, or can't get it sliced, just use the boneless leg. Serve with a raita for a refreshing contrast.

2 oranges

3/4 cup ghee, butter, or canola oil

1 teaspoon green cardamom pods

1/2 teaspoon whole cloves

Two 1 1/2-inch pieces cinnamon stick

5 bay leaves

1/4 teaspoon black peppercorns

1/2 teaspoon cumin seeds

1/2 teaspoon fennel seeds

A 3-inch piece fresh ginger, peeled and cut into thin strips

2 pounds leg of lamb, cut into large (1 1/2- to 2-inch) cubes, including, if possible, four 1- to 1 1/2-inch-thick bone-in slices from the shank end

1 cup plain yogurt, whisked until smooth

1/4 teaspoon ground mace

2 teaspoons salt, or to taste

6 cups water

3 3/4 cups basmati rice

1/2 teaspoon saffron threads

1 tablespoon milk

Cut the orange zest off the oranges in strips with a vegetable peeler, leaving most of the white pith behind. Cut the zest into long, thin strands and set aside.

Heat the ghee, butter, or canola oil in a large ovenproof casserole, preferably one with a lid, over medium heat until liquid. Add the cardamom, cloves, cinnamon stick, bay leaves, peppercorns, and cumin and fennel seeds, and cook, stirring, until the fennel and cumin begin to turn a golden brown and the cinnamon stick unfurls, 1 to 2 minutes.

Add the ginger and cook, stirring, 1 minute. Add the lamb pieces and cook, stirring every now and then, until the lamb begins to brown, about 10 minutes.

Add the reserved strands of orange zest and cook, stirring, 1 minute. Add the yogurt, mace, salt, and water. Bring to a boil, turn the heat down, and simmer, covered, until the meat is very tender, about 1 hour.

Preheat the oven to 350°F.

Remove the lamb to a bowl with a slotted spoon. Ladle out 3 cups of the cooking liquid (along with any spices that are in it) and add to the bowl with the lamb; set aside.

Put the rice in the casserole with the leftover cooking liquid and add water to cover by about 2 inches. Bring to a boil, turn the heat down, and simmer vigorously 6 minutes. Drain and discard the cooking liquid.

Return the lamb and its reserved cooking liquid to the casserole. Taste for salt. Add the drained, cooked rice and smooth the top.

Toast the saffron in a small frying pan over medium heat, stirring, until the saffron darkens to a maroon color, about 30 seconds. (Do not burn.) Put the saffron in a mortar and grind to a powder, or crush in a bowl with the back of a spoon. Add the milk and stir, then drizzle over the rice.

Cover the casserole with foil and then the lid, if there is one. Bake 45 minutes. Remove from the oven and let stand 10 minutes at room temperature. Stir the biriyani very gently to mix the meat and the rice and serve hot, with raita.

sweet pepper biriyani with cumin and fennel seeds

SIMLA MIRCHI KEE BIRIYANI

SERVES 6 TO 8

I came up with this recipe one night when I had a houseful of vegetarian friends who love to eat. Although Indian cuisine is known for its vegetarian food, before that night I didn't have a recipe for a really delicious vegetable biriyani. I had just made a batch of tomato chutney that day, so I used some to flavor the bell pepper mixture. A commercial tomato chutney works perfectly as well.

SPICE POWDER

1 tablespoon coriander seeds

1 teaspoon cumin seeds

1 teaspoon black mustard seeds (optional)

1 teaspoon fennel seeds

1 whole dried red chile

10^3/$_4$ cups water

2 cups basmati rice

^{1}/$_4$ cup canola oil

1 teaspoon cumin seeds

3 whole dried red chiles

1 large onion, cut into 1-inch dice

1^1/$_2$ teaspoons salt, or to taste

2 garlic cloves, minced

5 bell peppers of various colors (e.g., 2 red, 1 green,
     1 yellow, and 1 orange), stemmed, seeded,
     and cut into 1-inch cubes

1 medium tomato, chopped

2 tablespoons storebought tomato chutney

^{3}/$_4$ cup chopped fresh cilantro

For the spice powder, combine all of the spices in a spice grinder and grind to a powder. Set aside.

Bring 10 cups of water to a boil over high heat in a large saucepan. Add the rice and stir gently so that it doesn't stick to the bottom of the pan. Return to a boil, turn the heat down, and simmer vigorously, partially covered, 6 minutes. Drain, return the rice to the pan, and set aside until ready to use.

Combine the oil, cumin, and chiles in a large frying pan, wok, or *kadai* over medium-high heat. Cook, stirring, until the cumin seeds darken slightly, 1 to 2 minutes. Add the onion and salt and cook, stirring, until the onion is softened, about 5 minutes. Add the garlic and cook, stirring, 30 seconds. Add the reserved spice powder and cook, stirring, 30 seconds. Add the peppers and cook, stirring and scraping the bottom of the pan to pick up any spices that stick, about 1 minute. Add ^{1}/$_4$ cup of the water and continue cooking, stirring, until the peppers are softened and beginning to stick to the sides of the pan, 6 to 7 minutes.

Add the chopped fresh tomato and tomato chutney and stir to blend. Scrape the bottom and sides of the pan well to pick up any spices that stick. Then cook, stirring, 5 more minutes. Taste for salt.

Meanwhile, preheat the oven to 350°F. Spread about 2 cups of cooked rice over the bottom of a large ovenproof casserole, preferably one with a lid. Spoon about half of the pepper mixture over the rice and sprinkle with ^{1}/$_4$ cup of the cilantro. Cover that with about 1^1/$_2$ cups more rice, spreading the rice evenly. Layer the remaining pepper mixture over the rice and sprinkle with another ^{1}/$_4$ cup cilantro. Spread the remaining rice over the top. Drizzle the remaining ^{1}/$_2$ cup water in a thin stream around the edges of the casserole and then over the rice. Cover the dish tightly with foil and then with the lid, if there is one. Bake for 35 minutes. Let stand 10 minutes at room temperature, sprinkle with the remaining ^{1}/$_4$ cup cilantro, and serve hot.

my grand-uncle's khitcheree

MUNG DAL KEE KHITCHEREE

SERVES 4 TO 6

When we were kids, my parents decided to pack up and move all of us for three years to the city of Nagpur, in the state of Maharashtra. It was a way, or so they said, of accustoming the family to "the art of living." That meant that, instead of having a household of servants as we did at home in Delhi, we had to make do on our own. My mother cooked and we all had chores. On one occasion, several family members came to visit us, including my grand-aunt and grand-uncle from Delhi. Grand-uncle could not understand why my parents had chosen not to have help. But he eventually got into the spirit of things and made this rice and lentil khitcheree for dinner one night. One taste and we were all hooked. He made it with ghee, which, as I remember, was something of a luxury at the time because my mother was making it herself, churning the cream by hand into butter and then clarifying the butter into ghee.

Khitcheree is the chicken soup of India: a one-pot meal that is soulfully delicious, healthy, and addictive. I often make it as a break from periods of heavy eating out and entertaining. If you like, you can add vegetables, too: sauté diced potato along with the onions until the onions begin to wilt, and then add chopped cauliflower and green chile, and sauté another minute. Continue with the recipe as below. Serve with a raita and a chutney.

1¼ cups yellow split peas, or split yellow mung beans
    (moong dal), picked over, rinsed, and drained
¾ cup basmati rice
¼ cup ghee, butter, or canola oil
3 whole dried red chiles
1½ teaspoons cumin seeds
2 bay leaves
8 whole cloves
4 black peppercorns

½ teaspoon turmeric
⅛ teaspoon asafetida (optional)
¼ teaspoon ground black pepper
2 medium onions, halved through the root ends, each
    half cut in half again crosswise and then sliced
    ¼ inch thick (to make short, thick slices)
5¾ cups water
1½ teaspoons salt, or to taste
¼ teaspoon garam masala (page 250)

Combine the split peas or mung beans and rice in a bowl and add cold water to cover; let soak 20 minutes. Drain and set aside.

Combine the ghee, butter, or oil, the red chiles, cumin seeds, bay leaves, cloves, peppercorns, turmeric, asafetida, if using, and black pepper in a medium, heavy-bottomed casserole over medium-high heat. Cook, stirring, for 2 minutes.

Add the onions and cook, stirring, until they begin to wilt, about 3 minutes. Add the rice and split pea mixture and sauté, stirring gently so as not to break the rice, about 1 minute.

Add the water, salt, and garam masala and stir gently to mix. Bring to a boil, turn the heat down to low, cover, and simmer very gently 20 minutes. Stir gently. Then continue cooking, covered, until the rice and lentils are tender and the mixture is still wet, like a very thick, savory porridge, about 5 more minutes. Taste for salt and serve hot.

SIMPLE LAHORI CHICKEN CURRY WITH ONION AND TOMATO

LAHORI CHICKEN CURRY WITH WHOLE SPICES AND POTATOES

SOUTHERN-SPICED LAHORI CHICKEN CURRY

CHICKEN CURRY WITH GREENS AND GARAM MASALA

BRAISED CHICKEN IN WHITE SAUCE WITH GARAM MASALA

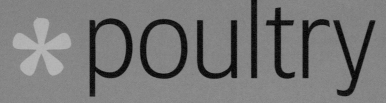

*poultry

BUTTER CHICKEN

BOMBAY CHICKEN CURRY WITH CORIANDER AND COCONUT MILK

COCONUT CHICKEN WITH CASHEWS

SOUTH INDIAN–STYLE CHICKEN WITH CURRY LEAVES AND BLACK PEPPERCORNS

CHICKEN STIR-FRY WITH MIXED SWEET PEPPERS

GROUND TURKEY WITH SPINACH AND WHOLE SPICES

TANDOORI ROAST CORNISH GAME HENS

Of all the meats, chicken, because of its mild taste, is

the ideal meat for curries. It doesn't get in the way of our spices and flavorings, and it adapts

well to any style of spicing. The Punjab region of northern India is particularly well known for

its chicken curries. The first recipe in this chapter—the Simple Lahori Chicken Curry with

Onion and Tomato—is a very simple, standard chicken curry from that region. The two

recipes that follow are variations: the first is another northern Indian curry, while the second

is spiced in the style of South India. Having cooked all three, you should feel quite confident

in Indian chicken cookery and be able to attack the rest of the chapter quite easily.

I've included several southern Indian chicken preparations, such as the Bombay Chicken

Curry with Coriander and Coconut Milk and Coconut Chicken with Cashews, which may be

less familiar to you but are made exactly the same way.

The curries in this chapter demonstrate how Indian cooks build flavor into their stews by

layering spices, aromatics, and other flavoring agents into the dish. The first step in some

recipes is to marinate the chicken in a combination of spices, usually including turmeric,

believed by Indians to have antiseptic properties, or lemon juice. This step infuses the

chicken with the flavor of the spices or simply freshens the taste and cuts fatty flavors.

For the sauce, many recipes begin by sautéing whole spices in oil. (Northern Indian cur-

ries typically use a garam masala—cinnamon, cloves, black pepper, cardamom, cumin,

coriander, and red chiles—while South Indian dishes use black mustard seeds, curry leaves, legumes, and fenugreek, sometimes in addition to the garam masala.) This step infuses the cooking oil with the essential oils of the spices, lending the dish a warm, long-lasting, but muted taste of those spices. I call this back heat—it goes and goes in your mouth long after you've swallowed the bite! Ground spices, added later on in the cooking, add a more immediate taste of the spice—there's a big bang of flavor as you're eating and then it's gone, and you're ready for the next bite.

Pureed or finely chopped onions usually go in after whole spices, sometimes with ginger and garlic. Onions give the sauce body as well as a subtle sweetness that balances the taste and heat of the spices. The onions are cooked for a long time to develop their sweetness and break them down to a soft, sauce-like consistency. (I like using red onions because they are sweeter than yellow onions.) Tomato and/or yogurt are often added next. Both give the sauce a bit of acidity that balances the onion, and, of course, tomato adds sweetness as well. Yogurt is chosen when the cook wants a creamy sauce without adding much fat. Yogurt also has a particular quality of sourness, adding a subtle background acidity that doesn't compete with the flavors of the spices. Lemon and mango powder, other souring agents, are bolder flavors that you taste more directly.

At this point, the foundation of the sauce has been laid. The chicken is added along with enough water to cover, and the stew is simmered until the chicken is very tender. Lemon may be added at the end to brighten the flavor of the sauce, and a handful of chopped fresh cilantro may be stirred in then, too, for the same reason. Indian chefs often add potatoes and other vegetables such as radishes and turnips to their chicken curries, too. This makes the dish seem more substantial, renders it more economical, and also gives nonmeat eaters something to eat with the sauce.

I like cooking with Cornish game hens; I find that they have better flavor than the larger chickens. If you like, you can use halved or quartered game hens in any of the recipes that call for chicken parts. All of the stews can be made with chicken thighs as well. You'll see that I've also adapted some traditional Indian recipes for boneless, skinless chicken breasts because they're so quick to cook.

In India we always skin our chickens so that the spices will easily penetrate the meat. We also remove as much fat as possible so that the flavor of the fat doesn't compete with the spices.

simple lahori chicken curry
with onion and tomato

SERVES 4

We have a saying in India that a person who hasn't seen Lahore has yet to be born. Lahore is a city in what is now Pakistan. The hub of land trade between India and the Middle East, it used to be called "the Paris of the East" because it was such an important center of high culture in India. The street foods and meat preparations of Lahore are still legendary. This chicken curry is a staple for Lahoris and a great introduction to chicken curries for the novice Indian cook. Serve it with rice and a raita.

A 4-pound chicken, cut into 8 to 10 pieces and skinned

3/4 teaspoon turmeric

3/4 teaspoon cayenne pepper

Salt

1 1/2 medium onions, roughly diced

5 garlic cloves

A 2-inch piece fresh ginger, peeled and cut in half crosswise

3 tablespoons canola oil

A 2-inch piece cinnamon stick

12 green cardamom pods

9 whole cloves

9 black peppercorns

2 large tomatoes, chopped

2 tablespoons tomato paste

1/4 cup plain yogurt, whisked until smooth

1 cup water

1/2 cup chopped fresh cilantro

Juice of 1 lemon

Combine the chicken, 1/2 teaspoon of the turmeric, 1/2 teaspoon of the cayenne, and 1/4 teaspoon salt in a bowl and stir to coat the chicken with the spices. Let stand while you make the sauce.

Finely mince the onions, garlic, and ginger in a food processor and set aside.

Combine 2 tablespoons of the oil, the cinnamon, cardamom, cloves, and black peppercorns in a large casserole over medium-high heat. Cook, stirring, until the cinnamon unfurls, 1 to 2 minutes. Add the minced onion mixture and 1 teaspoon salt, and cook, stirring, until the onion browns around the edges, 10 to 15 minutes.

Remove and discard the cinnamon and stir in the remaining 1/4 teaspoon turmeric and 1/4 teaspoon cayenne. Add the tomatoes and tomato paste and cook, stirring, 5 minutes. Transfer to a food processor or blender and puree until smooth; set aside.

Heat the remaining 1 tablespoon oil in the same pan over medium-high heat. Add the chicken and cook, stirring, 2 minutes. Add the yogurt 1 tablespoon at a time and stir well after each addition. Cook, stirring, 2 minutes to evaporate some of the moisture.

Add the pureed tomato mixture and bring to a boil. Stir in the water. Return to a boil, then reduce the heat and simmer, partially covered, until the chicken is cooked through, about 30 minutes. Stir and scrape the bottom of the pan every 5 to 8 minutes to keep the sauce from sticking. Then uncover and cook 5 more minutes to reduce and thicken the sauce. Stir in the cilantro and lemon juice. Taste for salt and serve hot.

lahori chicken curry with whole spices and potatoes

SERVES 4

This is a variation on the preceding chicken curry. It's very similar but includes potatoes to make it heartier, and a wider assortment of spices for more complexity.

A 4-pound chicken, cut into 8 to 10 pieces and skinned

3 medium red boiling potatoes, peeled and quartered

3/4 teaspoon turmeric

1/2 teaspoon cayenne pepper

Salt

1 1/2 medium onions, roughly diced

5 garlic cloves

A 2-inch piece fresh ginger, peeled and cut in half crosswise

3 tablespoons canola oil

A 1-inch piece cinnamon stick

12 green cardamom pods

9 whole cloves

10 black peppercorns

3 whole dried red chiles

1 teaspoon coriander seeds

1/2 teaspoon cumin seeds

1 fresh hot green chile, cut in half

2 large tomatoes, chopped

2 tablespoons tomato paste

1/4 cup plain yogurt, whisked until smooth

1 cup water

1/2 cup chopped fresh cilantro

Juice of 1 lemon

Combine the chicken, potatoes, 1/2 teaspoon of the turmeric, 1/4 teaspoon of the cayenne, and 1/4 teaspoon salt in a bowl and stir to coat the chicken and potato with the spices. Let stand while you make the sauce.

Finely mince the onions, garlic, and ginger in a food processor and set aside.

Combine 2 tablespoons of the oil, the cinnamon stick, cardamom, cloves, black peppercorns, red chiles, coriander, and cumin in a large casserole over medium-high heat. Cook, stirring, until the cinnamon unfurls, 1 to 2 minutes. Add the minced onion mixture, the green chile, and 1 teaspoon salt and cook, stirring, until the vegetables brown around the edges, 10 to 15 minutes.

Remove the cinnamon and green chile, and stir in the remaining 1/4 teaspoon turmeric and 1/4 teaspoon cayenne. Add the tomatoes and tomato paste and cook, stirring, 5 minutes. Transfer to a food processor or blender and puree until smooth; set aside.

Heat the remaining 1 tablespoon oil in the same pan over medium-high heat. Add the chicken and potatoes and cook, stirring, 2 minutes. Add the yogurt 1 tablespoon at a time and stir well after each addition. Cook, stirring, 2 minutes, to evaporate some of the moisture.

Add the pureed tomato mixture and bring to a boil. Stir in the water. Return to a boil, then reduce the heat and simmer, partially covered, until the chicken is cooked through, about 30 minutes. Stir every 5 to 8 minutes and scrape the bottom of the pan to keep the sauce from sticking. Then uncover and cook 5 more minutes to reduce and thicken. Stir in the cilantro and lemon juice. Taste for salt and serve hot.

southern-spiced lahori chicken curry

SERVES 4

Here is another variation on the simple Lahori curry on page 111. This time, I've spiced the curry with the southern Indian flavors of curry leaves, black mustard seeds, fenugreek, and coconut. These ingredients are critical to this dish—there are no substitutions—but they are well worth seeking out.

A 4-pound chicken, cut into 8 to 10 pieces and skinned
1 teaspoon ground black pepper
3/4 teaspoon turmeric
3/4 teaspoon cayenne pepper
Salt
3 tablespoons canola oil
20 fresh or 30 frozen curry leaves, torn into pieces
15 black peppercorns
9 whole cloves
6 green cardamom pods
3 whole dried red chiles
2 bay leaves
1 teaspoon black mustard seeds

1/4 teaspoon fenugreek seeds
1 1/2 medium onions, roughly diced
5 garlic cloves
A 2-inch piece fresh ginger, peeled and
    cut in half crosswise
1 fresh hot green chile, finely minced
1/4 cup unsweetened shredded coconut
2 large tomatoes, chopped
2 tablespoons tomato paste
1/4 cup plain yogurt, whisked until smooth
1 cup water
1/2 cup chopped fresh cilantro
Juice of 1 lemon

Combine the chicken, black pepper, 1/2 teaspoon of the turmeric, 1/2 teaspoon of the cayenne, and 1/4 teaspoon salt in a bowl and stir to coat the chicken with the spices. Let stand while you make the sauce.

Combine 2 tablespoons of the oil, the curry leaves, black peppercorns, cloves, cardamom, red chiles, bay leaves, mustard seeds, and fenugreek seeds in a large casserole over medium-high heat. Cook, stirring, until the mustard seeds begin to crackle, 1 to 2 minutes. Add the onions, garlic, ginger, green chile, and 1 teaspoon salt and cook, stirring, until the onions brown around the edges, 10 to 15 minutes.

Remove the bay leaves and green chile, and stir in the remaining 1/4 teaspoon turmeric, 1/4 teaspoon cayenne, and the coconut. Cook, stirring, 1 minute. Add the tomatoes and tomato paste and cook, stirring, 5 minutes. Transfer to a food processor or blender and puree until smooth; set aside.

Heat the remaining 1 tablespoon oil in the same pan over medium-high heat. Add the chicken and cook, stirring, 2 minutes. Add the yogurt 1 tablespoon at a time and stir well after each addition. Cook, stirring, 2 minutes, to evaporate some of the moisture.

Add the pureed tomato mixture and bring to a boil. Stir in the water. Return to a boil, then reduce the heat and simmer, partially covered, until the chicken is cooked through, about 30 minutes. Stir every 5 to 8 minutes and scrape the bottom of the pan to keep the sauce from sticking. Then uncover and cook 5 more minutes to reduce and thicken. Stir in the cilantro and lemon juice. Taste for salt and serve hot.

chicken curry with greens and garam masala

METHI MURGH

SERVES 4

This northern Indian dish is traditionally made with fenugreek greens but I like it with chopped fresh cilantro too, and cilantro is certainly easier to find. It is usually finished with ¼ cup heavy cream. I don't add the cream—the yogurt makes a creamy sauce on its own. But if you'd like the extra richness, stir the cream in at the end and return the sauce to a simmer before serving. Serve with Mushrooms in a Coriander-Scented White Sauce (page 66), Plain Basmati Rice (page 91), and toasted pita bread.

A 3½- to 4-pound chicken, cut into 8 to 10 pieces
   and skinned
½ teaspoon turmeric
½ teaspoon cayenne pepper
Salt
4 tablespoons canola oil
A 1-inch piece cinnamon stick
6 whole cloves
8 green cardamom pods
1 teaspoon coriander seeds

½ teaspoon cumin seeds
2 medium onions, cut into chunks
5 garlic cloves
A 2-inch piece fresh ginger, peeled and cut in half
½ firmly packed cup stemmed cilantro leaves,
   or ¼ cup dried fenugreek leaves (kasoori methi)
1 tablespoon ground coriander
1 teaspoon garam masala (page 250)
1 cup plain yogurt, whisked until smooth
1 cup water

Combine the chicken, turmeric, ¼ teaspoon of the cayenne, and ¼ teaspoon salt in a large bowl and stir to coat well with the spices. Let stand while you make the sauce.

Combine 3 tablespoons of the oil, the cinnamon stick, cloves, cardamom, coriander, and cumin in a heavy-bottomed casserole over medium-high heat. Cook, stirring, until the cinnamon unfurls, 1 to 2 minutes. Add the onions, garlic, ginger, and 1 teaspoon salt and cook, stirring, until the edges of the vegetables brown, 10 to 15 minutes. Remove the cinnamon stick and discard.

Add the cilantro or fenugreek leaves, ground coriander, garam masala, and the remaining cayenne and cook, stirring, 1 minute. Transfer to a food processor and puree. Set the onion puree aside.

In the same pan, heat the remaining 1 tablespoon oil over medium-high heat. Add the chicken and cook, stirring, 2 minutes. Add the yogurt a tablespoon at a time, stirring well after each addition to completely incorporate the yogurt. Then cook, stirring, 2 minutes to dry out the mixture.

Add the onion puree and the water, and bring to a boil. Turn the heat down and simmer, partially covered, until the chicken is tender, about 30 minutes. Stir every 5 to 8 minutes and scrape the bottom of the pan to keep the sauce from sticking. Uncover and cook 5 more minutes to reduce the sauce. Taste for salt and serve hot.

braised chicken in white sauce with garam masala

MURGH KURMA

SERVES 4

This is my rendition of a classic Mogul dish. It is a truly wonderful way to prepare chicken, delicately scented with garam masala and bathed in a lovely white yogurt-cream sauce that is luscious without being overly rich. Because Mogul culture valued the pristine, elegant look of white food, this kurma (meaning "braise") would have been spiced with bleached white cardamom pods and white peppercorns. I don't go in for that kind of drama in my cooking: I use everyday green cardamom and black peppercorns. Serve this with a Grape Raita (page 185) and some Quince Chutney (page 211). This kurma is also the base of Chicken Biriyani with Cream and Garam Masala on page 100.

3 medium red onions, quartered

3 garlic cloves, peeled

A 3-inch piece fresh ginger, peeled and sliced

1/3 cup canola oil

A 1-inch piece cinnamon stick

12 green cardamom pods, pounded in a mortar and pestle just to break open the shells

16 whole cloves

1/2 teaspoon cumin seeds

1/4 teaspoon coriander seeds

5 bay leaves

1/4 teaspoon white or black peppercorns

3 whole dried red chiles

1 teaspoon salt, or to taste

2 teaspoons ground coriander

1 cup plain yogurt, whisked until smooth

2 pounds boneless, skinless chicken breasts, cut into 2- by 1-inch pieces

3/4 cup hot water

1/2 teaspoon garam masala (page 250)

1/2 cup heavy cream, plus extra for drizzling

Combine the onions, garlic, and ginger in a food processor and process to finely mince; set aside.

Combine the oil, cinnamon stick, cardamom, cloves, cumin, coriander seeds, bay leaves, peppercorns, and red chiles in a large, heavy-bottomed casserole over medium-high heat. Cook, stirring, until the cinnamon unfurls and the spices brown lightly, 1 to 2 minutes. Add the minced onion mixture and the salt, and cook, stirring, until the onions turn a uniformly light brown color, about 15 minutes. Keep a cup of water beside the stove while the onion cooks. As the caramelized sugars begin to stick to the bottom of the pan, dribble in water, about 1 teaspoon at a time, and scrape the pan with the spoon to pull up all the sugars and keep them from burning. Do this as often as necessary until the onions are golden.

Add the ground coriander and cook, stirring, 1 minute. Add about 3 tablespoons of the yogurt and cook, stirring, until the yogurt is entirely blended and the moisture evaporated. Continue adding the yogurt, about 3 tablespoons at a time and cooking out the moisture after each addition, to use all of the yogurt.

Add the chicken and cook, stirring, until opaque, about 5 minutes. Add the hot water and stir. Bring to a boil, then turn the heat down to low. Cover and simmer gently (the onion mixture will be very thick) until the chicken is just cooked through, about 5 more minutes.

Stir in the garam masala and cook, stirring, 2 minutes. Stir in the heavy cream and remove from the heat. Let the kurma rest for at least 1 hour to allow the flavors to infuse the sauce.

When you are ready to serve, warm the kurma through over low heat and then drizzle with a little cream. Taste for salt and serve hot.

butter chicken

CHICKEN TIKKA MASALA

SERVES 4

This recipe is supposed to have been invented at a restaurant in Delhi called Moti Mahal (The Palace of Pearls). The restaurant opened in the 1940s shortly after India gained its independence. It is said to be India's first real, sit-down restaurant where Indians of all classes could, for the first time in India's history, dine indoors, publicly. This recipe is a standard in the repertoire of most Indian cooks, as it is in mine. You'll find it on most Indian restaurant menus in America too, where it's listed as *chicken tikka masala*. (Ironically, Indians always call it "Butter Chicken.")

I bake the chicken on a drip tray so that all of the moisture falls through and the chicken develops some crust and good flavor, but a baking sheet will work almost as well. This is delicious cooked on the grill, too, with a tablespoon of canola oil added to the marinade. Finely chopped cilantro adds flavor to the marinade and is a good use for the stems. Serve with toasted pita, rice, and a vegetable or Cucumber Raita (page 178).

MARINADE

4 garlic cloves

A 2-inch piece fresh ginger, peeled and coarsely
    chopped

1 small onion, coarsely chopped

1/4 teaspoon cayenne pepper

1/4 teaspoon garam masala (page 250)

1/4 cup plain yogurt

2 tablespoons finely chopped fresh cilantro stems
    (tender, light green parts only; optional)

4 boneless, skinless chicken breasts (about 2 pounds),
    cut crosswise into thirds

1 large red onion, cut into large chunks

4 garlic cloves

A 2 1/2-inch piece fresh ginger, peeled and cut into
    large chunks

1/3 cup canola oil

A 1-inch piece cinnamon stick

1 teaspoon salt, or to taste

1 tablespoon ground coriander

1 teaspoon ground cumin

1/2 teaspoon turmeric

1/4 teaspoon cayenne pepper

1 1/2 pounds tomatoes, pureed in a food processor

1/2 cup heavy cream

For the marinade, combine the ingredients in a food processor and puree.

Toss the chicken with the marinade in a bowl and refrigerate at least 1 hour and up to overnight, if you can.

When the chicken has marinated, puree the onion, garlic, and ginger in a food processor and set aside.

Combine the oil and cinnamon stick in a large saucepan or casserole over medium-high heat. Cook, stirring, until the cinnamon stick unfurls, 1 to 2 minutes. Add the onion puree and salt, and cook, stirring, until it turns light golden brown, about 20 minutes. Keep a cup of water beside the stove while the onion cooks. As the onion begins to stick, add water, about 1 teaspoon at a time, and scrape the bottom of the pan with the spoon to pull up the browned bits and keep the onion from burning.

Add the coriander, cumin, turmeric, and cayenne and cook, stirring, 1 minute. Add the pureed tomatoes, give the sauce a stir, and simmer until the oil separates, about 10 minutes. Add the cream, bring to a simmer, and take the sauce off the heat. Heat the oven to 350°F. Lift the chicken breasts out of the marinade and arrange them in a single layer on a drip tray or, in a pinch, a foil-lined baking sheet. Cover with aluminum foil and bake until tender, 15 to 20 minutes. Then put them into the pan with the sauce and stir gently. Warm over medium heat 5 minutes. Taste for salt and serve hot.

bombay chicken curry with coriander and coconut milk

SERVES 4

I adapted this recipe from one that was served to me by a friend of mine named Ashok Rao Kavi, a journalist from the state of Maharashtra on the western coast of India. The cuisine of Maharashtra is characterized by bold flavors and, because it borders the southern Indian states, by the use of southern Indian spice combinations such as mustard seeds, curry leaves, and coconut. The sauce of this curry is very flavorful, thin, and light. Serve it with Plain Basmati Rice (page 91).

SPICE POWDER

2 tablespoons coriander seeds

1/2 teaspoon black mustard seeds (optional)

12 black peppercorns

2 whole dried red chiles

1/4 teaspoon turmeric

A 1/2-inch piece cinnamon stick

6 whole cloves

6 green cardamom pods

1 large red onion, quartered

6 garlic cloves

A 2-inch piece fresh ginger, peeled and cut crosswise
    into thirds

3 tablespoons canola oil

1 teaspoon salt, or to taste

1 fresh hot green chile, sliced crosswise into thin rounds

12 fresh or 18 frozen curry leaves, torn into pieces
    (optional)

A 4-pound chicken, cut into 8 to 10 pieces and skinned

3/4 cup coconut milk

1/2 cup water

1/2 cup chopped fresh cilantro

For the spice powder, combine the ingredients in a grinder and grind to a powder. Set aside.

Combine the onion, garlic, and ginger in a blender and process to a puree; set aside.

Heat the oil in large casserole over medium-high heat. Add the onion puree and salt, and cook, stirring often, until golden brown, 10 to 15 minutes. Keep a cup of water beside the stove while the onion cooks. As the onion begins to stick, drizzle in water, about 1 teaspoon at a time, and scrape the bottom of the pan with the spoon to pull up the browned bits and keep the onion from burning.

Add the green chile and curry leaves, if using, and cook, stirring, 1 minute. Add the spice powder and salt, and cook, stirring, 2 minutes. Sprinkle in a few drops of water if the onion mixture begins to stick. Add the chicken pieces and cook, stirring constantly, until the meat is mostly opaque, 4 to 5 minutes.

Add the coconut milk and water, and bring to a boil. Reduce the heat and simmer, partially covered, stirring and scraping the bottom of the casserole every now and then to keep the sauce from sticking, until the chicken is tender, about 40 minutes.

Stir in 1/4 cup of the cilantro and simmer, uncovered, 5 more minutes. Taste for salt, sprinkle with the remaining 1/4 cup cilantro, and serve hot.

coconut chicken with cashews

MURGH KAJU

SERVES 4

This is an adaptation of a traditional Bora Muslim recipe that I learned from my friend Mustafa, a Bora from Bombay who lives just around the corner from me in Manhattan. Mustafa makes this with a commercial spice mix that his mother sends him from Bombay. I figured out what was in the mix and used those spices here. Ground cashews serve to bind the sauce.

You'll find cashews in dishes from all over India, but like almonds, they are generally associated with Mogul or Muslim cuisines. Serve this with pita and rice, and chilled sliced red onions tossed in fresh lemon juice and sprinkled with paprika.

1 cup raw or roasted cashews, plus 1/4 cup roasted
    cashews, for serving
4 whole dried red chiles
A 1-inch piece cinnamon stick
6 whole cloves
3 tablespoons coriander seeds
2 teaspoons cumin seeds
1 medium onion, coarsely chopped
8 garlic cloves

A 2-inch piece fresh ginger, peeled and sliced
1/2 cup unsweetened shredded coconut, or 1/4 cup
    ground raw or roasted cashews
1/3 cup canola oil
1 teaspoon ground black pepper
2 pounds boneless, skinless chicken thighs,
    cut crosswise into thirds
2 cups water
1 teaspoon salt, or to taste

Process 1 cup of the raw cashews to a powder in a food processor.

Combine the chiles, cinnamon stick, cloves, coriander, cumin, onion, garlic, ginger, coconut, and 3/4 cup of the ground cashews in a large saucepan or casserole over low heat. Cook, stirring, until the cashews and coconut have turned light golden, about 10 minutes. Cool and process to a paste in a food processor.

Wipe out the casserole and put it over medium heat. Add the oil, the spice paste, and the black pepper, and cook, stirring, until the mixture turns deep golden brown, about 10 minutes. Keep a cup of water beside the stove as the mixture cooks. As the spices begin to stick, add water, about 1 teaspoon at a time, and scrape the bottom of the pan with the spoon to pull up the browned bits and keep the spices from burning.

Add the remaining ground cashews and cook, stirring, 5 more minutes. Add the chicken and cook, stirring, until it turns opaque, about 5 minutes.

Add the water and the salt, bring to a boil, turn the heat down, and simmer, partially covered, until the chicken is tender, 15 to 20 minutes. Taste for salt and sprinkle with the remaining 1/4 cup roasted cashews. Serve hot.

south indian–style chicken with curry leaves and black peppercorns

DAKSHIN MURGH

SERVES 4

This is my version of a traditional southern dish called "pepper chicken." This isn't as fiery hot with black pepper as it ought to be; I didn't want to scare people away from a delicious recipe. I have eaten this chicken in Chettinad, in southern India where the weather is very hot, and this is perfect for those summer evenings when you want something spicy and interesting tasting, to invite your hunger. Serve with Stir-Fried Cabbage with South Indian Spices (page 51) and Onion Pachadi (page 186).

2 pounds chicken thighs, skinned
Salt
1 teaspoon ground black pepper
Juice of ½ lemon

SPICE MIX
14 fresh or 20 frozen curry leaves, torn into pieces
2 teaspoons black mustard seeds
1 teaspoon cumin seeds
¾ teaspoon fenugreek seeds
1 teaspoon black peppercorns

6 whole cloves
3 green cardamom pods

3 tablespoons canola oil
½ teaspoon black mustard seeds
3 whole dried red chiles
6 green cardamom pods
1 fresh hot green chile, sliced crosswise into rounds
12 fresh or 18 frozen curry leaves, torn into pieces
¼ cup unsweetened shredded coconut
1 (13½-ounce) can coconut milk

Toss the chicken with ¼ teaspoon salt, the ground pepper, and lemon juice and let stand at room temperature for 30 minutes.

For the spice mix, combine the spices in a frying pan over medium heat and cook, stirring, until fragrant, 1½ to 2 minutes. Grind to a powder in a spice grinder and set aside.

Combine the oil, mustard seeds, red chiles, cardamom, green chile, and curry leaves in a large saucepan or casserole over medium-high heat. Cover (the mustard seeds splatter and pop) and cook until you hear the mustard seeds crackle, 1 to 2 minutes. Add the ground spice mix and cook, stirring, 30 seconds. Add the shredded coconut and cook, stirring, 30 seconds. Add the chicken and cook, stirring, until opaque, about 5 minutes.

Add the coconut milk and ½ teaspoon salt. Bring to a boil, turn the heat down, and simmer, partially covered, until the chicken is tender, 25 to 30 minutes. Stir two or three times during the last 10 minutes of cooking and scrape the bottom of the pan to keep the sauce from sticking. Taste for salt and serve hot.

chicken stir-fry with mixed sweet peppers

SERVES 4

This recipe is inspired by a northern Indian street food called taka-tak, which is the name for any stir-fried dish of meat, chicken, or vegetable in which the foods are chopped with two large knives right on the griddle, making the sound "taka-taka." In India, stir-fries such as this one are rolled in handkerchief-thin rotis, but in America I serve it with a spoonful of Green Chutney (page 209), rolled in warm flour tortillas almost like a fajita.

1½ pounds boneless, skinless chicken breasts,
    cut crosswise into ½-inch-wide strips
1 tablespoon ground coriander
½ teaspoon cayenne pepper
¼ teaspoon turmeric
Pinch of coarsely ground black pepper
Juice of 1 lemon
3 tablespoons canola oil
1½ teaspoons cumin seeds
1 large onion, sliced

A 2-inch piece fresh ginger, peeled and finely grated
2 bell peppers (use 2 different colors), stemmed, cored,
    and cut lengthwise into ½-inch strips
1 teaspoon chopped garlic
1 fresh hot green chile, halved lengthwise and then
    sliced crosswise ¼ inch thick
1 teaspoon salt, or to taste
2 large eggs, whisked to blend
¾ cup chopped fresh cilantro

Sprinkle the chicken with the coriander, cayenne, turmeric, black pepper, and lemon juice in a bowl and stir to coat with the spices. Let stand while you prepare the rest of the dish.

Combine the oil and cumin in a large wok or frying pan over medium-high heat. Cook, stirring, until the cumin turns golden brown, 1 to 2 minutes. Add the onion and ginger, and cook, stirring, 3 minutes. Add the peppers, garlic, green chile, and salt and cook, stirring, until the peppers soften slightly, about 3 minutes.

Meanwhile, pour the eggs over the chicken in the bowl, add the cilantro, and stir to mix. Dump this mixture into the wok and cook, stirring, until the chicken is cooked through, 7 to 8 minutes. Serve hot.

ground turkey with spinach and whole spices

TURKEY-PAALAK KA KEEMA

SERVES 4

Keema literally means "minced." In fact, when someone in India verbally or physically bashes another person, the individual is often said to have made that person into *keema*. You can make this dish without the fenugreek leaves, too, if you don't have any, but fenugreek is so good in this recipe that I keep a small package in the freezer (where it keeps practically forever) to have on hand for this dish alone. Serve with raita and a homemade Indian bread such as Poori (pages 193 and 198) or Parathas (page 194), or with toasted pita bread.

10 ounces fresh spinach, stemmed and washed, or 10
    ounces frozen spinach, unthawed
¼ cup canola oil
A 2-inch piece cinnamon stick
8 whole cloves
8 green cardamom pods
3 whole dried red chiles
2 bay leaves
1 medium onion, thinly sliced

A 2-inch piece fresh ginger, peeled and finely minced
1 fresh hot green chile, split lengthwise
1½ pounds ground turkey
1 teaspoon salt, or to taste
1 cup plain yogurt, whisked until smooth
1 tablespoon dried fenugreek leaves (*kasoori methi;*
    optional)
½ teaspoon garam masala (page 250)

Bring 2 inches of water to a boil in a large saucepan. Add the spinach and stir. Cover and steam until fresh spinach is wilted, or frozen is thawed, stirring every now and then, about 5 minutes. Drain, cool under cold tap water, drain again, and then puree in a blender or food processor; set aside.

Combine the oil with the cinnamon stick, cloves, cardamom, red chiles, and bay leaves in a heavy-bottomed casserole over medium-high heat. Cook, stirring, until the cinnamon unfurls, 1 to 2 minutes.

Add the onion, ginger, and green chile and cook, stirring often, until the onion browns on the edges, about 10 minutes.

Add the turkey and cook, stirring, 3 minutes. Add the salt and then the yogurt, a few tablespoons at a time, stirring well after each addition. Stir in the fenugreek leaves, if using, and then the spinach puree. Cook, stirring every now and then, until the mixture is dry, about 5 minutes.

Stir in the garam masala, taste for salt, and serve hot.

tandoori roast cornish game hens

SERVES 4

A tandoor is a freestanding cylindrical clay oven that is wider in the belly and narrows at the top. You build a fire in the belly and lower the food, threaded onto skewers that are as long as the oven is tall, into the oven. A tandoor cooks food at a very high heat—from 550°F. to 850°F. The advantage to tandoori cooking is that it gives the food a crisp crust, using very little fat. I've adapted this technique to a conventional oven and grill.

For the best flavor, the hens should marinate overnight, but in a pinch you can marinate as little as 4 hours. Line the roasting pan with aluminum foil for easy clean-up. You can use chicken parts and grill or roast them for 30 to 40 minutes. Be sure to drain the yogurt before using, or the hens will never develop a good crust. And be forewarned—unlike restaurant tandoori, the meat will not be a bright red color since this recipe doesn't use food coloring.

2 Cornish game hens
1 tablespoon paprika
1/2 teaspoon salt
1/4 teaspoon turmeric
Juice of 1 lemon

MARINADE

1 small onion, quartered
4 garlic cloves
A 2-inch piece peeled fresh ginger, cut in half
1 teaspoon ground toasted cumin (see sidebar, page 39)
1 teaspoon ground black pepper
3/4 teaspoon ground cardamom

1/2 teaspoon cayenne pepper
1/4 teaspoon paprika
Pinch of ground cloves
Pinch of ground cinnamon
Pinch of garam masala (page 250)
1/2 cup plain yogurt, drained in a cheesecloth-lined strainer or coffee filter for 2 hours
3 tablespoons tomato paste
1 teaspoon canola oil

2 tablespoons canola oil
Lemon wedges, for serving

Pull and cut as much of the skin as possible off the hens. Make several deep slashes in the breasts and thighs.

Mix the paprika, salt, turmeric, and lemon juice in a bowl. Rub the mixture over the hens and then massage the birds with the spices for about 1 minute. Set aside, covered, for half an hour.

Meanwhile, put all of the marinade ingredients in a blender and process on low speed until smooth. Toss the hens in the marinade until coated. Put them in resealable plastic bags and refrigerate for at least 4 hours, overnight, or for up to 2 days.

Set the hens at room temperature for about 1 hour. Preheat the oven to 550°F. or preheat the grill.

Add one tablespoon of the oil to each of the bags with the hens, reseal the bags, and massage between your hands to incorporate the oil. Remove the hens from the marinade, put them on a rack in a foil-lined roasting pan, and roast until the juices run clear when the thickest part of the thigh is pierced with a skewer, about 30 minutes. Or grill, turning to brown all sides, until cooked through, about 30 minutes. Remove from the oven and let stand 5 minutes. Cut each hen in half and serve with lemon wedges.

SIMPLE LAMB CURRY WITH CORIANDER AND GARAM MASALA

LAMB CURRY WITH CORIANDER, GARAM MASALA, AND COCONUT

PARSI LAMB CURRY

LAMB STEW WITH TOMATO AND SOUTHERN INDIAN SPICES

meats

PORK VINDALOO

LAMB COOKED DELHI-STYLE

LAMB COOKED WITH ALMONDS

GROUND BEEF WITH SPINACH AND FRESH MINT

GROUND LAMB WITH ALMONDS, CARDAMOM, AND COCONUT

SAVORY LAMB PATTIES

GAEL'S TANDOORI LAMB CHOPS

MOGUL LAMB "FILET" IN A CREAM SAUCE WITH GARAM MASALA

Many of the recipes in this chapter (and the chicken chapter before this) are curries. There's always a lot of interest in my classes as to what exactly a curry is, where the word came from, and whether it is an English or an Indian word. As I understand it, it's a bit of both. The British indiscriminately called a lot of Indian dishes "curries." The word may be derived from the Indian word *tari* that, for northern Indians, means "sauce." On the other hand, for the people of southern India, *kari* is the word for the leaf of the curry plant, often used to flavor vegetable and meat dishes, including stews. In any event, the word *curry,* even for non-English speaking Indians, generally refers either to a sauce or to a dish of meats or vegetables cooked in sauce, eaten with rice. The sauce is typically thickened with onion, spices, and sometimes yogurt, poppy seeds, lentils, or nut flours.

There is no basic recipe for curry in Indian cuisine. If you flip through the recipes in this chapter and the one on poultry, you'll see that each curry is put together slightly differently. That said, there are some discernable, if mutable, patterns: if whole spices are used, they are fried first in oil to infuse the oil with their flavor. Onion, and often garlic and ginger, is added to the oil and cooked to evaporate the moisture and concentrate their flavors. Meat, ground spices, ground nuts, or poppy seeds used as thickening agents go in and the meat is cooked in this mixture to absorb all of those myriad, concentrated flavors. Yogurt may be added and cooked dry to thicken the sauce. The meat is covered with water and stewed until very tender. Some curries may be finished with a tempering oil (spice-infused oil) for even more flavor.

Most Indians who eat meat eat goat, which we call mutton (a holdover from the days of the British Raj). Indians like goat because it is both lean and tender, and both more mild-flavored and leaner than the lamb in India. Goat is almost impossible to get hold of outside of large international cities like New York, however, so I've written most of the recipes in this chapter for lamb. The curries can all be made with beef stew meat, too, or even with pork.

Meat is at its best when cooked on the bone. The bone adds flavor to the sauce, and Indians who eat meat love to hold the bones in their hands and suck the marrow out. But since it's difficult in America to find stewing meat cut with bone, I've developed all of the stews to work for either boneless chunks of lamb or pork. Be sure to cut as much of the fat off the meat as possible to ensure that its taste doesn't overpower the spices. Marinating it, sometimes with yogurt but sometimes with spices alone, flavors and tenderizes it. For large pieces such as lamb chops, deep slashes are cut into the meat to allow the marinade to penetrate easily. And then the meat is cooked until it's falling off the bone with a marvelously yielding texture.

All of these curries are immeasurably better several hours after they are made. The sauces get more flavorful, the meat more tender, and the flavors more integrated. So if you can, cook a few hours or even a day ahead, and then reheat.

simple lamb curry with coriander and garam masala

GOSHT KORMA

SERVES 4

This is a very common dish in Muslim homes around Lucknow in northern India. It is an everyday lamb stew thickened with pureed onion, and is very subtly spiced. (Add more cayenne if you'd like a hotter stew.) Serve with rice and Crispy Potatoes with Cumin (page 78). The recipe may be varied by adding different spices, as in the recipe that follows, or by cooking potatoes and/or other vegetables along with the lamb.

SPICE POWDER
12 black peppercorns
8 green cardamom pods
5 whole cloves

3 medium red onions
3 tablespoons canola oil
1 teaspoon salt, or to taste
4 garlic cloves
A 2-inch piece fresh ginger, peeled and
    cut into large chunks

2 pounds well-trimmed boneless leg of lamb,
    cut into 1- to 1 1/2-inch pieces
2 teaspoons ground coriander
1/4 teaspoon cayenne pepper, or to taste
1/2 cup plain yogurt, whisked until smooth
3 cups water
1/2 teaspoon garam masala (page 250)
1/4 cup heavy cream (optional)
1/4 cup chopped fresh cilantro

For the spice powder, combine all of the spices in a spice grinder and grind to a powder. Set aside.

Chop one of the onions, and cut the remaining two into large chunks.

Heat the oil in a large, heavy-bottomed casserole over medium-high heat. Add the chopped onion and the salt, and cook, stirring often, until the onion just begins to brown, about 10 minutes.

Meanwhile, combine the onion chunks, the garlic, and ginger in a food processor and process to a paste; set aside.

When the onion has browned, add the spice powder and the lamb. Cook, stirring often, until the lamb begins to brown, 6 to 7 minutes. (If the lamb doesn't brown, turn up the heat.) Add the pureed onion mixture and cook, stirring, until the mixture is dry and the oil begins to separate, about 10 more minutes.

Add the coriander and cayenne and cook, stirring, 2 more minutes. Add the yogurt a tablespoon at a time and stir well after each addition. Then cook, stirring often, until the mixture is dry again and the meat is beginning to stick to the bottom of the pan, about 5 minutes. Add the water and garam masala, stir well, and simmer, covered, until the lamb is tender, 35 to 40 more minutes.

Just before serving, add the cream, if using, and bring almost to a simmer. Taste for salt. Sprinkle with cilantro and serve hot.

lamb curry with coriander, garam masala, and coconut

DAKSHIN GOSHT KORMA

SERVES 4

This is a variation on the preceding recipe. It's made exactly the same way but uses a spice paste with curry leaves and coconut in place of the spice powder. Potatoes or another vegetable can be added to this recipe as well. Serve with Stir-Fried Green Beans with Coconut (page 48), Chilled Smoky Eggplant with Yogurt and Cilantro (page 64), or Stir-Fried Mixed Summer Squash (page 85).

SPICE PASTE

12 black peppercorns

8 green cardamom pods

5 whole cloves

16 fresh or 24 frozen curry leaves, torn into pieces

2 whole dried red chiles

1 bay leaf

¼ cup unsweetened shredded coconut, or
  ¼ cup ground blanched almonds

3 medium red onions

3 tablespoons canola oil

1 teaspoon salt, or to taste

4 garlic cloves

A 2-inch piece fresh ginger, peeled and cut into
  large chunks

2 pounds well-trimmed boneless leg of lamb,
  cut into 1- to 1 ½-inch pieces

2 teaspoons ground coriander

¼ teaspoon cayenne pepper, or to taste

½ cup plain yogurt, whisked until smooth

3 cups water

½ teaspoon garam masala (page 250)

¼ cup heavy cream (optional)

¼ cup chopped fresh cilantro

For the spice paste, combine the ingredients in a spice grinder and grind to a paste, using a little water if you need to. Set aside.

Chop one of the onions, and cut the remaining two into large chunks.

Heat the oil in a large, heavy-bottomed casserole over medium-high heat. Add the chopped onion and the salt and cook, stirring often, until the onion just begins to brown, about 10 minutes.

Meanwhile, combine the onion chunks, the garlic, and ginger in a food processor and process to a paste; set aside.

When the onion has browned, add the spice paste and the lamb. Cook, stirring often, until the lamb begins to brown, 6 to 7 minutes. (If the lamb doesn't brown, turn up the heat.) Add the pureed onion mixture and cook, stirring, until the mixture is dry and the oil begins to separate, about 10 more minutes.

Add the coriander and cayenne and cook, stirring, 2 more minutes. Add the yogurt a tablespoon at a time and stir well after each addition. Then cook, stirring often, until the mixture is dry again and the meat is beginning to stick to the bottom of the pan, about 5 minutes.

Add the water and garam masala, stir well, and simmer, covered, until the lamb is tender, 35 to 40 more minutes. Just before serving, add the cream, if using, and bring to a near-simmer. Taste for salt. Sprinkle with cilantro and serve hot.

parsi lamb curry

PARSI GOSHT NI CURRY

SERVES 4

Having been persecuted in their homeland, Parsis settled in India in the thirteenth century. They very quickly adapted to India's rituals and practices, creating a prosperous culture and enticing cuisine there. Parsi curries are famous for their near-perfect balance of sweet, sour, and hot tastes. This one is thickened with peanuts, and the addition of tamarind and brown sugar offsets the heat of the spices deliciously.

SPICE POWDER

1 teaspoon coriander seeds

1/2 teaspoon cumin seeds

2 tablespoons peanuts

1/4 cup canola oil

7 whole dried red chiles

12 fresh or 16 frozen curry leaves, torn into pieces

2 large red onions, sliced

1 teaspoon salt, or to taste

4 garlic cloves, finely minced

A 2-inch piece fresh ginger, finely minced or grated

1/2 cup ground peanuts, or 1/2 cup unsweetened shredded coconut

2 pounds boneless leg of lamb, well trimmed and cut into 1- to 11/2-inch cubes

4 medium red boiling potatoes, peeled and quartered

3 cups water

1 tablespoon tamarind concentrate, or juice of 2 small lemons

1/2 cup warm water (if using tamarind)

2 large tomatoes, pureed in the food processor

1 tablespoon brown sugar

For the spice powder, combine the ingredients in a spice grinder and grind to a powder; set aside.

Combine the oil with the dried chiles and curry leaves in a large, heavy-bottomed casserole over medium-high heat. Cook, stirring, 1 minute. Add the onions and salt and cook, stirring, until the onions turn a uniformly golden brown color, about 15 minutes. Keep a cup of water by the stove as the onions cook. As the caramelized sugars from the onions begin to collect on the bottom of the pan, add water, about a teaspoon at a time, and stir, scraping the bottom of the pan to pick up the browned bits and keep the onions from burning. Do this as often as necessary.

Add the garlic and ginger and cook, stirring, 1 minute. Continue to sprinkle in water if the mixture sticks. Add the spice powder and cook, stirring, 1 more minute, adding water as needed. Add the ground peanuts or coconut and cook, stirring, 1 more minute. Add the lamb and potatoes and cook, stirring, until the lamb is opaque, about 2 more minutes.

Add the 3 cups water and stir well to blend. Bring to a boil, reduce the heat, and simmer partially covered, stirring occasionally, 25 minutes.

Meanwhile, if using tamarind, measure the warm water into a small bowl or measuring cup. Add the tamarind concentrate and stir to dissolve it. Rinse the measuring spoon and your fingers in the water to dissolve all of the sticky tamarind. Set this tamarind water aside.

When the lamb has cooked, add the tamarind water, if using, the tomatoes, and brown sugar. Simmer, uncovered, until the lamb is very tender, 15 to 20 more minutes. Taste for salt, stir in the lemon juice, if using, and serve hot.

lamb stew with tomato and southern indian spices

LAMB KOIRAMBHA

SERVES 4 TO 6

This is my version of a southern Indian lamb stew, cooked in a tomato sauce flavored with a complex and rather exotic mixture of tastes that are common to South Indian cooking. I have added fennel seed, which is more commonly found in the north—I find that the fennel smoothes out the meaty flavor of lamb. While there's no substitute for curry leaves and fenugreek, you can omit these spices (as well as the coconut) and still have a superb, rich-flavored tomato-lamb stew.

Serve this with plain rice and a southern Indian onion raita, Onion Pachadi (page 186).

1 large onion, quartered

5 garlic cloves, peeled

A 2-inch piece fresh ginger, peeled and cut into chunks

¼ cup canola oil

2 bay leaves

A 2-inch piece cinnamon stick

10 fresh or 16 frozen curry leaves, torn (optional)

2 teaspoons cumin seeds

2 teaspoons fennel seeds

½ teaspoon fenugreek seeds (optional)

1 teaspoon salt, or to taste

1 large tomato, pureed

1 teaspoon turmeric

2¼ pounds boneless leg of lamb, well trimmed and cut into 1-inch cubes

2 teaspoons store-bought curry powder

1 teaspoon cayenne pepper

1 teaspoon ground black pepper

1 (8-ounce) can tomato sauce

1 cup water

¼ cup coarsely chopped fresh cilantro

TEMPERING OIL

1 teaspoon cumin seeds

½ teaspoon fennel seeds

3 whole dried red chiles

2 teaspoons canola oil

3 teaspoons unsweetened shredded coconut (optional)

Combine the onion, garlic, and ginger in a food processor and process to a paste; set aside.

Combine the oil, bay leaves, cinnamon stick, and curry leaves, if using, in a large, heavy-bottomed casserole and cook over medium-high heat, stirring, until the cinnamon unfurls, about 1 minute. (Stand back if using curry leaves; they spit when the oil gets hot.)

Add the cumin and fennel seeds, and fenugreek seeds, if using, and cook, stirring, until the cumin turns golden brown, 1 to 2 minutes. Add the onion puree and salt, and cook, stirring, until the raw smell of the garlic disappears, about 2 minutes. Add the tomato puree and turmeric, and cook, stirring every now and then, for 3 minutes. Add the lamb, turn the heat to high, and cook, stirring every now and then, 5 minutes.

Add the curry powder, cayenne, and black pepper and stir well. Add the tomato sauce and stir well. Then add the water, bring to a boil, reduce the heat, and simmer, covered, until the lamb is tender, about 1 hour.

Uncover and cook about 5 more minutes to thicken the sauce. Stir in the cilantro.

For the tempering oil, combine the cumin, fennel seeds, and red chiles in a spice grinder and grind to a powder. Just before serving, heat the oil with the ground spices in a small frying pan or *kadai* over medium heat and cook, stirring, until the spices are fragrant, 1 to 2 minutes. Stir into the stew and taste for salt. Serve hot.

pork vindaloo

SERVES 4

This recipe, given to me by a Parsi friend, is a version of the famous, fiery Goan stew unique to Christians of that area. Made with onions and ripe tomatoes, and soured with vinegar, the sauce has a mildly sweet-and-sour taste. Pork shoulder is meltingly tender. I also make this stew with cubed leg of lamb (you can use beef or chicken, too); cook the lamb for about 45 minutes.

Traditionally a vindaloo is quite, quite hot, and this recipe is as well. But don't miss the dish if you don't like spicy food; just cut the number of chiles in half. Use tomatoes that are so ripe they are too soft for salads, or canned tomatoes. The pork needs to marinate 2 to 4 hours before cooking. Serve with rice.

SPICE PASTE

1 teaspoon cumin seeds
1 teaspoon coriander seeds
10 whole dried red chiles
A 1/2-inch piece cinnamon stick
8 whole cloves
6 green cardamom pods
10 black peppercorns
1/2 teaspoon turmeric
6 garlic cloves, minced
A 2-inch piece fresh ginger, peeled and minced
2 tablespoons white vinegar

Juice of 1/2 lemon
1/4 teaspoon salt

2 pounds boneless pork shoulder, well trimmed and
    cut into 1-inch cubes
2 very ripe medium tomatoes, quartered, or
    1 (14.5-ounce) can whole peeled tomatoes, drained
2 medium onions, quartered
3 tablespoons canola oil
1 teaspoon salt, or to taste
1/4 to 1/2 cup water

For the spice paste, combine the cumin, coriander, red chiles, cinnamon, cloves, cardamom, and peppercorns in a spice grinder and grind to a coarse powder. Dump out into a large ceramic or glass bowl and stir in the turmeric, garlic, ginger, vinegar, lemon juice, and 1/4 teaspoon salt.

Add the pork and stir with a spatula to coat the meat with the paste. Cover and let marinate in the refrigerator at least 2 hours or up to 4 hours.

Meanwhile, combine the tomatoes and onions in a food processor and puree; set aside.

Heat the oil in a large, heavy-bottomed casserole over medium-high heat. Add the pork with its marinade and cook, stirring often, for 10 minutes.

Add the tomato-onion puree and salt, and stir well. Bring to a boil. Add water as needed to cover the meat. Return to a boil, turn the heat down, and simmer, covered, until the meat is tender, about 1 hour. Taste for salt and serve hot.

lamb cooked delhi-style

DILI WAALA GOSHT

SERVES 6

Foods prepared in the centuries-old city of Delhi are still connected to a bygone era. This traditional dish is light in feel, spicy, and a perfect meat dish to eat with simple boiled basmati rice. This recipe is easy to make: there is very little chopping and the spices are all cooked whole.

2¼ pounds leg of lamb, trimmed of fat and
    cut into 1-inch pieces
5 cups water
1 cinnamon stick
6 green cardamom pods
½ teaspoon turmeric
Salt
¼ cup canola oil
5 whole dried red chiles

2 teaspoons cumin seeds
¾ teaspoon fennel seeds
6 whole cloves
5 garlic cloves, finely minced
2 inches fresh ginger, finely minced
½ teaspoon cayenne pepper
1 cup plain yogurt, whisked until smooth
Juice of ½ lemon
½ cup finely chopped cilantro leaves

Combine the lamb, water, cinnamon, cardamom, turmeric, and ¼ teaspoon salt in a large casserole. Bring to a boil, turn down the heat and simmer, uncovered, until the lamb is tender, about 1 hour. Remove the lamb with a slotted spoon. Reserve 1 cup of the broth; discard the rest.

Heat the oil with the red chiles in a large, heavy-bottomed casserole over medium-high heat and cook, stirring, until the chiles turn a very dark brown, about 3 minutes. Remove the pan from the heat and discard the chiles.

Return the pan to medium-high heat. Add the cumin, fennel, and cloves and cook, stirring, for 30 seconds. Add the lamb and cook, stirring, until it begins to brown, 2 to 3 minutes. Add the garlic, ginger, and cayenne and cook, stirring, for 1 minute. Add the yogurt, 2 tablespoons at a time, stirring well after each addition.

Pour in ¾ cup of the reserved broth, the lemon juice, and 1 teaspoon salt. Bring to a boil, reduce the heat, and simmer for 2 minutes. Add the remaining broth if needed to thin the sauce. Taste for salt and serve hot, garnished with cilantro leaves.

lamb cooked with almonds

BADAAMI GOSHT

SERVES 6

Here, lamb is poached in a spiced broth, then cooked again with almonds and yogurt. It makes for a wonderful, unusual dish with a subtle, nutty, and creamy sauce. This simple recipe is perfect for those times when guests come for a meal at short notice.

You can make the recipe with chicken as well: Use a 3½- to 4-pound chicken, skinned and cut into 8 to 10 pieces, and reduce the cooking time to 30 to 35 minutes.

2¼ pounds leg of lamb, trimmed of fat and
    cut into 1-inch pieces
5 cups water
1 cinnamon stick
6 green cardamom pods
½ teaspoon turmeric
Salt
¼ cup canola oil
5 whole dried red chiles

1 teaspoon cumin seeds
½ teaspoon fennel seeds
6 whole cloves
½ cup finely ground blanched almonds
5 garlic cloves, finely minced
2 inches fresh ginger, finely minced
½ teaspoon cayenne pepper
1 cup plain yogurt, whisked until smooth

Combine the lamb, water, cinnamon, cardamom, turmeric, and ¼ teaspoon salt in a large casserole. Bring to a boil, turn down the heat and simmer, uncovered, until the lamb is tender, about 1 hour. Remove the lamb with a slotted spoon. Reserve 1 cup of the broth; discard the rest.

Heat the oil with the red chiles in a large, heavy-bottomed casserole over medium-high heat and cook, stirring, until the chiles turn a very dark brown, about 3 minutes. Remove the pan from the heat and discard the chiles.

Return the pan to medium-high heat. Add the cumin, fennel, and cloves and cook, stirring, for 30 seconds. Add the ground almonds and cook for a minute to give them some color.

Add the lamb and cook, stirring, until it begins to brown, 2 to 3 minutes, then add the garlic, ginger, and cayenne and cook, stirring, for 1 minute. Mix in the yogurt, 2 tablespoons at a time, stirring well after each addition.

Add ¾ cup of the reserved broth and 1 teaspoon salt. Bring to a boil, reduce the heat and simmer for 2 minutes. Add the remaining broth if needed to thin the sauce. Taste for salt and serve hot.

ground beef with spinach and fresh mint

HARA KEEMA

SERVES 4

This is a great dish for the summer. The fresh taste of the mint makes it taste light even for a beef dish, and because it's a dry curry, it doesn't warm you up the way a steaming, brothy beef stew does. This is also very good, and a little different tasting, with ground lamb. Both are excellent served with Bhaturas (page 192) or pita and a Cucumber Raita (page 178).

GREEN PASTE
10 ounces fresh spinach, stemmed and washed
1/2 cup fresh cilantro sprigs
1/4 cup fresh mint leaves

1/4 cup canola oil
A 1-inch piece cinnamon stick
8 green cardamom pods
6 whole cloves
4 garlic cloves, finely minced

A 2-inch piece peeled fresh ginger, grated
1 large onion, halved, then halved again and
** sliced 1/2 inch thick**
1 fresh hot green chile, cut crosswise into
** 1/2-inch rounds**
1 teaspoon salt, or to taste
1 1/2 pounds lean ground beef
1/2 teaspoon ground black pepper
1 cup plain yogurt, whisked until smooth
1/2 teaspoon garam masala (page 250)

For the green paste, bring 2 inches of water to a boil in a large saucepan over high heat. Add the spinach and stir. Cover and steam, stirring every now and then, until wilted, about 5 minutes. Puree in a blender (with any remaining water) along with the cilantro and mint leaves. Set aside.

Heat the oil with the cinnamon stick, cardamom, and cloves in a large, heavy-bottomed casserole over medium-high heat, and cook, stirring, until the cinnamon unfurls, about 2 minutes.

Add the garlic and ginger and cook, stirring, 1 minute. Add the onion, green chile, and salt and cook, stirring, until the onion begins to brown around the edges, 8 to 10 minutes.

Stir in the beef and black pepper and cook, stirring, 5 minutes. Add the yogurt 2 tablespoons at a time and stir well after each addition. Simmer gently, stirring every now and then, 5 minutes. Add the green paste, bring to a boil, reduce the heat, and simmer 5 more minutes.

Stir in the garam masala and cook 1 more minute. Taste for salt. Serve hot.

ground lamb with almonds, cardamom, and coconut

SAFED KEEMA

SERVES 4 TO 6

A lamb dish with a creamy white sauce like this one, bound with ground almonds, could only be a Mogul recipe from North India. It's traditional in such dishes to use white cardamom pods and peppercorns so as not to mar the perfect white color of the sauce, but don't worry—green cardamom and black pepper taste pretty much the same. This has a wonderful, rather exotic flavor, tasting subtly of coconut and cardamom, with the creamy richness of almond in the background.

¼ cup blanched almonds

¼ cup canola oil

10 green cardamom pods

1 large onion, sliced

5 garlic cloves, finely minced

1 teaspoon salt, or to taste

1½ pounds ground lamb

1 cup plain yogurt, whisked until smooth

1 teaspoon ground cardamom

1 teaspoon ground pepper, preferably white

½ teaspoon garam masala (page 250)

1 fresh hot green chile, cut in half lengthwise

½ cup heavy cream

½ cup unsweetened shredded coconut, or ¼ cup ground, blanched almonds

Grind the almonds as fine as possible in a spice grinder; set aside.

Heat the oil in a large, heavy-bottomed pan over medium-high heat. Add the cardamom pods and cook, stirring, until they puff, 1 to 2 minutes. Add the onion, garlic, and salt and cook, stirring, until the onion begins to brown around the edges, 8 to 10 minutes.

Stir in the lamb and cook, stirring, for 5 minutes. Add the yogurt 2 tablespoons at a time and stir well after each addition. Cook, stirring every now and then, 5 minutes.

Stir in the ground cardamom, white or black pepper, garam masala, and green chile. Add the almond powder and stir well. Simmer 3 minutes.

Remove the green chile and stir in the cream and coconut or the additional ¼ cup ground almonds. Bring to a simmer and cook 2 minutes. Taste for salt and serve hot.

savory lamb patties

MURGH TIKKIS

SERVES 4

This is a dish a friend of mine first prepared for a party in Bombay. My friends ate them inside buns that weren't very different from the hamburger buns you can find in supermarkets, and many people in India eat these patties like burgers: topped with cheese, sliced onions, and tomatoes.

1 pound ground lamb

1 jalapeño pepper, finely minced

1 medium red onion, finely minced

3 garlic cloves, finely minced

1 inch fresh ginger, finely minced

¼ cup finely chopped fresh cilantro leaves, plus extra for garnish

¼ cup finely chopped fresh mint leaves (optional)

½ teaspoon Worcestershire sauce

½ teaspoon white vinegar

Salt

Ground black pepper

1 slice of stale white bread, soaked in water and squeezed dry

1 egg, beaten, with pinches of salt and pepper added for seasoning

Bread crumbs for coating

In a heavy-bottomed pan over medium–low heat, sauté the lamb in its own fat until most of the liquid has evaporated. Transfer to a large bowl and set aside to cool.

In a separate bowl, mix together the onion, garlic, ginger, cilantro, mint (if using), Worcestershire, and vinegar, then add the mixture to the large bowl of lamb and combine. Season the lamb mixture to taste with salt and black pepper. Mash the soaked white bread in your hands and add it to the lamb mixture.

Form the ground spiced lamb into patties. The shape and size depends on your mood and the number of guests.

Roll each patty in the egg and then in a bowl filled with bread crumbs. Place on a platter and repeat until all the lamb has been coated.

In a nonstick frying pan, fry the patties until crisp and nicely golden. You can use a little canola or butter if you want more color on them. Keep the cutlets warm in a 350°F oven until all of them are done, then serve right away, garnished with cilantro.

gael's tandoori lamb chops

BURRAH KABAB

SERVES 4

Burrah literally means "big," so this is a recipe for people who like big kebabs. (Our good friend Gael Greene, for whom this recipe is named, is a particular fan.) There is a mosque in Old Delhi called Jama Masjid that is the largest mosque in India. The streets around it are peppered with stalls selling street foods. One such stall is Karim's, one of my favorite places to take friends and especially first-time visitors to India. Karim's is famous for many of their lamb preparations, and this is one of them. Hemant Mathur serves these chops at the Indian restaurant Amma, in New York City.

The kababs taste of the warm flavors of garlic, cumin, nutmeg, and mace, balanced by the sharpness of vinegar and lemon. The chops need to marinate overnight to absorb the marinade, so if you spend a few minutes to toss together the marinade the night before, the next night's dinner will take almost no time at all to put together.

The papaya paste acts as a tenderizer, but if you can't find it, the chops are tender enough without it. Be sure to drain the yogurt for at least 2 hours before using or the lamb will never develop that savory crust during cooking.

2 pounds rib lamb chops, cut 1 to 1½ inches thick

1 tablespoon paprika

½ teaspoon cayenne pepper

¼ teaspoon ground mace

¼ teaspoon ground nutmeg

1 tablespoon garam masala (page 250)

1 tablespoon toasted cumin seeds, coarsely ground (see sidebar, page 39)

8 medium garlic cloves, minced very fine or ground to a paste

A 3-inch piece fresh ginger, peeled and minced very fine or ground to a paste

¼ cup malt vinegar

Juice of 1 lemon

1 teaspoon salt

¾ cup yogurt, drained in a cheesecloth-lined strainer or a coffee filter for 2 hours

2 tablespoons canola oil

3 tablespoons melted butter

Cut three or four deep slashes in each of the chops.

Mix all of the remaining ingredients except the oil and melted butter in a nonplastic bowl large enough to hold the chops. Add the chops and toss to coat in the marinade. Put the chops with the marinade in a large, resealable plastic bag and refrigerate overnight.

Preheat the oven to 550°F. or preheat the grill.

Add the oil to the bag with the chops, reseal, and massage the bag between your hands to oil the chops. Remove the chops from the marinade. If roasting in the oven, put the chops in a single layer on a rack in a foil-lined baking pan and roast 20 minutes; remove from the oven and let rest 5 minutes; then turn the chops, drizzle with the butter, and roast 10 more minutes. If grilling, grill 5 minutes on each side; let rest 5 minutes off the grill, then brush with the butter and grill 5 more minutes on each side.

mogul lamb "filet" in a cream sauce with garam masala

GOSHT PASANDA

SERVES 4

This is a lovely recipe and rather unusual if you know Indian food only from restaurants. *Pasanda,* which means "filet," is a classic Mogul preparation in which thin pieces of lamb filet are pounded, sautéed in a wet spice mixture, then finished in the oven with a creamy yogurt sauce spiced with a whole garam masala (see page 250). The trick to this recipe is to sauté, not boil, the lamb in the spice mixture. In order to do so, the pureed onion mixture and then the yogurt are cooked almost dry before the meat is added. This guarantees meat that is beautifully tender with an intensely flavored sauce. The ingredient list may seem a bit long, but the dish itself doesn't take long to make and it's an exquisite one for a special occasion.

There are two versions of this recipe that I know of. In this one, the sauce is made with yogurt and/or cream. The other is made with onion and tomato. I like this recipe better. When you want a more tomatoey sauce, add a pureed ripe tomato to the lamb after it is cooked. And use ghee, if you have it, or butter; it adds a distinct richness to the sauce. If you don't have Indian poppy seeds, you can make the recipe without; just don't try to substitute American poppy seeds.

The dish is finished in the oven, on a very low heat, so that the lamb steams very gently in the sauce. If you have a diffuser or an asbestos pad, you can finish it over the lowest possible flame on top of the stove.

Serve with Parathas (page 194) or just pita bread, warmed in the toaster oven.

MARINADE
¼ teaspoon salt
¼ teaspoon ground garam masala (page 250)
¼ teaspoon ground ginger
¼ teaspoon ground black pepper
¼ teaspoon ground cardamom
Juice of ½ lemon

1½ pounds well-trimmed boneless leg of lamb, sliced as thin as possible, the slices cut into strips about 2¼ inches long and 1 inch wide
4 tablespoons ghee, butter, or canola oil
1 medium onion, finely chopped
1 teaspoon salt, or to taste
4 garlic cloves

A 1½-inch piece fresh ginger, peeled and cut into large chunks
¼ cup slivered blanched almonds
2 tablespoons warm water
A 1-inch piece of cinnamon stick
2 black or 6 green cardamom pods
2 bay leaves
6 whole cloves
1 cup plain yogurt, whisked until smooth
1 very ripe medium tomato, pureed (optional)
¼ cup heavy cream
1 teaspoon ground garam masala
½ teaspoon ground cardamom
½ teaspoon ground black pepper
¼ teaspoon cayenne pepper
1 tablespoon julienned fresh ginger, for garnish

For the marinade, combine the ingredients in a large bowl. Add the lamb and toss. Refrigerate for 1 hour to marinate. Heat 3 tablespoons of the ghee, butter, or oil in a large, heavy-bottomed casserole, preferably oven-proof, over medium-high heat. Add half of the chopped onion (reserve the rest) and the salt and cook, stirring, until it turns light brown, 10 to 15 minutes. If the onion starts to burn on the edges before it browns, turn the heat down a little. Keep a cup of water beside the stove as the onion cooks. If the caramelized sugars begin to stick to the bottom of the pan, add water, about 1 teaspoon at a time, and scrape the pan with the spoon to pull up all the sugars and keep them from burning. Do this as often as necessary until the onion is golden. Remove from the heat.

Preheat the oven to 275°F.

Meanwhile, combine the cooked onion, reserved chopped onion, garlic, ginger, almonds, and warm water in a blender and blend to a smooth paste; set aside.

Add the remaining 1 tablespoon ghee, butter, or oil to the pan over medium-high heat. Add the cinnamon, cardamom, bay leaves, and cloves and cook, stirring, until the cinnamon unfurls, 1 to 2 minutes.

Add the onion paste and cook, stirring, until most of the water has evaporated and it has turned a deep tan color, about 5 minutes. Continue to sprinkle in water as needed as the paste begins to brown and stick to the bottom of the pan.

Add the yogurt about 1 tablespoon at a time and stir well after each addition. Then cook, stirring, until the mixture is dry again, about 5 minutes. Add the marinated lamb and cook, stirring, until the oil begins to separate out of the sauce, about 5 more minutes. (The lamb may begin to brown.) Add the pureed tomato, if using, and bring to a boil.

Transfer to the casserole. Drizzle the cream around the edges of the dish. Sprinkle with the ground garam masala, cardamom, black pepper, and cayenne. Cover and bake 10 minutes. Stir everything together and taste for salt. Garnish with the ginger, if using, and serve hot.

SALMON CURRY

HALIBUT IN A HOT-AND-SOUR SAUCE

SALMON "EN PAPILLOTE" WITH A COCONUT-CILANTRO CHUTNEY

 fish and shellfish

HALIBUT "EN PAPILLOTE" WITH A MINT-CILANTRO CHUTNEY

SPICY FRIED SALMON

MANGALORE FRIED SHRIMP

GOAN SHRIMP BALCHAO

TANDOORI PRAWNS

India is surrounded on three sides by ocean and numerous rivers flow through the country. Of course, all of the coastal regions of India have their traditional, local seafood dishes. Seafood in Bombay is typically roasted in the tandoor, which makes it incomparably delicious. I've adapted a recipe for tandoori prawns for the grill and a conventional oven. Bombay also has a tradition of steaming fish in a wrapping of banana leaves. I've adapted some of those recipes for the oven, too, baked "en papillote."

The east and west coasts of India are famous for their seafood dishes. On both coasts they make curries like the Salmon Curry on page 150, with whatever fish is freshly caught. The coastal shrimp is also excellent in curry dishes. On the eastern coast of India, Bengal is famous for its mustard-based fish dishes; the Brahmans of Bengal (who are otherwise vegetarian) call seafood *jal torai,* "zucchini of the seas." In Tamil Nadu, the southeastern tip of India, seafood is flavored with tamarind and curry leaves. And on the western coast of Malabar, curry leaves and coconut are the local seasonings while in Goa, seafood preparations are characterized by the use of coconut, chiles, and vinegar.

You'll see that most of the following recipes begin by marinating fish in salt, lemon juice, and sometimes turmeric. This is a traditional Indian technique that minimizes "fishiness" so that even people who aren't sure they like fish love the flavor.

salmon curry

SERVES 4

For this recipe, I have used a traditional sauce from Kerala in southern India, in a brand-new way. I cook the fish on top of, rather than in, the sauce so that it doesn't overcook. The sauce is very chunky, more like a chutney than a sauce. Serve this with Crispy Potatoes with Cumin (page 78), Plain Basmati Rice (page 91), and a raita.

Juice of 1 lemon
4 skinless salmon fillets (1½ to 2 pounds total),
    each about 1 inch thick
1½ teaspoons tamarind concentrate, or
    juice of 2 lemons
½ cup warm water (if using tamarind)

SPICE PASTE
2 teaspoons canola oil
2 teaspoons black mustard seeds
½ teaspoon fenugreek seeds (optional)
4 green cardamom pods
A ½-inch piece cinnamon stick
4 whole cloves

4 whole dried red chiles
10 fresh or 14 frozen curry leaves, torn into pieces
1 cup unsweetened shredded coconut
¾ cup water

3 tablespoons canola oil
12 fresh or 16 frozen curry leaves, torn into pieces
3 whole dried red chiles
1 large onion, very finely chopped
1 teaspoon salt, or to taste
¾ teaspoon turmeric
1 large ripe tomato, finely chopped
¾ cup water

Squeeze the lemon juice over the salmon and marinate for an hour in the refrigerator. Rinse and pat dry with paper towels.

Meanwhile, if using the tamarind, measure the warm water into a small bowl or measuring cup. Add the tamarind concentrate and stir to dissolve it. Rinse the measuring spoon and your fingers in the water to dissolve all of the sticky tamarind. Set this tamarind water aside.

For the spice paste, combine the oil, mustard seeds, fenugreek, if using, cardamom, cinnamon, cloves, red chiles, and curry leaves in a small frying pan over medium-high heat. Cover (the mustard seeds splatter and pop) and cook until you hear the mustard seeds begin to crackle, 1 to 2 minutes. Remove from the heat, stir in the coconut, and transfer to a blender. Add the water and blend to a paste. Set the paste aside.

Combine the oil with the curry leaves and red chiles in a large, heavy-bottomed casserole or deep frying pan over medium-high heat. Cook, stirring, until the chiles begin to brown, 1 to 2 minutes. Add the onion and ½ teaspoon of the salt, and cook, stirring, until the onion turns a sandy brown color, about 10 minutes.

Add the turmeric and cook, stirring, 30 seconds. Add the chopped tomato and the reserved tamarind water, if using. Bring to a boil, turn the heat down, and simmer on low heat for 3 minutes.

Stir in the spice paste, the water, and the remaining ½ teaspoon salt. Bring to a boil, reduce the heat, and simmer until the sauce thickens, 1 to 2 minutes. Stir in the lemon juice, if using.

Lightly sprinkle the salmon with salt and arrange it in a single layer on top of the sauce. Cover and simmer very gently until the fish is just cooked through, 8 to 10 minutes. Serve hot.

halibut in a hot-and-sour sauce

SERVES 4

This is a wonderful dish that I've adapted from a Goan recipe. Traditionally, it's made with prawns and you can certainly use prawns, shrimp, or even scallops; I like the fire and spice of the sauce with halibut. This is usually cooked with a lot more cayenne (up to 2 teaspoons!) than you'll find listed in this recipe; I've softened the heat substantially. But if you like really hot food, go ahead and add more. Serve with Spicy Peas Sautéed with Ginger (page 69), Cumin-Scented Rice Pilaf (page 91), and a raita.

SPICE POWDER

1 teaspoon cumin seeds
1 teaspoon fenugreek seeds (optional)
1 teaspoon ground ginger
1 teaspoon turmeric
1 teaspoon sugar
1/4 teaspoon cayenne pepper

1 tablespoon tamarind concentrate, or
    juice of 2 lemons
1/2 cup warm water (if using tamarind)
2 tablespoons canola oil
2 whole dried red chiles

1 teaspoon cumin seeds
2 green cardamom pods
1 large onion, finely chopped
1 garlic clove, finely chopped
Salt
4 large, very ripe tomatoes, peeled, seeded, and finely
    chopped by hand or in a food processor
2 cups water
1 1/2 to 2 pounds halibut steak (1 inch thick), boned and
    cut into 2-inch pieces
2 limes
1 bunch fresh cilantro, roughly chopped

For the spice powder, grind the cumin and fenugreek, if using, to a powder in a spice grinder. Stir in the remaining ingredients and set aside.

If using tamarind, measure the warm water into a small bowl or cup. Add the tamarind concentrate and stir to dissolve it. Rinse the measuring spoon and your fingers in the water to dissolve all of the sticky tamarind. Set this tamarind water aside.

Combine the oil with the chiles, cumin, and cardamom in a large casserole over medium-high heat. Cook, stirring, until fragrant, 1 to 2 minutes. Add the onion, garlic, and 3/4 teaspoon salt and cook, stirring, 1 minute. Add the spice powder and cook, stirring, 1 minute. Add the tomatoes, bring to a simmer, and cook 3 minutes.

Add the tamarind water, if using, and 1 cup of the water, bring to a boil, and simmer vigorously until reduced by about one-half. Add the remaining 1 cup water and simmer again until reduced by about one-half. (The sauce will be very thick; about the consistency of a chutney.) Stir in the lemon juice, if using.

Sprinkle the halibut with salt. Turn the heat down to low, add the halibut, cover, and cook until the fish is cooked through, 6 to 8 minutes.

Meanwhile, grate the zest from 1 lime and juice both limes.

When the fish is cooked, fold in the cilantro. Spoon into a serving bowl, drizzle the lime juice over the top, and sprinkle with the zest. Serve hot.

salmon "en papillote" with a coconut-cilantro chutney

PATRA NI MACHHI

SERVES 4

I've adapted this dish from a celebrated Parsi dish of fish steamed in banana leaves. I can't eat it without thinking of the Parsis of Bombay, among whom I lived while I was in school there. They are an extraordinarily civilized people, as educated as any on earth and beautifully dressed. But when you go to a Parsi banquet, you see another side of the culture. The people are so enraptured by the food that a sort of brawl breaks out when the buffet is opened. This is one of my favorite Parsi dishes; the fresh, citrusy taste of the cilantro, with the mint and coconut, tastes just heavenly with salmon.

4 skinless salmon fillets, 6 to 8 ounces each (about 1 inch thick)
1 teaspoon salt

CILANTRO-COCONUT CHUTNEY
2/3 cup grated fresh coconut, or 2/3 cup unsweetened shredded coconut mixed with 1/3 cup milk
3 fresh hot green chiles
3/4 teaspoon cumin seeds

6 garlic cloves
2 cups fresh cilantro leaves
1/3 cup fresh mint leaves (optional)
3/4 teaspoon tamarind concentrate or juice of 2 small lemons
1 teaspoon fresh lemon juice (if using the tamarind)

Canola oil, for brushing

Sprinkle the fish all over with the salt and refrigerate 30 minutes.

Meanwhile, for the chutney, combine the ingredients in a food processor and process until well chopped. Preheat the oven to 450°F.

When the fish has marinated 30 minutes, rinse and pat it dry.

Cut a piece of aluminum foil about 15 inches long and lay it on a work surface, one of the short sides facing you. Brush the bottom half with a little oil. Spoon about one-eighth of the chutney on the bottom half of the foil rectangle and spread it out to a horizontal rectangle about the size of the salmon fillet. Set one fillet on top of the chutney and cover with another eighth of the chutney. Fold the top half of the foil rectangle over the salmon so that the top and bottom edges meet. Fold the bottom edge up about 1/4 inch, and then fold it up twice more. Do the same on both sides to completely seal the salmon in the foil package. Repeat to make three more packages.

Put the packages in a single layer on a baking sheet and bake until the foil just begins to puff, about 11 minutes. Cut the packages open and slide the fish and chutney out onto plates. Serve hot.

variation

For salmon cooked "en papillote" with tomato chutney, follow the directions above, but instead of the Cilantro-Coconut Chutney, use a store-bought tomato chutney—using a tablespoon underneath the fillet and a tablespoon on top. Cook exactly the same way.

GRATING FRESH COCONUT

Coconuts may be available at your supermarket. If not, you'll find them sold in markets in Hispanic and Asian neighborhoods. To grate fresh coconut meat, twist or hammer a screwdriver or a sharpening steel into two of the "eyes" of the coconut and pour out the coconut juice. (This sweet juice is not a substitute for coconut milk, the thick, rich liquid that you buy in cans in the supermarket and use in curry recipes. It does, however, make a lovely, sweet, and very refreshing drink if you strain and chill it well.)

Bake the coconut in a 350°F. oven to make the white flesh pull away from the brown husk. Then wrap the coconut in a towel and bang with a hammer in several places to split it open. Use a regular screwdriver to separate the white flesh from the hard brown shell. Then use a vegetable peeler to peel off the thin layer of brown skin. Grate the coconut on a grater or in a food processor.

halibut "en papillote" with a mint-cilantro chutney

MACHI GULNAR

SERVES 4

This dish comes from the famous Mogul city of Oudh, which, like Lucknow and Delhi, is the home of a lively and successful fusion of Mogul and local cultures. Peter Beck, chef of the restaurant Tamarind in New York City, has popularized this dish in New York. The fish is baked "en papillote" with a chutney, as in the preceding recipe, but here the fillets are split and stuffed with the chutney. (If splitting the fish in half is daunting, you can just coat the top and bottom of the fish with the chutney, as in the previous recipe, and bake it "en papillote"; the cooking time is the same.) I use cream cheese in the chutney to replace strained yogurt (yogurt that has been drained to remove as much liquid as possible, so that it is thick, like cream cheese) that binds the ingredients and gives the mixture a luscious texture. Serve this fish with your favorite dal, a vegetable stir-fry, and raita.

4 skinless halibut fillets, 6 to 8 ounces each (about
  1 inch thick)
2 teaspoons salt
Juice of 1 lemon
¼ cup plain yogurt
½ teaspoon garam masala (page 250)

MINT-CILANTRO CHUTNEY
2 cups fresh cilantro leaves
1 bunch scallions, white parts only, trimmed
A 1-inch piece fresh ginger, peeled and cut into
  large pieces

4 garlic cloves
3 fresh hot green chiles, stemmed and seeded,
  if you like
½ cup fresh mint leaves (optional)
⅓ cup cream cheese
¾ teaspoon cumin seeds
½ teaspoon sugar
¼ teaspoon salt, or to taste
Juice of 1 lemon

Sprinkle the halibut all over with 1 teaspoon of the salt and the lemon juice and refrigerate 10 minutes. Rinse and pat the fish dry on paper towels. Stir together the yogurt, garam masala, and remaining 1 teaspoon of salt. Pour over the fish and refrigerate 45 more minutes. Meanwhile, for the chutney, combine the ingredients in a blender and process until well blended.

Preheat the oven to 450°F. Cut a piece of aluminum foil about 15 inches long and lay it on a work surface, one of the short sides facing you. Brush the bottom half with a little oil. Set one fillet on top of the greased foil. Cut the fillet in half crosswise and remove the top half. Spoon 1 to 2 tablespoons chutney over the bottom half and cover with the top half. Spoon 1 to 2 more tablespoons chutney on top of the fish. Fold the top half of the foil rectangle over the halibut so that the top and bottom edges meet. Fold the bottom edge up about ¼ inch, and then fold it up twice more. Do the same on both sides to completely seal the halibut in the foil package. Repeat to make three more packages.

Put the packages in a single layer on a baking sheet and bake until the foil just begins to puff, about 10 minutes. Cut the packages open and slide the fish and chutney out onto plates. Serve hot.

spicy fried salmon

SOOKHEE MASALEDAAR MACHEE

SERVES 4

This simple recipe is from northern India, where it is often served as a snack in the late evenings as friends sit and enjoy cocktails; it so happens that most Indians love their Black Label Scotch at that hour. I think salmon tastes particularly good breaded this way, but you can substitute any other fish, or use larger pieces. Serve with Green Chutney (page 209) and a raita.

8 garlic cloves, ground to a paste with ¼ teaspoon cumin seeds

A 2-inch peeled fresh ginger, finely minced

2½ teaspoons ground coriander

¼ teaspoon salt

Pinch of cayenne pepper

1½ tablespoons fresh lime juice

1½ pounds skinless salmon fillet, cut into 2-inch pieces, about ⅓ inch thick

2 cups bread crumbs, seasoned with ¼ teaspoon salt and pinch of cayenne

1¼ cups ghee or canola oil

Lemon wedges, for serving

Stir together the garlic–cumin paste, ginger, coriander, salt, cayenne, and lime juice. Rub over the salmon and refrigerate 2 hours.

Spread the bread crumbs on a large plate. Coat the salmon squares in the crumbs.

Heat the ghee or canola oil in a large, heavy-bottomed frying pan over medium heat until "shimmering." Add as many salmon pieces as will comfortably fit in one layer and cook until well browned on both sides and cooked through, about 2½ minutes total. (If the salmon browns faster than that, turn the heat down.) Remove the salmon to a plate lined with paper towels. Continue until all of the salmon has been cooked. Serve hot, with the lemon wedges.

mangalore fried shrimp

SERVES 4

This dish is from the southern Indian coastal state of Karnataka, where seafood is an important part of the diet. The shrimp has extraordinary flavor. I sometimes vary the recipe by adding 1½ tablespoons unsweetened shredded coconut along with the mustard seeds, or 2 to 6 chopped small fresh green chiles with the scallion. Serve with Green Chutney (page 209) or lemon wedges, Lemon Rice (page 92), and a raita.

1 pound medium shrimp, peeled and deveined
½ teaspoon cayenne pepper
¼ teaspoon turmeric
¼ teaspoon mustard powder
2 teaspoons fresh lemon juice
4 teaspoons canola oil

½ teaspoon cumin seeds or black mustard seeds
6 fresh or 10 frozen curry leaves, torn into pieces
(optional)
3 tablespoons finely chopped scallion
Salt to taste

Rinse the shrimp and pat them dry on paper towels. Put them in a bowl and sprinkle with the cayenne, turmeric, mustard powder, and lemon juice. Stir gently to coat the shrimp evenly with the spices. Cover and refrigerate for 30 minutes.

When the shrimp have marinated, combine the oil, cumin or mustard seeds , and curry leaves, if using, in a large wok, frying pan, or *kadai* over medium-high heat. Cover, if using mustard seeds (the seeds splatter and pop), and cook until the cumin darkens and/or you hear the mustard seeds crackle, 1 to 2 minutes.

Add the shrimp and cook, stirring, 30 seconds, stirring often.

Add the chopped scallion and cook, stirring, until the shrimp turn pink all over, about 1 minute. Sprinkle with salt and serve hot.

goan shrimp balchao

SERVES 4

We serve this dish at Amma, my restaurant in midtown Manhattan. This dish has a mixture of Indian and European flavors, since it comes from the Goa region of India, once a Portuguese colony. Its appeal is in the contrast between the sweetness of the butter-sautéed shrimp and the smoky red chile–spiced tomato sauce. The sauce should be hot and tangy and the shrimp sweet and perfectly cooked.

SPICE PASTE
1 teaspoon cayenne pepper
½ teaspoon garam masala (page 250)
1 inch fresh ginger root, chopped
3 cloves of garlic
2 teaspoons rice wine vinegar

1 pound shrimp, shelled, deveined, and dried
4 whole dried red chiles
2 tablespoons canola oil
1 medium red onion, finely chopped
3 garlic cloves, finely minced
Salt
1 teaspoon sugar
10 curry leaves (optional)
2 medium tomatoes, finely chopped
1 tablespoon butter

In small food processor, finely blend the spice paste ingredients. Set aside. Salt the shrimp lightly and set aside while you prepare the sauce.

In a heavy-bottomed pan fry the red chiles in the canola oil, until dark brown in color, but not burnt, a minute at most. Add onions and sauté over medium-high heat until brown. Add the garlic, salt to taste, and sugar and fry for a minute more. Add the curry leaves, if using, and the tomatoes, and cook until the tomatoes lose some of their moisture.

Melt the butter in a frying pan over medium heat, and sauté the shrimp until firm and pink, barely a couple of minutes, depending on size. Ladle the sauce into a bowl and top with the shrimp, or add the sauce to the pan with the shrimp and toss before serving.

tandoori prawns

A tandoori oven cooks with a searing heat that cannot really be equaled in the home kitchen. But I've found a way to approximate the tandoori effect with prawns, using the oven or the grill. If using a grill, preheat it well before cooking. If using an oven, cook the shrimp on a rack over a foil-lined pan; the marinade will burn where it falls in the pan and foil makes it immeasurably easier to clean up. You'll need to buy prawns or very large shrimp (called "colossal" or "U-8's" in the industry); the little ones cook before the marinade has a chance to become a delectable coating. Serve with a dal, Cumin-Scented Rice Pilaf (page 91), and a raita. Since this recipe doesn't use food coloring, the dish does not have the bright red color of restaurant tandoori.

MARINADE

3 tablespoons minced fresh ginger

3 tablespoons minced garlic

3 tablespoons all-purpose flour or chickpea flour
   (besan)

1 teaspoon cumin or carom seeds

1 teaspoon ground white pepper

1 teaspoon garam masala (page 250)

1/2 teaspoon turmeric

1/2 cup lemon juice

2 cups plain yogurt, drained over a bowl in a
   cheesecloth-lined strainer or a coffee filter for
   at least 2 hours

12 "colossal" shrimp (about 2 pounds), shelled

1 teaspoon cumin seeds

Salt

3 tablespoons butter, melted

1 lemon, cut in half

For the marinade, stir together the ginger, garlic, all-purpose or chickpea flour, cumin or carom seeds , white pepper, garam masala, and turmeric in a bowl large enough to hold the shrimp. Stir in the lemon juice and then the yogurt, 1/4 cup at a time, stirring until smooth after each addition.

Add the shrimp and toss to coat with the marinade. Refrigerate for at least 2 hours.

Toast the cumin in a dry frying pan over medium heat, stirring, until fragrant and lightly browned, 2 to 3 minutes. Grind to a powder and set aside.

Preheat the oven to 550°F., or heat the grill. If using the oven, put the shrimp in a single layer on a rack in a foil-lined baking pan, sprinkle with salt, and roast 10 minutes; remove from the oven and let rest 15 minutes, then brush with the melted butter and roast another 10 minutes. If grilling, grill 3 minutes each side; let rest 15 minutes off the grill, then brush with the butter and grill 10 more minutes.

Arrange the shrimp on a platter, sprinkle with the reserved toasted cumin, and squeeze the lemon over. Serve hot.

SPINACH, ONION, AND POTATO PAKORAS

PUFF PASTRY SAMOSAS WITH GREEN PEAS

ANN'S CHEESE TOASTS

CHICKPEA SALAD

CRISP TORTILLA CHIPS WITH CHICKPEAS AND YOGURT

*appetizers
and snacks

WARM BREAD SALAD WITH MUSTARD, CUMIN, AND TOMATO

"SCRAMBLED" TOFU WITH INDIAN SPICES

PAPADUM

SPINACH-POTATO PATTIES

WARM POTATO SALAD

Most of the recipes in this book are for dishes that are to be eaten during regular mealtimes. This chapter, however, is devoted to foods that we Indians serve with cocktails, as appetizers, or as afternoon snacks—that is, any time friends or family gather outside of formal meals. Every child in India grows up with the expectation of coming home in the afternoon, with friends, to these kinds of snacks. And then when we grow up, we expect to visit our friends and neighbors and be served these same foods.

The whole idea of these dishes is that they can be put together almost instantaneously when people drop by unannounced—a usual and constant occurrence in India. We call this food *nashta*. It's something like the Jewish "nosh," which, interestingly enough, it sounds like. So, with a little forethought, these recipes can be put together with minimum preparation for an afternoon snack, lunch, brunch, or even a light dinner. The trick is to have a few things on hand, such as frozen peas and/or spinach, a package of frozen puff pastry, a can of chickpeas, yogurt, a couple of homemade or store-bought chutneys, and cold boiled potatoes.

These dishes are basically assembled foods. Boiled potatoes are chopped up, then fried and seasoned with spices and one or several chutneys. Peas are stirred with a chutney, wrapped in puff pastry, and baked. Or some starch—potatoes, chickpeas, bread cubes, or diamonds of crisp, deep-fried flatbread—is tossed together with spices and chutneys, perhaps with yogurt and a vegetable, too, to make a quick bite. These recipes are simple enough to put together that you can be entertaining people in your kitchen while you cook.

Incidentally, these are also the foods that are becoming popular in restaurants and on some corners of large American cities as Indian street food. In India, street vendors travel with carts of prepared foods that, upon request, they toss together with spices, chiles, and other seasonings, and serve up as warm or cold *chaats. Chaat* literally means "to lick." When I think of these foods, my mouth begins to water and I drool just remembering the last time I tasted one. You can ask that these made-to-order snacks be seasoned exactly as you like so that each preparation is slightly different from the next.

Chaat masala is a spice mixture traditionally used in some of these chaats—*aloo chaat,* on page 175, for example. It is a rather complex mix of ground, toasted spices meant to tickle a palate that is fatigued, overheated, or overindulged. The mix is sprinkled over the finished dish or tossed into it. I have substituted other spices for *chaat masala* in my recipes in the interest of simplicity, but you may want to buy some (you can find it at an Indian grocery store) and experiment with it.

Many of these snacks rely on green and tamarind chutneys for seasoning or as a condiment for serving. You'll find recipes for these two chutneys in the chutney chapter, but if your goal is speed, you can always buy them ready-made at a good supermarket or Indian grocery store.

spinach, onion, and potato pakoras

PALAK PAKORAS

MAKES ABOUT 30 PAKORAS

Traditionally, pakoras are made with one vegetable at a time, and each vegetable is fried in a specific shape. But my mother, who invented this recipe to feed an army of starving teenagers (we'd bring our friends home with us), would make them with spinach, onion, and potato all together. And she used less batter than is usual, so that they were irregularly shaped, quick to make, lighter, and I think more interesting than the traditional version. They make wonderful hors d'oeuvres for parties. But when I'm feeling greedy for them, I've been known to make them for dinner, accompanied by a hard-boiled egg for protein, so that I can eat as many as I like without fear of ruining my appetite for the main course.

These are unquestionably best straight out of the oil, but in a pinch you can reheat leftovers on a baking sheet at 180°F. or in a toaster oven. Save the broken bits that fall off of the pakora to eat crumbled on top of yogurt.

SPICE POWDER
1 teaspoon coriander seeds
1 teaspoon cumin seeds
1 teaspoon garam masala (page 250)
1/2 teaspoon cayenne pepper
1/2 teaspoon fennel seeds

6 firmly packed cups chopped, stemmed spinach
1 medium red boiling potato, peeled and very finely diced
1 medium red onion, cut into medium dice

1 fresh hot green chile, very finely chopped
1/3 cup chopped fresh cilantro
2 cups chickpea flour (besan)
1 teaspoon salt
1/2 teaspoon baking powder
1 3/4 cups water
Canola oil, for deep-frying
Green Chutney (page 209) or store-bought (sold as cilantro or mint chutney), to serve

For the spice powder, combine the spices in a mortar and pestle or spice grinder and grind very coarsely. Combine the spice powder with the vegetables, chile, cilantro, flour, fenugreek, salt, and baking powder and stir to coat everything with the flour. Add the water and stir to make a batter.

Pour about 3 inches of oil into a large saucepan or medium *kadai* and heat to 360°F. over medium heat. (To gauge the temperature of the oil without using a thermometer, drop a piece of bread about 1-inch square into the hot oil over medium heat, turning often; when the oil reaches 360°F., the bread should begin to brown almost immediately and turn golden brown—like a crouton—in about 30 seconds.) Use a scant 1/4 cup measure or large serving spoon to measure out about 3 tablespoons of the pakora mixture and slide it into the hot oil. Immediately turn the heat down to medium. Spoon several more pakoras into the oil (four or five total) and cook for 1 minute. Turn the *pakoras* over with a slotted spoon and cook for 1 more minute. Then turn the heat back up to high and continue cooking, turning twice, until evenly browned all over, 5 to 6 minutes. Remove to a paper-towel-lined platter with a slotted spoon. Repeat to cook all of the pakoras. Serve with chutney.

puff pastry samosas with green peas

MATAR KEE PATTY

MAKES 9 TURNOVERS

These are quick samosas using a frozen, commercial puff pastry instead of the traditional samosa dough. You can use cubed boiled potatoes in place of the peas, too, or combine the two vegetables if you like. I have fond memories of standing in line in school at our lunch break to buy myself some samosas like these. When I moved to the United States (where I was still in school), this was the first Indian recipe I made.

I always have homemade chutneys in the refrigerator to serve with this; a couple of store-bought chutneys will work, too, and make the recipe even easier. You'll need only three sheets of pastry for this recipe. Put the remaining pastry back in the freezer for the next time you want to make samosas.

2 tablespoons canola oil

1 teaspoon cumin seeds

1 (9- to 10-ounce) package frozen petite peas

¼ teaspoon salt

2 tablespoons Green Chutney (page 209), or
    store-bought (sold as cilantro or mint chutney)

1 tablespoon Tamarind Chutney (page 210),
    or store-bought

1 pound frozen puff pastry, thawed

1 egg whisked with a pinch of salt, for glaze

Preheat the oven to 400°F.

Combine the oil and cumin in a large frying pan over medium-high heat. Cook, stirring, until the cumin begins to brown, 1 to 2 minutes. Add the peas and the salt, and cook, covered, until the peas soften, 5 to 6 minutes. Remove from the heat and stir in the chutneys. Let cool.

Lay a sheet of puff pastry on a lightly floured work surface. Cut the sheet into thirds along the lines of the folds. Roll out one-third to a 6- by 12-inch rectangle. Cut the rectangle crosswise into thirds to make three smaller rectangles. Brush all around the edges of each with egg glaze. Spoon a generous tablespoon of peas in the center. Fold the top of the rectangle down so that it meets the bottom layer 1 to 1½ inches above the bottom edge and makes a triangle. Fold the bottom up and tuck the overhang over. Press gently to seal. Put on a baking sheet and brush with the egg glaze. Repeat to make two more turnovers. Then roll out and fill six more turnovers.

Bake until crisp, 18 to 20 minutes. Serve hot.

ann's cheese toasts

SERVES 4

One evening, when I had just started out as a young cooking teacher in America, I was telling two of my students about these cheese toasts that Panditji used to make. One of the students, Ann, dismissed the idea, saying that grilled cheese was an American institution and no other culture could possibly make them better. So that night I made these for the two of them. They both were very quiet for the rest of the evening, and next time I saw them they were bubbling with stories about their friends' reactions when they made these Indian grilled cheese sandwiches. Since then, I've always referred to them as Ann's cheese toasts. We often make a dinner out of them when she comes by to visit. You can also make these toasts using English muffins or bagels.

1 pound whole-milk mozzarella cheese, coarsely grated

1/2 cup finely chopped onion

1 medium tomato, very finely chopped and then squeezed in your hand to eliminate most of the liquid

2 fresh hot green chiles, seeded and finely diced

1/2 cup chopped fresh cilantro

1/2 cup mayonnaise

1/2 teaspoon cayenne pepper

Ground black pepper to taste

10 slices whole wheat bread, toasted

Preheat the broiler. Stir together all of the ingredients except the bread in a mixing bowl, mashing to make a fairly smooth mixture.

Spread the mixture on the toasted bread slices and put them in a single layer on baking sheets. Broil until the cheese mixture has melted and is lightly browned, 3 to 5 minutes. Serve hot.

chickpea salad

CHOLE KEE CHAAT

SERVES 4

This hot and tart North Indian classic is often served during holidays as an appetizer or a side dish. You can add to the spiciness by using more red pepper powder and fresh green chiles to your taste. It tastes good at room temperature, but has a great bite served chilled on a hot summer afternoon.

2 cups drained canned chickpeas

2 medium potatoes, boiled in skin, cooled, and chopped into small cubes

1 small hot green chile, finely chopped

1/2 small red onion, very finely chopped

3 teaspoons ground toasted cumin (see sidebar, page 39)

2 teaspoons lemon juice

1/4 teaspoon garam masala (page 250)

1 teaspoon cayenne pepper

1/2 teaspoon ground black pepper

1 tablespoon chopped fresh mint leaves or 1 teaspoon dry mint leaves

2 tablespoons chopped fresh cilantro

3 tablespoons Green Chutney (page 209) or store-bought

2 tablespoons Tamarind Chutney (page 210) or store-bought

Lemon or lime juice

Salt

Mint or cilantro leaves, for garnish

In a large bowl, mix the chickpeas, potatoes, green chile, and onions with the cumin, garam masala, cayenne, and black pepper. Toss a few times to make sure the spices are evenly distributed.

Add the mint and cilantro leaves, the two chutneys, and the lemon or lime juice to taste and toss again. Sprinkle with salt to taste. Garnish with mint or cilantro leaves to serve.

crisp tortilla chips with chickpeas and yogurt

LUCKNOWI CHAAT

SERVES 4 TO 6

In India, this salad is made with a roti dough that is rolled into a thin round, cut into diamonds, and deep-fried. Here in America, flour tortillas work fine and are even quicker because they're already rolled. I keep a tightly sealed container of the deep-fried tortillas in my refrigerator, and I always have boiled potatoes so that I can put this together very quickly.

The salad must be eaten immediately while the tortillas are still crisp. It is traditionally seasoned with black rock salt (*kaala namak*), a grayish-pink salt prized for its spicy, tangy taste. It's available anywhere you can buy Indian groceries. Regular table salt is fine.

12 large flour tortillas (preferably whole wheat)
Canola oil, for deep-frying
1¼ teaspoons cumin seeds
2 cups plain yogurt
¼ cup plus 1 tablespoon chopped fresh cilantro
1 fresh hot green chile, finely chopped
1 teaspoon sugar
½ teaspoon salt or Indian black salt *(kaala namak)*
½ teaspoon cayenne pepper

1 medium red boiling potato, simmered in water to
    cover until tender
1 (14½-ounce) can chickpeas, drained and rinsed
4½ tablespoons Green Chutney (page 209)
    or store-bought, plus extra for serving
3½ tablespoons Tamarind Chutney (page 210)
    or store-bought, plus extra for serving
Pinch of cayenne pepper, for garnish
Julienned fresh ginger, for garnish

Cut the tortillas into 1-inch strips. Then cut the strips on the diagonal to make diamond shapes that are about 1 inch wide and 2 inches long.

Pour about 3 inches of oil into a large saucepan or medium *kadai* and heat to 360°F. over medium heat. (To gauge the temperature of the oil without using a thermometer, drop a piece of bread about 1 inch square into the hot oil over medium heat, turning often; when the oil reaches 360°F. the bread should begin to brown almost immediately and turn golden brown—like a crouton—in about 30 seconds.) Turn the heat down to low, add the tortillas in two batches, and cook, stirring every now and then with a slotted spoon, until puffed and golden brown, 4 to 5 minutes. Drain on paper towels.

Toast the cumin in a dry frying pan over medium heat, stirring, until fragrant and lightly browned, 2 to 3 minutes. Grind to a powder and set aside.

Stir together the yogurt, ¼ cup of the cilantro, the green chile, 1 teaspoon of the toasted cumin, the sugar, salt, and cayenne in a large bowl; set aside.

Peel the potato. Slice it about ¼ inch thick and then cut into 1-inch cubes. Put the potato in a second bowl and add the chickpeas. Add 2 tablespoons of the green chutney and 1 tablespoon of the tamarind chutney and toss.

Assemble the tortilla chips, potato-chickpea mixture, yogurt mixture, and the chutneys on a work surface along with a large bowl or 8-inch baking dish. To assemble the *chaat,* sprinkle a handful of the tortilla chips over the bottom of the bowl or dish. Sprinkle a handful of the potato-chickpea mixture on top. Drop a handful of chips into the bowl filled with yogurt, stir to coat the chips, lift them out of the yogurt, and layer them on top of the potatoes. Drizzle 1/2 tablespoon tamarind chutney over the top, then drizzle with 1/2 tablespoon green chutney. Repeat this layering process three more times to use all of the tortilla chips, potato-chickpea mixture, and yogurt mixture. Pour any yogurt remaining in the bowl over the top. Drizzle the remaining 1/2 tablespoon each of the chutneys over the top and sprinkle with the remaining tablespoon cilantro. Sprinkle with the remaining 1/4 teaspoon toasted cumin and the cayenne, and garnish with the julienned ginger, if using. Serve immediately (before the tortilla chips get soggy) with more chutney on the side.

warm bread salad with mustard, cumin, and tomato

SERVES 4

For this Indian-style bread salad, I simmer toasted bread cubes with chopped fresh tomato and a spiced yogurt dressing until the bread gets juicy and savory. I use whole wheat bread because I like the texture, but you can use any good-quality bread.

12 slices whole wheat bread, cut into 1/2-inch dice

2 tablespoons canola oil

1 1/2 teaspoons black mustard seeds (optional)

1 teaspoon cumin seeds

1 large onion, sliced about 1/4 inch thick, slices cut in
    half crosswise

2 fresh hot green chiles, seeded and finely diced

1 teaspoon salt, or to taste

1 cup frozen peas, unthawed

1/2 teaspoon cayenne pepper

1/3 cup plain yogurt, stirred until smooth

2 medium tomatoes, chopped

Juice of 1/2 lime

Preheat the oven to 375°F. Spread the bread squares out in a single layer on a baking sheet and toast in the oven until the outside of the bread is dry, 6 to 7 minutes. Remove from the oven and set aside.

Combine the oil, mustard seeds, if using, and cumin seeds in a large wok or frying pan over medium-high heat. Cook, stirring, until the cumin darkens, 1 to 2 minutes. (Cover the pan if using mustard seeds—they splatter and pop—and cook until you hear the mustard seeds crackle.)

Add the onion, green chiles, and salt and cook, stirring every now and then, until the onion is softened but not brown, about 5 minutes. Add the peas, cover, and cook until soft, 3 to 4 minutes.

Stir in the cayenne and then, immediately, the yogurt. Add the toasted bread and gently stir to coat the bread with the oil and spices. Then stir in the tomatoes, cover, and cook until the bread is juicy, 4 to 5 minutes. Stir in the lime juice and taste for salt. Spoon the salad into a serving bowl and serve warm.

"scrambled" tofu with indian spices

SERVES 4

When tofu is mashed and then sautéed with onion and spices, it absorbs the taste of both and forms a texture very much like scrambled eggs. I sometimes make this for an informal dinner—it's substantial enough for that—but in India it's traditionally served as a snack. Cook it in two pans or in two batches so that the liquid from the tofu evaporates. This recipe divides very nicely in two.

2 (14-ounce) packages firm tofu, drained and patted dry
1/4 cup canola oil
2 teaspoons cumin seeds
1 teaspoon black mustard seeds (optional)
2 fresh hot green chiles, seeded and finely diced

2 cups chopped red onion
Salt
1 green bell pepper, seeded and finely diced
2 medium tomatoes, chopped
1 cup chopped fresh cilantro

Put the tofu in a bowl and mash it in your hand to break it up into smallish clumps (like scrambled eggs).

Divide the oil between two large frying pans or handled woks, and put them over medium-high heat. Divide the cumin and mustard seeds, if using, between the pans and cook, stirring, until the cumin turns golden brown and/or the mustard seeds crackle, 1 to 2 minutes. (Cover the pan if using mustard seeds; they splatter and pop.)

Add half of the chiles to each pan and cook, stirring, 30 seconds. Add half of the onion and 1/2 teaspoon salt to each pan and cook, stirring, until the onion begins to brown, 6 to 7 minutes.

Add half of the bell pepper to each pan and cook, stirring, until it softens, about 2 minutes. Divide the tofu between the pans and cook, stirring, to evaporate the liquid, 3 to 4 minutes.

Add half of the tomatoes to each pan and cook 2 minutes. Stir half of the cilantro into each pan, taste for salt, and serve.

papadum

These lentil-bean wafers, called papadum in the south and papad in the north, are eaten throughout India as a snack the way one would eat potato chips or popcorn here in America. They may also be served along with or at the end of the meal. In India, for a snack, we would make a quick salad of onion and hot peppers tossed with lemon juice, served on top of roasted papadum. Now, I often end up eating them late at night, watching a film in bed.

In the past, papadum were made in the home. Now packages of papadum are sold in grocery stores. All you have to do is cook them quickly to make them crisp. Most of us northern Indians prefer them roasted, but in the south, papadum are always deep-fried.

I like the Lijjat or Bikaneri Papad brands of papadums. Both are available at Indian grocery stores and online. Serve papadum on its own, as a snack, with any of the rice dishes, or with a simple dal and rice.

To roast the papadum on a gas stove, turn the flame to medium-high. Grasping a papadum with flat tongs, hold it over the flame so that the flame just touches it and roast, turning constantly to ensure even roasting, until the papadum loses its pale plastic look and turns an off-white color with some black spots, 30 seconds to a minute. Serve immediately.

If you have an electric stove, you'll need to deep-fry the papadum: Pour over 2 inches of oil into a large saucepan or medium *kadai* and heat to 360°F. over medium heat. (To gauge the temperature of the oil without using a thermometer, drop a piece of bread about 1-inch square into the hot oil over medium heat, turning often; when the oil reaches 360°F., the bread should begin to brown almost immediately and turn golden brown all over like a crouton in about 30 seconds.) Slide a papadum into the hot oil and cook until it puffs and turns a sandy beige color (if it browns it's overcooked), 3 to 5 seconds. Remove from the oil with tongs and drain on paper towels while you fry the rest of the papadums.

spinach-potato patties

PALAK KEE TIKKI

MAKES ABOUT 10 CAKES

Panditji makes these the traditional way—deep-fried—but I find it simpler to cook them in a small amount of oil in a nonstick pan. The patties can be made in the morning, refrigerated, and then sautéed for dinner.

I recently made these for a friend's grandmother in West Virginia who didn't have much in the way of Indian spices. I was able to get hold of only some cilantro, cayenne, and black pepper, but the patties turned out great anyway. In India, we'd eat these sandwiched between two slices of bread spread with tamarind or green chutney.

2 pounds red boiling potatoes, simmered in water
    to cover until tender, 20 to 30 minutes
4 firmly packed cups finely chopped, stemmed,
    washed spinach
1 fresh hot green chile, finely chopped
1/4 cup chopped fresh cilantro
1 teaspoon garam masala (page 250)
1/2 teaspoon cayenne pepper

1/2 teaspoon ground black pepper
1 1/4 teaspoons salt
Juice of 1/2 lemon
1 cup dried bread crumbs
2 tablespoons canola oil
Tamarind Chutney (page 209) or Green Chutney
    (page 210) or store-bought, for serving

Combine all of the ingredients except the bread crumbs, oil, and chutney in a large bowl and mix well with your hands, squeezing the ingredients together. (There will still be small chunks of potato in the mixture.)

Spread the bread crumbs on a plate or in a shallow bowl.

Scoop out about 1/2 cup of the spinach-potato mixture and dump it into the bowl with the bread crumbs. Roll it with the palm of your hand to make a ball and coat with the bread crumbs. Then press down to flatten to a 3-inch cake. Press the bread crumbs evenly onto the patty and put it in a baking dish. Continue to shape the rest of the mixture. When you've covered the bottom of the baking dish with a first layer, cover with plastic wrap and layer the rest of the patties on top. Chill at least 1 hour.

When you're ready to cook, heat 1 tablespoon of the oil in a large frying pan over high heat. When the pan is hot, swirl the pan to coat with the oil. Place five patties in the pan, and cook until well browned on one side, about 4 minutes. Turn and brown 4 more minutes. Turn and cook 1 more minute. Remove to a serving platter. Heat the remaining tablespoon oil in the pan and cook the remaining patties. Serve with chutney.

warm potato salad

ALOO CHAAT

SERVES 4

This is Delhi street food at its best. You'd buy it from a vendor selling made-to-order snacks *(chaats)* from a cart stocked with a variety of prepared foods that he tosses together at the whim of the customer. It would be plated on a large, dried leaf with a toothpick as a utensil. According to your specification, the vendor would add more or less of one of the chutneys, more or less spice and hot chile.

I often serve *aloo chaat* at parties as one of several appetizers. It also makes a good lunch, with an egg; if you find yourself eating it that way, count on serving only two from this recipe. Traditionally this is made with *chaat masala,* a rather complex spice mixture, but I've simplified the recipe by omitting it and adjusting the quantities of chutneys to compensate.

1 1/2 pounds (about 4) red boiling potatoes
3 tablespoons canola oil
2 tablespoons Green Chutney (page 209) or
    store-bought (sold as cilantro or mint chutney)
2 tablespoons Tamarind Chutney (page 210) or
    store-bought
1 tablespoon chopped fresh cilantro
1/2 fresh hot green chile, chopped (optional)

1 teaspoon ground toasted cumin (see sidebar,
    page 39)
1/2 teaspoon cayenne pepper
1/4 teaspoon garam masala (page 250)
1/4 teaspoon ground black pepper
Juice of 1/2 lemon
1/4 teaspoon salt

Simmer the potatoes in water to cover until tender, 25 to 30 minutes. Chill, then peel and cut into 1-inch cubes.

Heat the oil in a large nonstick pan over medium-high heat. Add the potatoes and cook, covered, turning the potatoes with a spatula every 3 or 4 minutes, until lightly browned, about 15 minutes. Drain on paper towels.

Put the potatoes in a bowl with all of the remaining ingredients and toss to combine. Serve hot or at room temperature.

CUCUMBER RAITA

MIXED RAITA

MINT AND ONION RAITA

PINEAPPLE RAITA

 raitas

EGGPLANT RAITA

GRAPE RAITA

ONION PACHADI

ZUCCHINI PACHADI

Creamy and tart, a raita is a kind of cold yogurt salad that cools the palate during a spicy meal. Raitas are simple to make by stirring yogurt until smooth and creamy and then flavoring it with raw or cooked vegetables or fruit, and sometimes with an aromatic tempering oil as well. A raita is an excellent way to add protein to a meal, fast. For example, if you have leftover stir-fried potatoes and cauliflower in the refrigerator—not really enough for dinner by itself—you can boil some rice and make a raita in just a few minutes and have a satisfying meal of varied tastes.

I've organized this chapter by starting with the simplest and most familiar raita, made with cucumber, and then moving on to those that are just slightly more complex. Some of the raitas are called *pachadi*—this is just the South Indian word for "raita." Raitas should be lightly salted—just enough to bring out the flavor of the salad. The salt must be added just before serving, however, so that the vegetables don't weep and dilute the raita. Tempering oil should traditionally be added just before serving, but I don't—I make the whole recipe at once and chill it, and I'm entirely satisfied with the results. You may use nonfat, low-fat, or full-fat yogurts in these recipes. Chill the raita well before serving if you have the time. All of these raitas are wonderful served with any Indian meal.

cucumber raita

KHEERE KA RAITA

SERVES 4 TO 6

This is the most common raita in India, and in America, too! Cucumbers are particularly cooling to the palate in the heat of the summer. As a child, I remember feeling comforted if I could at least find a cucumber raita on a restaurant menu—the other options all looked too exotic!

To make a southern Indian–style cucumber raita, called a *pachadi*, stir in a tempering oil at the end (see Variation).

2¼ cups plain yogurt
1 large cucumber, peeled and shredded
1 fresh hot green chile, seeded and finely chopped

½ teaspoon ground toasted cumin (see sidebar, page 39)
¼ teaspoon cayenne pepper
¼ teaspoon salt, or to taste

Whisk the yogurt in a bowl until smooth and lightened. Add the shredded cucumber, green chile, toasted cumin, and cayenne and stir. Chill well and stir in the salt just before serving.

variation

To make a southern Indian raita, combine 2 teaspoons canola oil, 1 teaspoon black mustard seeds, 1 teaspoon hulled black gram beans *(urad dal),* 12 fresh or 16 frozen curry leaves, and ½ teaspoon asafetida in a small frying pan or *kadai* over medium-high heat. Cover and cook until you hear the mustard seeds crackle, 1 to 2 minutes. Pour over the yogurt and mix well.

mixed raita

SERVES 4 TO 6

This is one of the first Indian dishes I made when I came to the United States. It tasted good, and was easy to make with ingredients from American supermarkets. Add more tomatoes and onion for a chunkier raita and more milk if you'd like to experiment with a thinner consistency.

1 teaspoon cumin seeds

1 teaspoon coriander seeds

1 teaspoon black peppercorns

2½ cups plain yogurt

1 small cucumber, peeled and finely chopped

1 small red onion, finely chopped

1 small tomato, chopped

2 fresh hot green chiles, finely minced

1 teaspoon chopped fresh mint

1 teaspoon cayenne pepper

¼ teaspoon salt, or to taste

¼ cup chopped fresh cilantro

Combine the cumin, coriander, and peppercorns in a small frying pan and toast over medium heat until the seeds begin to brown and become fragrant, 1 to 2 minutes. Grind to a powder in a spice grinder and set aside.

Whisk the yogurt in a bowl until smooth and lightened. Add the cucumber, onion, tomato, chiles, and mint and stir to mix well. Stir in the ground spices and the cayenne. Chill well. Stir in the salt just before serving and sprinkle with the chopped cilantro.

mint and onion raita

PODINA AUR PYAAZ KA RAITA

SERVES 4 TO 6

This is another very simple raita. For some reason, I prefer the flavor of dried to fresh mint in it. This is fortunate— it means that I can make this raita all year long without having to keep fresh mint on hand. You can make this without the onion, or add a chopped tomato or cucumber. Or, to make an *aloo ka raita,* replace the onion with 1 large boiled potato, cut into ¼-inch cubes.

2¼ cups plain yogurt

1 large red onion, diced

2 teaspoons dried mint, or ¼ to ½ cup fresh mint
   (preferably spearmint), chopped

2 fresh hot green chiles, seeded and finely chopped

½ teaspoon ground toasted cumin (see sidebar,
   page 39; optional)

¼ teaspoon ground black pepper

⅛ teaspoon cayenne pepper

¼ teaspoon salt, or to taste

Whisk the yogurt in a bowl until smooth and lightened. Stir in the remaining ingredients except the salt. Chill well and then stir in the salt just before serving.

pineapple raita

I first ate this raita when vacationing with my family in Kerala, in the south of India, as a young teenager. The sour taste of the yogurt balances the sweetness of the fruit in a particularly appealing way. This is an excellent choice for a summer meal. Add the pineapple just before serving; if the fruit sits in the raita, it will turn bitter.

3 cups plain yogurt

1 tablespoon sugar

½ teaspoon cayenne pepper

¼ teaspoon ground toasted cumin (see sidebar,
    page 39)

¼ teaspoon ground black pepper

¼ teaspoon salt, or to taste

1 cup finely chopped fresh pineapple

Whisk the yogurt in a bowl until smooth and lightened. Stir in the sugar, cayenne, cumin, and black pepper. Chill well.

Just before serving, stir in the salt and pineapple.

eggplant raita

BURRANI

This raita is traditionally eaten with biriyanis, as well as with most other northern Indian rice dishes, especially in households with close ties to the Moguls. The eggplant gives the yogurt a silky texture and a sweetness that is balanced by the black pepper.

¼ cup ghee or canola oil

1 pound eggplant, peeled and cut crosswise into
  ¼-inch cubes

1 medium red onion, sliced

2 garlic cloves, ground to a paste

4 cups plain yogurt

½ teaspoon ground black pepper

Pinch of cayenne pepper

¼ cup finely chopped fresh mint (optional)

¼ teaspoon salt, or to taste

Pinch of ground toasted cumin (see sidebar, page 39)

Pinch of paprika

Heat the ghee or oil in a large frying pan over medium-high heat until shimmering. Working in batches if necessary, add as many eggplant cubes as will fit into the pan in a single layer and cook until lightly colored on both sides, about 5 minutes total for each batch. Drain on paper towels and set aside.

Add the onion to the pan and cook, stirring, until golden brown, 8 to 10 minutes.

Add the garlic and cook, stirring, 1 minute. Remove the onion and garlic from the pan with a slotted spoon and drain on paper towels.

Whisk the yogurt with the pepper, cayenne, and mint, if using, in a bowl until smooth and lightened.

Stir in the eggplant and the onion–garlic mixture, and chill well. Stir in the salt and sprinkle with ground cumin and paprika just before serving.

grape raita

I recently rediscovered this delightfully unusual raita from Bukhara, a restaurant in Delhi that has the reputation among some as being the finest in the world. I like it best with tiny Champagne grapes, if you can find them, but any seedless variety works. When I have a great deal of leisure, I peel and halve the grapes, but neither is necessary. I particularly love this with a lamb or chicken biriyani.

3 cups plain yogurt
1½ cups seedless grapes, halved
2 teaspoons ground toasted cumin (see sidebar, page 39)
2 teaspoons sugar
½ teaspoon cayenne pepper or paprika

TEMPERING OIL
3 tablespoons canola oil
2 teaspoons cumin or black mustard seeds
1 teaspoon fennel seeds
6 fresh or 10 frozen curry leaves, torn into pieces (optional)

¼ teaspoon salt, or to taste

Whisk the yogurt in a bowl until smooth and lightened.

Stir in the grapes, and then the cumin, sugar, and cayenne or paprika.

For the tempering oil, heat the oil with the cumin or mustard seeds in a small frying pan or *kadai* over medium–high heat. Cook until the cumin seeds darken or the mustard seeds crackle, 1 to 2 minutes. (Cover the pan if using mustard seeds; they crackle and pop.) Add the fennel seeds and curry leaves, if using, and cook uncovered, stirring, 5 to 10 more seconds. (Stand back if using curry leaves; they spit when they hit the hot oil.) Pour over the yogurt and chill well.

Just before serving, stir in the salt.

onion pachadi

SERVES 6

Pachadi is simply the south Indian word for "raita," so this is a raita that is flavored with southern Indian spices. I end up making this quite often at least because I always have yogurt and onions at home. The onions are cooked just long enough to soften their strong taste but retain their texture. You can make this without the South Indian spices, too.

3 cups plain yogurt
1/2 teaspoon sugar

TEMPERING OIL
2 tablespoons canola oil
1 teaspoon black mustard seeds
1/2 teaspoon fenugreek seeds
1/2 inch fresh ginger, peeled and finely chopped
Pinch of asafetida

1 whole dried red chile, or fresh hot green chile, chopped
6 fresh or 10 frozen curry leaves, torn into pieces (optional)
1 medium red onion, finely chopped
2 tablespoons unsweetened shredded coconut (optional)

1/4 teaspoon salt, or to taste
2 tablespoons chopped fresh cilantro

Whisk the yogurt in a bowl until smooth and lightened. Whisk in the sugar and set aside.

For the tempering oil, heat the oil in a small frying pan or *kadai* over medium-high heat. Add the mustard and fenugreek seeds, cover, and cook until you hear the mustard seeds crackle, 1 to 2 minutes. Add the ginger, asafetida, and red chile, if using, and cook uncovered, stirring, 1 minute. Add the curry leaves and green chile, if using, and the onion and cook, stirring, until the onion softens, 2 to 3 minutes longer. (Stand back; the curry leaves spit when they hit the hot oil.) Remove from the heat and stir in the coconut, if using.

Pour the tempering oil over the yogurt and stir to combine. Chill well and stir in the salt just before serving. Serve garnished with chopped cilantro.

zucchini pachadi

SERVES 4 TO 6

When I find great-looking fresh zucchini or yellow squash in the farmer's market, I invariably use it in this southern-spiced pachadi. I'm not really a fan of squashes, and this is one way that I do enjoy eating them.

2¼ cups plain yogurt
1 medium zucchini, shredded
1 fresh hot green chile, seeded and finely chopped

TEMPERING OIL
1 teaspoon canola oil
1 teaspoon black mustard seeds (optional)
12 fresh or 16 frozen curry leaves, torn into pieces (optional)
3 whole dried red chiles
½ teaspoon asafetida (optional)

¼ teaspoon salt, or to taste

Whisk the yogurt in a bowl until smooth and lightened. Add the shredded zucchini and green chile and mix well.

For the tempering oil, combine the oil, mustard seeds and curry leaves, if using, red chiles, and asafetida, if using, in a small frying pan or *kadai* over medium-high heat, and cook, stirring, 1 to 2 minutes. (Cover the pan if using mustard seeds; they splatter and pop.) Pour over the yogurt and mix well. Chill well and stir in the salt just before serving.

CHAPATIS

BHATURAS

POORIS WITH POTATOES, PEAS, AND CILANTRO

*flatbreads
and crackers

PARATHAS

PARATHAS STUFFED WITH POTATO, CHILES, AND CILANTRO

CORNMEAL POORIS WITH POTATO AND CUMIN SEEDS

CRISP SEMOLINA CRACKERS WITH CUMIN

One of the most popular classes I teach is one on Indian breads. I find that people are dying to learn how to make them. There is a common misconception that Indian breads are difficult to make. Watching my students, I can see that this isn't so. My coauthor's twelve-year-old daughter, Joanna, became a great devotee of bhaturas—rich, puffy breads and one of my favorites—on the day that Stephanie and I tested them. She insisted on rolling and frying them herself, and now she makes the breads, from start to finish, all by herself. If you get past your initial intimidation and gain a little experience, making them will become second nature for you, too. Following Joanna's example, you might want to start with the bhaturas: they are clearly relatively easy to work with.

You'll also need to buy an Indian rolling pin—a slender stick of wood that narrows at both ends; it's much easier to make Indian breads with an Indian rolling pin because you have more control over the thickness of the dough as you roll. About half of these breads are made with unbleached all-purpose flour, and the other half with a mixture of half whole wheat and half all-purpose flour in place of Indian chapati flour.

Indian breads really need to be eaten hot. So when I make them, I stand at the stove and cook and serve until all of the breads are made. My guests often feel uncomfortable about this—they want me to sit down at the table and eat. So I gather everyone in the kitchen and get everybody involved in the bread making. It becomes a fun, interactive part of the party in which people eat and learn to cook something new at the same time.

chapatis

MAKES ABOUT 14

Chapatis, a kind of plain, griddle-cooked flatbread, are comfort food to the Indian soul and one of the few foods that you'll find, with only a little variation, throughout India. At our home in Delhi, we called them *phulkas,* which means "to swell up," because the bread puffs up like a balloon as it cooks. As a child, I loved getting my perfect, crisp ball of bread, spread with ghee, so that I could punch holes in it and watch the steam escape. Even now in New York, my partner, Chuck, and I are happiest settling into a simple meal of dal, a vegetable dish, and chapatis.

Usually, chapatis are made on a gas stove—they are cooked first on a griddle and then directly over the gas burner. My grandmother, however, makes excellent chapatis on her electric stove, so I've included instructions for cooking chapatis her way, too. You'll need a pair of flat tongs so as not to break the fragile chapatis when you flip them.

1 cup whole wheat flour plus 1 cup unbleached
    all-purpose flour, or 2 cups chapati flour
1 to 1¼ cups water

All-purpose flour, for rolling
Butter, for serving

Mix the flour(s) in a large bowl. Add ½ cup of the water to the flour and mix with your hand to combine. Add another ¼ cup water and mix again. Continue adding water, a little at a time, until the dough forms a ball. (The dough should take about 1 cup water.)

Now knead the dough vigorously on a clean, unfloured work surface until the dough is moist, soft, and slightly sticky, but doesn't cling to clean hands or the work surface, about 5 minutes. If the dough is dry, dip your fingers into some water and knead the water into the dough. Put the dough into a clean bowl, cover with a clean, damp kitchen towel pressed directly onto the surface, and let rest at least 10 minutes and up to 30 minutes.

When the dough has rested, prepare a small bowl of all-purpose flour and also flour your work surface. Break off a piece of dough a little smaller than a golf ball. Toss it in the bowl of flour and then roll it between the palms of your hands to make a ball. Set the ball on the work surface and flatten it into a 2-inch disk. Now roll the disk, flouring the work surface and the dough round as needed, into a thin round 5 to 6 inches in diameter. Put the chapati on a plate and cover with a sheet of plastic wrap. Continue to roll all of the dough into chapatis and stack them on the plate, pieces of plastic wrap between them.

Heat a griddle or frying pan (preferably cast-iron) over medium-high heat.

Place a chapati on the heated griddle or in the pan over medium-high heat and cook until the top darkens slightly and you see bubbles begin to form underneath the surface of the dough, about 1 minute. Now flip the chapati with a spatula and cook the other side until you see more bubbles, about 30 seconds.

If working on a gas stove, turn a second burner to high. Using a pair of flat tongs, carefully pick up the chapati by the edge and put it directly onto the burner. Cook until the chapati balloons and browns, 10 to 15 seconds. Then carefully turn the chapati, using the tongs to pick it up by the very edge, and cook until the underside browns and the bread balloons again, 10 to 15 more seconds. Remove the chapati from the fire with the tongs, or slide it off the griddle, put it on a plate, and rub with butter. Serve immediately while you continue cooking the remaining chapatis.

If working on an electric stove, cook the chapati on the griddle or in the pan until bubbles have begun to form on both sides. Then continue cooking the chapati, pressing down the edges of the round with a wad of paper towels as it balloons and turning the chapati in a clockwise motion, until the chapati is well browned and swells like a balloon. Turn and do the same on the other side.

bhaturas

MAKES 12 BHATURAS

Bhaturas are very similar to pooris except that they are made with an egg, yogurt, and a little sugar so they taste a little bit like puffed fried pancakes. As a child I remember being amazed that a bread could taste so good. Panditji always made bhaturas to go with Sour Chickpeas with Garam Masala and Toasted Cumin (page 38); it's a heavenly match.

2 cups all-purpose flour

1 teaspoon baking powder

1 teaspoon salt

1 teaspoon sugar

1 large egg

½ cup plain yogurt

3 to 4 tablespoons warm water

1 tablespoon ghee or softened butter

Canola oil, for deep-frying

Combine the flour, baking powder, salt, and sugar in a large bowl and stir to mix. Make a well in the center of the dry ingredients.

Add the egg, yogurt, and warm water to the well and stir with a spoon or your hand to combine. Then pull in the dry ingredients with the spoon or your hand and mix until a soft dough is formed. Turn out onto an unfloured work surface and knead 5 minutes to make a smooth dough that is soft but not sticky.

Rub the ghee or butter onto the palms of your hands and knead it into the dough. Cover the dough with a wet paper towel and let rest at room temperature for 3 hours.

When you are ready to cook the breads, divide the dough into 12 equal pieces and roll each into a ball between the palms of your hands. Set the dough balls on a baking sheet and cover with a damp paper towel.

Heat 2 inches of oil in a *kadai* or large saucepan over medium heat to 325°F. (To gauge the temperature of the oil without a thermometer, drop a piece of bread about 1-inch square into the hot oil over medium heat, turning often; when the oil has reached 325°F., the bread should begin to brown within about 10 seconds and turn golden brown all over—like a crouton—in about 45 seconds.)

Set one of the balls on an unfloured work surface and flatten into a 2-inch disk. Roll the disk into a thin round, 4 to 5 inches in diameter. (Make sure the rounds are thin—about ⅛ inch thick; if they are too thick, they won't puff properly.) Put the bhatura on a plate and cover with a sheet of plastic wrap. Continue to roll all of the remaining dough into bhaturas and stack them on the plate, pieces of plastic wrap between them.

Gently slide a dough round into the hot oil. The round will bob to the surface. Press down on it with a slotted spoon to keep it submerged in the oil so that it will brown evenly. When it is a light golden brown and puffed (this should take 15 to 30 seconds), gently turn the bhatura and cook to brown the other side. Remove with the slotted spoon to the paper-towel-lined plate. Serve immediately. Continue in the same way to cook all of the bhaturas.

pooris with potatoes, peas, and cilantro

MATAR KEE POORIYAN

MAKES ABOUT 16 POORIS

Pooris are crisp deep-fried "balloons" of bread. These and the cornmeal pooris that follow are made with potatoes, so the dough is very soft and tender. You can roll and cook these pooris one by one, or roll all of the dough into rounds, layer the rounds on an oiled tray with pieces of plastic wrap between the layers to keep them from sticking to one another, and then cook them.

2 cups all-purpose flour, plus extra for rolling

1 teaspoon ground toasted cumin (see sidebar, page 39)

½ teaspoon cayenne pepper

2 teaspoons salt

3 tablespoons canola oil, plus extra for deep-frying

1 pound boiling potatoes, boiled in their skins until tender (25 to 30 minutes), cooled, and peeled

1 cup fresh or frozen green peas, cooked in water until tender (about 5 minutes) and pureed in a food processor or blender

2 fresh hot green chiles, very finely chopped

¼ cup finely chopped fresh cilantro

Combine the flour, cumin, cayenne, and salt in a large bowl. Add the 3 tablespoons oil and rub the mixture between your hands until the fat is completely incorporated into the dry ingredients and the mixture is the consistency of fine cornmeal. Squeeze the potatoes in your hand to roughly mash them and add them to the bowl. Add the pureed peas, the chiles, and cilantro. Mix with your hand to make a soft, moist dough. Place in a clean bowl and cover with a clean, damp kitchen cloth or paper towel pressed directly onto the surface. Let the dough rest for about 10 minutes or up to 30 minutes.

Heat about 2 inches of oil in a small wok, *kadai,* or large saucepan over medium heat to 375°F. (To gauge the temperature of the oil without a thermometer, drop a piece of bread about 1-inch square into the hot oil over medium heat, turning often; when the oil is hot enough, the bread should begin to brown almost immediately and turn golden brown all over—like a crouton—in about 30 seconds.) Set a bowl of flour on the work surface and line a plate with paper towels.

Break off a piece of dough a little smaller than a golf ball. Toss it first in the bowl of flour and then roll between the palms of your hands to make a ball. Set the ball on the work surface and flatten to a 2-inch disk. Now roll the disk, flouring the work surface and the dough as needed, into a thin round 5 to 6 inches in diameter. (Make sure the rounds are thin—about ⅛ inch thick; if they are too thick, they won't puff properly.) Pat off the excess flour as well as possible; any flour clinging to the pooris will fall into the oil and eventually burn. Put the poori on a plate and cover with plastic wrap. Repeat to roll all of the remaining dough into pooris and stack them on the plate, pieces of plastic wrap between them.

Gently slide one of the dough rounds into the hot oil. The round will bob to the surface. Press down on it gently with a slotted spoon to keep it submerged in the oil so that it will brown evenly. When it is brown and puffed (this should take just 15 to 30 seconds), gently turn the poori and brown the other side. Remove with the slotted spoon to the paper-towel-lined plate. Serve immediately. Continue to cook all of the pooris.

parathas

Parathas are a type of griddle-cooked flatbread made with essentially the same dough as chapatis. Because of the way they are shaped and cooked in oil, however, they have a crisp, flaky texture, unlike that of chapatis. Serve them with any Indian meal.

Parathas travel very well. When I drove through Canada with friends last year, I made parathas, pooris (pages 193 and 198), Crispy Potatoes with Cumin (page 78), and My Grand-Uncle's Khitcheree (page 107) for the trip to eat with pickles (no self-respecting Indian travels without pickles). The parathas stayed perfectly soft during the long trip. When we got hungry, we stuffed them with the potatoes and pickles for a delicious on-the-road snack.

1 cup whole wheat flour plus 1 cup unbleached
   all-purpose flour, or 2 cups chapati flour
1 teaspoon salt
1 to 1¼ cups water

All-purpose flour, for rolling
Canola oil, for rolling and cooking
Butter, for serving

Mix the flour(s) and salt in a large bowl. Add ½ cup of the water to the flour mixture and mix with one hand to combine. Add another ¼ cup water and mix again. Continue adding water, a little at a time, until the dough forms a ball. (The dough should take about 1 cup water.)

Now knead the dough vigorously on a clean, unfloured work surface until the dough is moist, soft, and slightly sticky, but doesn't cling to clean hands or the work surface, about 5 minutes. If the dough is dry, dip your fingers into some water and knead the water into the dough. Put the dough into a clean bowl, cover with a clean, damp kitchen towel pressed directly onto the surface, and let rest at least 10 minutes or up to 30 minutes.

When the dough has rested, set out a bowl of all-purpose flour on your work surface, along with a small bowl of oil with a spoon. Lightly flour your work surface.

Break off a piece of dough about the size of a golf ball. Toss it first in the bowl of flour and then roll between the palms of your hands to make a ball. Set the ball on your work surface and flatten into a 2-inch disk. Now roll the disk, flouring the work surface and the dough round as needed, into a thin round 5 to 6 inches in diameter.

Use the back of the spoon to coat the top of the dough round with a little oil. Sprinkle the round with flour.

Place the point of a small knife in the center of the round and cut down to make a slit from the center to the edge of the dough round. Then, starting with one side of the slit and working your way around the center, roll the dough onto itself to form a cone. Pick the cone up, place it pointed side down in the palm of your left hand, and squash it into a disk with your right hand.

Lightly flour the work surface again. Roll out the disk to a round 5 to 6 inches in diameter. Pat it between your hands to brush off the excess flour. Put the paratha on a plate and cover with a sheet of plastic wrap. Continue in this same way to roll the remainder of the dough into parathas and stack them on the plate with sheets of plastic wrap between them.

Heat a griddle or a frying pan, preferably cast-iron, over medium-high heat.

Place a paratha on the ungreased heated griddle or in the pan and cook until the dough darkens slightly and you see bubbles begin to form underneath the surface of the dough, 30 seconds to 1 minute. Now flip the paratha with a spatula and cook until you see bubbles form again.

With the back of the spoon, coat the top of the paratha with oil. Flip and coat the other side with oil. Now continue cooking, pressing gently on the bread with the back of the spoon and moving the spoon around in a circular motion to press the bread onto the pan for even browning. When the bottom of the bread has browned, flip and repeat. Do this a few times until both sides of the parathas are golden brown and very crisp, 2 to 3 minutes total.

Remove the paratha from the pan and spread with butter. Serve immediately, and continue to cook all of the parathas.

variations

Knead ¼ teaspoon cayenne pepper and ¼ cup chopped fresh cilantro into the dough. Roll and cook as above. Knead ¼ teaspoon toasted cumin seeds into the dough. Roll and cook as above.

parathas stuffed with potato, chiles, and cilantro

ALOO KEE PARATHE

MAKES ABOUT 12 PARATHAS

These parathas always make me think of Nani, my maternal grandmother, who lives in San Francisco. She makes these scrumptious breads like no one else: hers are crisp on the outside and oozing with potato and butter. As her own special touch, she rips a small hole in the top of the bread as it cooks and uses her fingers to stuff butter inside. This makes the potato filling as buttery and flavorful as the crisp bread that encloses it. Try doing this, if you like, but use a knife instead of your fingers so that you don't burn yourself.

A typical light lunch in Nani's household is parathas served with plain yogurt and mint chutney, and nothing else. I myself eat these parathas by the stack, with chutney or, believe it or not, ketchup. For a richer, softer bread, substitute milk for ¹/₂ cup of the water in the dough.

1 cup whole wheat flour plus 1 cup unbleached
    all-purpose flour, or 2 cups chapati flour
Salt
1 to 1¹/₄ cups water
1¹/₂ pounds boiling potatoes, boiled in their skins until
    tender (25 to 30 minutes) and cooled
¹/₄ cup very finely chopped red onion
1 fresh hot green chile, very finely chopped
1¹/₂ tablespoons very finely chopped fresh cilantro

¹/₂ teaspoon cayenne pepper
¹/₂ teaspoon garam masala (page 250)
¹/₄ teaspoon cumin or ¹/₂ teaspoon carom seeds
    (ajawain)
Juice of ¹/₂ lemon or lime
All-purpose flour, for rolling
Canola oil, for cooking
Butter, for serving

Mix the flour(s) and 1 teaspoon salt in a large bowl. Add ¹/₂ cup of the water to the flour mixture and mix with your hand to combine. Add another ¹/₄ cup water and mix again. Continue adding water, a little at a time, until the dough forms a ball. (The dough should take about 1 cup water.)

Now knead the dough vigorously on a clean, unfloured work surface until the dough is moist, soft, and slightly sticky, but doesn't cling to clean hands or the work surface, about 5 minutes. If the dough is dry, dip your fingers into some water and knead the water into the dough. Put the dough into a clean bowl, cover with a clean damp kitchen towel pressed directly onto the surface, and let rest at least 10 minutes or up to 30 minutes.

Meanwhile, peel the potatoes and mash them roughly in your hands in a bowl. Add 1 teaspoon salt, the onion, chile, cilantro, spices, and lemon or lime juice and mix well to form a fairly smooth mixture (there will be small lumps in it).

When the dough has rested, set out a bowl of all-purpose flour and a small bowl of canola oil, with a spoon, on your work surface. Lightly flour your work surface as well.

Break off a piece of dough about the size of a golf ball. Toss it first in the bowl of flour and then roll it between the palms of your hands to make a ball. Set the ball on your work surface and flatten to a 2-inch disk. Now roll the disk, flouring the work surface and the dough round as needed, into a thin round 4¹/₂ to 5 inches in diameter.

Mound about ¼ cup of the potato mixture into the center of the dough round. Bring the edges of the round up over the top of the filling and press them together to make a pouch. Press down on the "neck" of the pouch with the palm of one hand to make a slightly rounded disk. Turn the disk in the bowl of flour and roll it out again into a round about 6 inches in diameter. Pat it between your hands to brush off the excess flour. Put the paratha on a plate and cover with a sheet of plastic wrap. Continue to roll all of the remaining dough into parathas and stack them on the plate with sheets of plastic wrap between them.

Heat a griddle or frying pan (preferably cast-iron) over medium-high heat.

Place the dough round on the heated ungreased griddle or in the pan and cook until the dough darkens slightly and you see bubbles begin to form underneath the surface of the dough, 30 seconds to 1 minute. Now flip the paratha with a spatula and cook until you see bubbles form again.

With the back of the spoon, coat the top of the paratha with oil. Flip and coat the other side with oil. Now continue cooking, pressing gently on the bread with the back of the spoon and moving the spoon around in a circular motion to press the bread onto the pan for even browning. When the bottom of the bread has browned, flip and repeat. Do this a few times until both sides of the paratha are golden brown and very crisp, 2 to 3 minutes total.

Remove the paratha from the pan and spread with butter. Serve immediately. Then continue in this way until all of the parathas have been cooked.

cornmeal pooris with potato and cumin seeds

PAALAK KEE POORIYAAN

MAKES ABOUT 12 POORIS

These pooris are so tasty and satisfying that sometimes I just eat them by themselves with yogurt and chutney, or pickles. I also love them with spinach (try the Indian Cheese in an Herbed Green Sauce on page 80 or Spinach with Potatoes on page 82). My coauthor, Stephanie, loves these with chickpea dishes.

¾ cup yellow or white cornmeal

¾ cup all-purpose flour, plus extra for rolling

⅛ teaspoon cumin or ¼ teaspoon carom seeds (ajawain)

1 teaspoon salt

1 teaspoon canola oil, plus extra for deep frying

1 pound boiling potatoes, boiled in their skins until tender (25 to 30 minutes), cooled, and peeled

Combine the cornmeal, flour, cumin or carom seeds, and salt in a large bowl. Add the 1 teaspoon oil and rub the mixture between your hands to distribute the fat completely throughout the dry ingredients. Squeeze the potatoes in your hand to coarsely mash them and add them to the bowl. Then mix everything with your hand to make a soft, moist dough. Place in a clean bowl and cover with a clean damp kitchen cloth or paper towel pressed directly onto the surface. Let the dough rest for at least 10 minutes or up to 30 minutes.

Heat about 2 inches of oil in a small wok, *kadai,* or large saucepan over medium heat to 375°F. (To gauge the temperature of the oil without a thermometer, drop a piece of bread about 1-inch square into the hot oil, over medium heat, turning often; when the oil is hot enough, the bread should begin to brown almost immediately and turn golden brown all over—like a crouton—in about 25 seconds.) Set a bowl of flour on the work surface and line a plate with paper towels. Lightly flour your work surface.

Break off a piece of dough a little smaller than a golf ball. Toss it first in the bowl of flour and then roll between the palms of your hands to make a ball. Set the ball on your work surface and flatten into a 2-inch disk. Now roll the disk, flouring the work surface and the dough as needed, into a thin round 5 to 6 inches in diameter. (Make sure the rounds are thin—about ⅛ inch; if they are too thick, they won't puff properly.) Pat off the excess flour as well as possible; any flour clinging to the pooris will fall into the oil and eventually burn. Put the poori on a plate and cover with a sheet of plastic wrap. Continue to roll out all of the remaining dough into pooris and stack them on the plate, pieces of plastic wrap between them.

Gently slide a dough round into the hot oil. The round will bob to the surface. Press down on it gently with a slotted spoon to keep it submerged in the oil so that it will brown evenly. When it is golden brown and puffed (this should take 15 to 30 seconds), gently turn the poori and cook to brown the other side. Remove with the slotted spoon to the paper-towel-lined plate. Serve immediately. Continue in the same way to cook all of the pooris.

crisp semolina crackers with cumin

MATHRI

MAKES ABOUT 18 CRACKERS

We kids could tell that Diwali, the Indian New Year, was close by when we would come home and find my grandmother sitting in a chair at the door to the kitchen, and my mother and Panditji taking direction from her in the making of *mathri*. During the two weeks before the holiday, there's a constant stream of visitors who bring gifts to the family, and we would serve them these crunchy crackers, with pickles, roasted nuts, and dried fruits.

I like taking these crackers to friends as a hostess gift. Stacked high and tied with raffia in transparent wrapping, it's the perfect gift with a jar of homemade chutney or pickles. Serve *mathri* whenever you would crackers.

2 cups farina (such as Cream of Wheat)
1 cup all-purpose flour
1 teaspoon salt

¾ teaspoon cumin or carom seeds *(ajawain)*
¼ cup ghee or solid vegetable shortening
¾ cup water

Mix the farina, flour, salt, and carom or cumin seeds in a large bowl. Add the ghee or shortening, and rub the mixture between your hands until the fat is completely incorporated into the dry ingredients and the mixture is the texture of cornmeal.

Add about ½ cup of the water and knead it into the dough. Then continue adding water, 1 tablespoon at a time, until the dough just holds together. You'll need ½ and ¾ cup water total. Continue kneading 4 to 5 minutes until you have a smooth, rather dry dough.

Pull off a piece of dough about the size of a golf ball, roll it into a ball, and press it between the palms of your hands to flatten it into a disk about 2½ inches in diameter. Roll it on an unfloured work surface to a round about 5 inches in diameter. Place on a cookie sheet. Continue rolling the crackers and placing them in a single layer on the cookie sheet. When the sheet is full, prick the crackers all over with the tines of a fork to keep them from puffing during cooking. Stretch a piece of plastic wrap over the crackers, and continue to make and prick the next layer.

Heat the oil in a small wok, *kadai*, or large saucepan over medium heat to 375°F. on a deep-fat thermometer. (To gauge the temperature of the oil without a thermometer, drop a piece of bread about 1-inch square into the hot oil over medium heat, turning often; when the oil has reached 375°F., the bread should begin to brown almost immediately and turn golden brown all over—like a crouton—in about 30 seconds.) Then turn the heat down as low as possible. Gently drop one of the crackers into the oil and cook, pressing gently on the cracker with a slotted spoon or spider to keep it submerged in the oil and turning it now and then for even cooking, until the cracker is golden brown on both sides, about 1 to 1½ minutes. Use a thermometer to measure the heat of the oil once or twice during cooking; the oil should stay at about 325°F. (You can also gauge the temperature by the time it takes for the cracker to rise to the surface: when you drop the cracker into the oil, the oil will bubble and then rise to the surface in 5 to 10 seconds.)

Drain the crackers on a cookie sheet lined with paper towels. Then stack them in an airtight container, wrapped in a paper towel to absorb moisture. Crackers will keep easily for up to a month.

SWEET-AND-SOUR EGGPLANT PICKLE

GREEN CHILE PICKLE

SPICY ORANGE PICKLE

SOUR LEMON PICKLE

SPICY MANGO PICKLE

*pickles and chutneys

GREEN CHUTNEY

TAMARIND CHUTNEY

APPLE OR QUINCE CHUTNEY

KASHMIRI WALNUT CHUTNEY

COCONUT CHUTNEY

SPICY MANGO CHUTNEY

PINEAPPLE CHUTNEY

Indians don't just love the taste of food; we *live* for the taste. With their varied and intense tastes, pickles and chutneys offer a way to satisfy your greed for lots and lots of different flavors, all at once. Both pickles and chutneys are made with an astonishing variety of fruits, vegetables, grains, herbs, and aromatics (we even pickle meats). Pickles are also used medicinally in India; my grandmother used to give me a little taste of Sour Lemon Pickle when I had a stomachache and, to this day, I still use it.

Like salsas, pickles and chutneys add a tasty complexity to any meal, Indian or otherwise. They can also make the meal: a reheated dal and a vegetable dish is a serviceable but uninteresting dinner. The addition of a couple of different pickles and chutneys makes it a feast. Serve chutneys and pickles with anything that needs a little kick, such as eggs, sandwiches, or grilled meats and seafood. You can make your own or buy one of the several varieties sold in Indian and Asian grocery stores, and even in a well-stocked supermarket these days.

Indian pickles use a lot of the same ingredients as American pickles: salt, vinegar, coriander seeds, mustard seeds, turmeric, cinnamon, cloves, and ginger. Most home pickles are made in the summer, with summer produce.

It's always been my contention that the best way to taste the different pickles in India is to take a train from the northern to the southern parts of the country. Everyone brings pooris (pages 193 and 198), an unleavened, deep-fried bread, usually filled with a kind of potato that is particularly suited to travel because it doesn't get hard over time. The pooris are pretty much the same no matter where the passenger is from, but the pickles vary by region. Inevitably, as the passengers open their lunches, everyone peers over the seats to see what pickles their fellow passengers have brought with them. Regardless of the mood before the lunches were opened, once the pickles appear there is always much conversation and sharing of pickles.

Though it's traditional to prepare pureed chutneys (like Green Chutney and Coconut Chutney) by grinding the ingredients between two large pieces of stone, it's obviously much easier to use a food processor or blender. The advantage to the traditional technique is that one can grind the ingredients without adding very much water at all. This gives the chutneys an intense flavor and long shelf life. So use as little water as possible when pureeing, even if it means stopping and starting the food processor or blender several times and stirring and scraping down the sides, so that the ingredients "catch" in the blade and puree.

Pickling was traditionally a way to preserve foods in a culture without refrigeration. We don't have this problem now, but I still recommend serving pickles the way we have always served them in India: spoon out a small amount into a bowl with a clean spoon. Never use a spoon that's already been used (even for the same pickle) and never put leftover pickles back in the jar. Any moisture or impurities can cause the pickle to spoil. All pickles and chutneys can be made in quantity and canned; I do this a lot, particularly when tomatoes, mangoes, quinces, and apples are in season. Follow the jar manufacturer's instructions for sterilizing and canning and store in the refrigerator once open. To keep oil-cured pickles (like Green Chile Pickle and Sweet-and-Sour Eggplant Pickle) fresh, make sure that there is always a layer of oil on the top of the pickle to protect it from air and moisture.

sweet-and-sour eggplant pickle

MAKES 1 QUART

This recipe was handed down to my mother by our family's landlord in Nagpur, a small city in the state of Maharashtra in western India where we lived for a few years. My mother dried pickles under the tamarind tree in our yard there. This pickle is a guaranteed hit with Indians and non-Indians alike, perhaps because of its appealing sweet-and-sour taste. This pickle is best made with Japanese eggplants because they have fewer seeds.

1 pound Japanese or small Italian eggplants, or 1 large ($1^1/_4$- to $1^1/_2$- pound) eggplant, stemmed

2 teaspoons salt

1 cup rice wine vinegar

$1^1/_2$ cups loosely packed light brown sugar

1 cup canola oil

$^1/_2$ tablespoon chopped garlic

$^1/_2$ tablespoon chopped fresh ginger

1 tablespoon cayenne pepper

If using Japanese eggplants, cut them in half lengthwise and then crosswise into 2-inch sections. If using small Italian eggplants, quarter them lengthwise and then cut crosswise into 2-inch sections. If you can only find a large eggplant, cut off the straight-sided upper half of the eggplant and cut it lengthwise into six pieces; cut each piece in half crosswise. Then set the bottom half of the eggplant on one end and cut off the rounded, outside edges in $4^1/_2$-inch-thick slices, discarding the central core. Cut the outer pieces in half lengthwise and then crosswise into 2- to $2^1/_2$- inch sections.

Sprinkle the eggplant slices with salt on a paper-towel-lined tray and let stand 2 hours. Meanwhile, in a small bowl, pour the vinegar over the brown sugar and let stand to soften.

Wipe the salt off the eggplant with paper towels. Heat the oil in a 12-inch frying pan over medium heat. Working in two batches, cook the eggplant, turning, until lightly browned and softened, 3 to 4 minutes. (Do not overcook or the eggplant will fall apart.) Drain on paper towels.

Remove the pan from the heat and stir the garlic, ginger, and cayenne into the oil. Return the eggplant to the pan and swirl the pan to coat the eggplant with the spices. Let stand off the heat 5 minutes. Then add the vinegar-sugar mixture, bring to a simmer, and cook until the syrup is very bubbly and thick enough to coat the back of a spoon, but not caramelized, about 15 minutes. Let stand until cooled completely to room temperature, spoon into a sterilized 1-quart jar, and refrigerate.

green chile pickle

MAKES 2 PINTS

This is a very hot pickle, eaten in tiny quantities, guaranteed to jazz up anything that needs a bit of flavor. Because the pickle is so hot, it's important to slice the chiles very thinly, so that you can take just a bit at a time onto your plate. The pickle may be eaten within four to five days, but is best after about 1 week.

3 tablespoons black mustard seeds

1 teaspoon asafetida

1 teaspoon fenugreek seeds

**1 pound serrano chiles, washed and dried completely,
    then stemmed and thinly sliced**

2 teaspoons turmeric

¼ cup salt

1 cup light (not toasted) sesame oil

Juice of 4 to 6 lemons

Combine the mustard seeds, asafetida, and fenugreek seeds in a small frying pan and toast over medium heat, stirring often, until very fragrant, about 3 minutes. Transfer to a spice grinder and grind to powder.

Put the sliced chiles in a large nonaluminum bowl. Add the ground spice mixture, turmeric, and salt and stir to coat the chiles with the spices. Spoon the mixture into two sterilized pint jars, cap, and set aside overnight at room temperature.

The next day, heat the oil to smoking in a small saucepan over medium heat. Pour slowly over chiles in the jars; the chiles will sizzle and foam. Cap the jars and set them on a sunny windowsill for 1 day.

The next day, add enough lemon juice to cover the chiles. Cap the bottles again and set in the sun for 3 to 4 more days. Refrigerate and eat within 2 to 3 weeks.

spicy orange pickle

MAKES 3 PINTS

This pickle is of my own creation, but it is reminiscent of a style of pickle made in Hyderabad in southern India. I serve it as an accompaniment to any Indian meal, or for a light lunch, with warmed pita bread and raita.

1½ teaspoons black mustard seeds

1 teaspoon fenugreek seeds

6 whole dried red chiles

¾ teaspoon asafetida (optional)

4 medium oranges

½ cup canola oil

¼ cup light (not toasted) sesame oil

8 fresh hot green chiles, sliced crosswise into
thin rounds

A 2-inch piece fresh ginger, peeled and minced

1 tablespoon cayenne pepper

¼ teaspoon turmeric

½ cup salt

Combine ½ teaspoon of the mustard seeds, the fenugreek, red chiles, and asafetida in a small, heavy-bottomed frying pan over medium heat and toast, stirring, until the mustard seeds begin to crackle, 1 to 2 minutes. Let cool to room temperature and then grind to a fine powder in a spice grinder and set aside.

Put the oranges in a large saucepan and add cold water to barely cover. Bring to a boil, reduce the heat, and simmer 15 minutes. Let the oranges cool to room temperature in their cooking liquid; drain and reserve the cooking liquid. Cut each orange into eight wedges.

Combine the canola and sesame oils in a large, heavy-bottomed frying pan over medium-high heat. Add the remaining 1 teaspoon mustard seeds and cook, covered, until you hear the seeds begin to crackle, 1 to 2 minutes. Add the fresh chiles, ginger, cayenne, and turmeric and cook, stirring, 2 minutes. Add the orange wedges and cook, stirring, 1 more minute.

Now add the reserved orange cooking liquid, bring to a boil, reduce the heat, and simmer 5 minutes.

Add the salt and reserved ground spice mixture and simmer 2 more minutes. Let the pickle cool to room temperature. Then spoon the oranges and their liquid into three sterilized pint jars and refrigerate.

sour lemon pickle

This pickle is best made in the summer when the strong summer heat can intensify the flavor of the lemon. It is set out daily in the sun for the first three weeks and brought in every night, then aged for several months or even several years. (I have a jar in my cupboard that I brought with me from India; it's at least 40 years old.) This pickle will enliven any simple meal, such as a simple dal served with boiled rice. Lemon pickle is also traditionally used as medicine to cure stomach ailments.

12 lemons, rinsed and well dried, hard stem
    ends removed
2 teaspoons black peppercorns
1 teaspoon cumin seeds
5 green cardamom pods
4 whole cloves
A 1/2-inch piece cinnamon stick

1 tablespoon cayenne pepper
1/8 teaspoon ground mace
1/8 teaspoon ground nutmeg
2 teaspoons carom seeds (*ajawain;* optional)
1 teaspoon red pepper flakes
2 teaspoons ground ginger
1/2 cup plus 1 tablespoon salt

Cut the lemons in half lengthwise and then cut each half lengthwise into six to eight wedges. Save any juices you get from cutting the lemons; set aside. Lay the wedges out on two paper towel–lined trays and let dry all day in a sunny spot.

Grind the peppercorns, cumin, cardamom, cloves, and cinnamon to a powder in a spice grinder. Transfer to a large bowl and add the cayenne, mace, nutmeg, carom seeds, if using, red pepper flakes, ground ginger, and salt. Add the reserved lemon juice and mix well. Now add the lemon wedges and mix, pressing the spice mixture onto the flesh of the lemons.

Pack the lemons into one sterilized quart jar and one sterilized pint jar. Cap the jars and set them in a sunny spot for 5 weeks, turning the jars up and down several times, once a day. Let the pickles age at least another month before eating. Refrigerate after opening.

spicy mango pickle

MAKES 1 QUART

This pickle, from the desert state of Rajasthan in the northwestern part of India, has a predominantly sour taste from unripe mangoes that's smoothed and mellowed by the warm taste of the spices. Indians find this taste addictive and eat a lot of this pickle. Mango pickle is particularly good with parathas, which, with yogurt and perhaps Green Chile Pickle (page 204), make a complete and absolutely delicious meal.

This is best made with unripe, Indian mangoes—reputed to be the best mangoes in the world and sold in Indian and Asian stores during the early summer when they're in season—but you can use any unripe mangoes that you find in your supermarket.

3 medium green (unripe) mangoes, peeled and cut into small cubes
½ cup kosher salt
3 tablespoons turmeric
1 teaspoon fennel seeds

1 tablespoon black mustard seeds, coarsely ground in a mortar and pestle or spice grinder
½ tablespoon fenugreek seeds, coarsely ground in a mortar and pestle or spice grinder
½ cup cayenne pepper
1 cup canola oil

Put the mango cubes in a nonaluminum bowl and sprinkle with the salt and half of the turmeric. Toss to coat all of the mango cubes. Spoon the mango into a clean jar, cap, and set in a sunny spot for 2 days, turning the jars up and down several times twice a day.

On the third day, empty the jar into a nonreactive colander and drain for about 30 minutes.

Spread the mango out on muslin or an old kitchen towel and let stand for 2 hours. (The turmeric will stain, so use something that you won't mind seeing yellow.)

Combine the remaining turmeric with the fennel seeds, ground mustard seeds, ground fenugreek seeds, and cayenne in a nonreactive bowl. Add the mangoes and half of the oil. Stir to mix well.

Spoon into a dry, sterilized quart jar and press down lightly to compact the mangoes. Add the remaining oil and tightly cap the jar. Set in a sunny spot for 10 to 12 days, turning the jars up and down several times once every few days. After the twelfth day the pickle is ready for use, but it tastes better as it ages. Refrigerate after opening.

green chutney

HAREE CHUTNEY

MAKES 1 1/2 CUPS

Almost every North Indian home makes a version of this recipe that is unique to the family. In many homes, it's served with every meal. I love this chutney; the last time I was in India I was ecstatically happy for the simple reason that every single day I was able to eat fresh green chutney made with mint, cilantro, and green mango.

This recipe is easy to vary. You can omit the mint and use cilantro alone. Or use chopped green mango if you can find it; it gives the chutney a delicious sour taste. Increase the number of chiles (I have been known to add up to 10) to make a hot pepper chutney. Or you can make a mint chutney by increasing the mint and using less cilantro (but do include *some* cilantro or the chutney will taste somewhat bitter).

1 1/2 cups firmly packed chopped fresh cilantro

1/2 cup firmly packed mint leaves

2 or 3 fresh hot green chiles, stemmed

A 2-inch piece fresh ginger, peeled and cut into chunks

1/2 red onion, quartered

Juice of 2 lemons

1 tablespoon sugar

1/2 teaspoon salt

1/4 cup water

Combine all of the ingredients in a blender and process to a puree. (This won't blend easily; you'll need to stop and start the blending and stir the ingredients often to get the mixture to catch. You can add a bit more water to facilitate the process but the flavor of the chutney will be milder.) Refrigerate and eat within 4 to 5 days.

tamarind chutney

MAKES ABOUT 1 1/4 CUPS

Tamarind makes a sweet-and-sour chutney with the consistency of a hot fudge sauce. It's an important element in the street and snack foods of northern India. I also serve it with many snacks and appetizers such as Puff Pastry Samosas with Green Peas (page 165), and Papadum (page 173).

1 tablespoon canola oil

1 teaspoon cumin seeds

1 teaspoon ground ginger

1/2 teaspoon cayenne pepper

1/2 teaspoon fennel seeds

1/2 teaspoon asafetida (optional)

1/2 teaspoon garam masala (page 250)

2 cups water

1 1/4 cups sugar

3 tablespoons tamarind concentrate

Combine the oil and spices in a medium saucepan over medium-high heat and cook, stirring, for 1 minute.

Add the water, sugar, and tamarind concentrate. Bring to a boil, turn the heat down, and simmer until it turns chocolaty brown and is thick enough to coat the back of the spoon, 20 to 30 minutes. (While still warm, it will look like a thin chocolate sauce and it will thicken a bit as it cools.) Store in the refrigerator in a tightly closed container for up to 2 weeks.

apple or quince chutney

MAKES ABOUT 1 PINT

In the Himalayan state of Himachal Pradesh, fruits are used in a variety of savory preparations. I ate this as a young man traveling through that region, eating with the local residents. There, it was made with apples, but I like making it in America with quince as well when it is in season in the fall. This chutney—sweet, hot, and tart—goes particularly well with fish because it doesn't mask the flavor.

1 tablespoon canola oil

1 teaspoon coriander seeds, coarsely ground
   in a spice grinder

1 teaspoon ground ginger

1/2 teaspoon cayenne pepper

1/4 teaspoon ground cloves

1 fresh hot green chile, very finely minced

2 pounds Granny Smith apples or quince, peeled,
   cored, and cut into 1/2-inch cubes

1 cup sugar

1/4 cup cider vinegar

1/4 cup dried currants

Combine the oil, coriander, ginger, cayenne, cloves, and green chile in a medium saucepan over medium-high heat. Cook, stirring, until fragrant, 1 to 2 minutes.

Add the remaining ingredients, bring to a boil, lower the heat to medium-low, and cook, partially covered, until thickened, 20 to 30 minutes.

Ladle the chutney into a dry, sterilized quart jar and process according to manufacturer's instructions. Cool and then chill.

kashmiri walnut chutney

AKHROT KEE CHUTNEY

MAKES ABOUT 1 PINT

In India, the best walnuts come from Kashmir, that beautiful valley nestled in the Himalayas. The oil from the walnuts gives this mildly sweet-and-sour chutney a rich, nutty taste that is balanced by the acidity of the yogurt. The texture is dense with the ground nuts. I've found that this is often a good chutney to serve to friends who are just beginning to eat and cook Indian food because its taste is mild and rather neutral. It goes with anything: cheese sandwiches, cold meats, and particularly, any northern Indian dish such as Braised Chicken in a White Sauce with Garam Masala (page 116), or Tandoori Roast Cornish Game Hens (page 127), or Coconut Chicken with Cashews (page 121).

1 cup shelled walnuts

4 or 5 dried whole red chiles

1/2 cup plain yogurt, stirred until smooth

1/4 teaspoon garam masala (page 250)

1/2 teaspoon salt, or to taste

1 teaspoon confectioners' sugar

Combine the walnuts and chiles in a food processor and grind to a paste.

Add the yogurt, garam masala, salt, and sugar and process for another minute. Spoon into an airtight container and refrigerate.

coconut chutney

MAKES ABOUT 1 PINT

I often find coconut heavy tasting, but in this chutney, its richness is cut with the acidity of the yogurt and the bright tastes of cilantro, mint, and fresh ginger. This is a heavenly combination of tastes, very refreshing, that cleans and reawakens the palate after every bite. The chutney is particularly delicious with fish.

**1 cup fresh grated coconut, or 1 cup shredded
   unsweetened coconut mixed with ¼ cup milk**
½ cup plain yogurt
A 1-inch piece fresh ginger, peeled
1 tablespoon chopped onion
1 fresh hot green chile, chopped
¼ cup fresh cilantro leaves
2 tablespoons fresh mint leaves

TEMPERING OIL
2 tablespoons ghee or canola oil
1 teaspoon black mustard seeds
1 teaspoon yellow split peas
1 teaspoon hulled black gram beans (*urad dal;* optional)
¼ teaspoon cumin seeds
¼ teaspoon black peppercorns
⅛ teaspoon asafetida
15 fresh or 20 frozen curry leaves, torn into pieces
1 whole dried red chile
½ teaspoon salt, or to taste

Combine all of the ingredients except for the tempering oil in a blender and blend to a paste. This won't blend easily; you'll need to stop and start the blending and stir the ingredients often to get the mixture to catch. (If you need a little more liquid, add a spoonful of yogurt.) Set aside in the blender.

For the tempering oil, heat the ghee or canola oil with the mustard seeds and yellow split peas in a very small frying pan or saucepan over medium-high heat. Cover and cook, stirring, until you hear the mustard seeds crackle, 1 to 2 minutes. (Mustard seeds splatter and pop.) Add the *urad dal,* if using, and the rest of the ingredients except the salt and cook, stirring, until the cumin turns light brown, about 1 more minute.

Pour the tempering oil into the blender with the coconut mixture and process to mix. Pour into a serving bowl and stir in the salt. Refrigerate and serve chilled.

spicy mango chutney

MAKES ABOUT 2 PINTS

In the summers, my mother used to make mango chutney several times a week during the peak of mango season. It tastes nothing like the commercial Major Grey's Chutney that you find in supermarkets: while the taste of Major Grey's is predominantly sweet, this chutney tastes rather of spice and the brown sugar serves to give it a deep, mellow taste. The flavors of green chile, black mustard seeds, and fennel linger in your mouth from one bite to the next.

I particularly like this with Spicy Peas Sautéed with Ginger (page 69). Green unripe mangoes are available during the summer at Indian and Asian grocery stores, but you can use any unripe mango.

2 pounds green (unripe) mangoes, pitted, peeled, and
    cut into julienne
2 teaspoons salt
1/2 teaspoon turmeric
1 cup water
1 fresh hot green chile, finely chopped
1/2 cup loosely packed light brown sugar
2 teaspoons cornstarch dissolved in
    2 tablespoons water

TEMPERING OIL
1 tablespoon ghee or canola oil
1 teaspoon black mustard seeds
1 teaspoon fennel seeds
1/2 teaspoon nigella seeds (*kalaunji;* optional)
3 whole dried red chiles
1 teaspoon cayenne pepper
Pinch of asafetida

Toss the mangoes with the salt and turmeric and set aside.

Bring the water to a boil in a medium, heavy-bottomed saucepan. Add the mangoes and green chile, turn the heat down to medium, and simmer until the mangoes are barely tender, about 15 minutes.

Add the brown sugar, turn the heat to high, and boil for 5 minutes. Add the cornstarch mixture and cook, stirring, until the sauce thickens, about 5 more minutes. Remove from the heat.

For the tempering oil, heat the ghee or oil with the mustard seeds in a small frying pan or *kadai* over medium-high heat. Cover and cook, until you hear the mustard seeds crackle, 1 to 2 minutes. Add the fennel and nigella seeds, if using, and cook, stirring, until the fennel turns light brown, about 1 minute. Add the red chiles, remove from the heat, and let sizzle until they turn a nice dark brown. Stir in the cayenne and asafetida and pour over the chutney. Stir well. Spoon into two sterilized pint jars and process according to manufacturer's instructions.

pineapple chutney

ANANAAS KEE CHUTNEY

MAKES 2 PINTS

This is a sweet chutney from eastern India. You'd find it served at meals in Assam, Bengal, and other eastern states. The sweetness of the chutney provides a fine contrast to the pungency of the mustard oil used in the cooking of that region. Eaten with flatbreads, it provides a welcome respite to an otherwise spicy meal.

1/4 cup dried apricots, quartered

1 cup fresh pineapple, very finely diced or grated

1 tablespoon golden raisins

1 1/2 lightly packed tablespoons light brown sugar

2 tablespoons fresh orange juice

1 tablespoon orange zest

1/2 teaspoon salt, or to taste

1/2 teaspoon cayenne pepper

1/2 teaspoon ground black pepper

1 tablespoon orange liqueur (optional)

Soak the apricots in hot water to cover for 3 hours. Drain and set aside.

Combine all of the remaining ingredients except the orange liqueur in a medium heavy-bottomed saucepan. Bring to a boil, turn the heat down, and simmer over low heat, stirring constantly, until almost all of the liquid has reduced and the chutney has thickened, 15 to 20 minutes.

Stir in the orange liqueur, if using, and take the chutney off the heat. Cool and refrigerate until cold. This will last 1 to 2 weeks in the refrigerator.

COCONUT-BANANA CARAMEL CUSTARD

CHAI POTS DE CRÈME

GINGERSNAP PUDDING

LEMON CURD

SUSAN AUNTY'S ORANGE FLAN

 sweets

LEMON PAVLOVA WITH FRESH BERRIES

VANILLA PUDDING

BLUEBERRY-LEMON PIE

BANANA PUDDING

NANI'S QUICK AND EASY KULFI

RICE PUDDING

HOLY VERMICELLI PUDDING

CHRISTMAS BANANA BREAD

Indians' affection for sweets is legendary, and I am no exception. In my home, the meal isn't complete without some kind of dessert. In this chapter are the desserts that I serve at my table when I'm entertaining in the contemporary Indian style. They run the gamut from Indian, to continental, to American. Many of them I learned from my mother, who is an excellent baker; her cakes are famous among our friends and family.

Just as there have been centuries of Western invasion of India, a tradition has also arisen of Western desserts served in concert with Indian sweets. At a formal Indian meal one is served at least two desserts: one Indian and one Western, to suit everyone's palate. I do the same. Western desserts complement Indian food beautifully, particularly fruit desserts, because they are light and fresh-tasting, refreshing and enlivening the palate after a meal that is heavy with spices. You'll see that most of the recipes in this chapter are non-Indian desserts: a simple vanilla pudding, a lemon pie with fresh blueberries, or banana bread. I've chosen desserts that are easy to make (because I insist on dessert with even the simplest meal!), although some are quite impressive for entertaining, too, such as the lemon pavlova with blueberries, delicate pots de crème flavored with the spices of Indian chai, and a caramel-coated orange flan.

At the end of the chapter you'll find recipes for a few Indian desserts that I consider to be indispensable: a rice pudding, a vermicelli pudding, and the Indian version of ice cream, called *kulfi.* These recipes are all based on a simple technique of simmering cream to reduce it until it thickens to a pudding-like consistency. Traditionally, the cook tends the pudding for hours. I don't think anyone has the time to do that anymore, but I love these desserts. So I've developed recipes that are as painless as possible (you need only stir the cream once every half hour or so) in the hope that one day, when you're at home for several hours, you'll set a pot on the stove and try one of these recipes. The *kulfi* recipe, my grandmother's brilliant shortcut version, requires no cooking at all.

From a practical standpoint, dessert is at least as important as the rest of the meal. It is the last taste that people go away from the table with, and they will remember it beyond anything that came before. But sweets have a larger symbolic and spiritual significance for me as well. They play an important ceremonial role in the diverse religions of my country. Religious holidays and ceremonies are often accompanied by a particular type of sweet, such as the Holy Vermicelli Pudding, served in celebration of the last day of the fast of Ramadan. And their taste brings back a child's memories of a time when even the most humble sweet, used as a part of a celebration or festival, took on the allure of a heavenly magic. May they bring you great pleasure.

coconut-banana caramel custard

SERVES 6 TO 8

I made this dessert with my coauthor Stephanie, and my partner, Chuck, in mind. Chuck loves bananas and Steph loves coconut. In any event, custard and caramel always taste delicious together, and the banana and coconut milk give the dessert a particularly creamy texture.

1 1/2 cups sugar (1 1/4 cups if using sweetened coconut)
1 large overripe banana
1/2 cup shredded unsweetened coconut or shredded sweetened dried coconut
1/2 teaspoon freshly ground nutmeg

1/8 teaspoon salt
6 large eggs
1 cup coconut milk
1 (12-ounce) can evaporated milk
1 teaspoon pure vanilla extract

Preheat the oven to 325°F. Line a 13 x 9 x 2-inch baking dish with a doubled dish towel.

Heat 3/4 cup of the sugar in a small, heavy-bottomed saucepan over low heat, stirring often, until the sugar has melted and caramelized to golden brown, about 5 minutes. (It is essential to stir so that the sugar browns evenly.) Pour the caramel into a 9 x 5-inch loaf pan. Tilt the pan to cover the bottom and part of the sides with the caramel. Set aside.

Combine the banana, the remaining 3/4 cup sugar (1/2 cup sugar, if using sweetened coconut), the shredded coconut, nutmeg, and salt in the bowl of an electric mixer and beat until smooth. Beat in the eggs until well mixed. Gradually beat in the coconut milk and then the evaporated milk. Beat in the vanilla and beat until the custard is well mixed.

Pour the custard into the prepared loaf pan. Set the pan in the baking dish and then put the dish into the preheated oven. Use a cup to add hot tap water to almost fill the baking dish. Bake until a toothpick inserted in the center comes out clean and the top is a light brown color, about 1 hour, 15 minutes.

Remove the loaf pan from baking dish and set it on a wire rack to cool. (Let the water in the baking dish cool before removing it from the oven.) Refrigerate the custard for at least 5 hours.

To serve, set the loaf pan over direct heat until the bottom gets hot, about 1 minute. (This is to melt the caramel so that the flan will unmold.) Run a knife around the edges to loosen the flan. Invert a serving dish on top of the loaf pan and then turn the mold upside down onto the plate. Remove the pan. Cut into slices and serve.

chai pots de crème

SERVES 6

As a young teenager I spent many afternoons baking with our neighbor next door. Armed with my great love for sweets and baking skills newly acquired from my mother (who had quite a reputation as a baker), we experimented with many recipes. Some were disasters, but this recipe was one of our great successes. Spicy, creamy, and delicate, this sweet works especially well as an ending to an Indian meal; the subtle play of its sweet spice complements highly aromatic savory dishes.

CUSTARD

1 cup whipping cream

1 cup half-and-half

1 tablespoon loose Darjeeling or Earl Grey tea

A 1-inch piece cinnamon stick, broken in half

6 green cardamom pods, pounded in a mortar and
    pestle just to break open the shells

5 whole cloves

A 1-inch piece fresh ginger, peeled and cut into chunks

4 black peppercorns

3 large egg yolks

1 large egg

¼ cup granulated sugar

¼ cup brown sugar

Zest of 1 lemon

WHIPPED CREAM

1 cup whipping cream

4 teaspoons granulated sugar (or 1 tablespoon,
    if not using garam masala)

⅛ teaspoon garam masala (page 250; optional)

For the custard, combine the cream, half-and-half, tea, cinnamon, cardamom, cloves, ginger, and peppercorns in a medium saucepan. Bring to a boil, remove from the heat, cover, and let steep 15 minutes.

Preheat the oven to 325°F. Line a 13 x 9 x 2-inch baking dish with a dish towel. Place six 6-ounce ramekins in the baking dish and set aside.

Combine the egg yolks, whole egg, sugars, and lemon zest in the bowl of an electric mixer and beat on high speed until the mixture has thickened and leaves a ribbon trail when you lift the beaters from the bowl, about 2 minutes.

Strain the spice-infused cream into a medium bowl. With the mixer running on low speed, gradually pour the warm cream into the egg mixture and mix to combine.

Carefully divide the custard among the six ramekins and put the baking dish in the oven. Use a cup to pour enough hot tap water into the baking dish to come halfway up the sides of the ramekins. Cover the pan with aluminum foil and punch several holes in the foil to allow the steam to escape. Bake until the custards are just set and the centers still jiggle when shaken, about 30 minutes.

Remove the ramekins from the hot water and let cool on a rack. (Turn off the oven and let the water in the baking dish cool before removing it from the oven.) Then chill until completely cold.

For the spiced whipped cream, beat the whipping cream with the sugar and garam masala, if using, in a medium bowl to soft peaks. Spoon a dollop of this spiced cream on top of each chilled custard and serve.

gingersnap pudding

SERVES 6 TO 8

I used to make my own rich gingersnaps for this pudding, but having discovered the Charles and Laurel brand, available at most supermarkets, I use them now instead. Serve this hot during the winter with vanilla ice cream, or chill it for a summer dessert to serve with a cold caramel sauce.

4 large eggs
4 ounces cream cheese
1 1/2 cup sugar
1/2 cup raisins

Zest of 1 large lemon
2 1/4 cups half-and-half
1/3 cup water
8 large gingersnaps

Preheat the oven to 350°F. Remove all but the bottom rack from the oven.

Combine the eggs, cream cheese, 1/2 cup of the sugar, the raisins, and lemon zest in a mixing bowl and beat until light and creamy. Beat in the half-and-half until smooth; set this pudding mixture aside.

Combine the remaining 1 cup sugar and the water in a small, heavy-bottomed saucepan. Bring to a simmer and remove from the heat. Stir until the sugar is dissolved and the syrup is clear. Then return to the heat and boil, swirling the pan every now and then, until the syrup caramelizes to a deep brown color, 4 to 5 more minutes. Pour immediately into a 2 1/2-quart metal charlotte mold or a 9 × 5-inch loaf pan, and tip the mold to coat it with the caramel. Let the mold cool a few minutes.

To assemble the pudding, pour about 1 cup of the pudding mixture into the cooled mold. Crumble two of the cookies and sprinkle over the custard. Place a third cookie on top, in the center. Then cut a fourth cookie into 1/2-inch strips and use those to cover the rest of the space.

Spoon another cup of the pudding mixture over the cookies. Set another cookie in the center and cut a second into strips to fill the gaps, as before. Repeat with another cup of the pudding mixture and the last two cookies. Finish with the remaining pudding mixture.

Line an 8-inch square baking dish, or a 13 × 9 × 2-inch baking dish if using a loaf pan, with a doubled kitchen towel. Put the mold or loaf pan in the baking dish and put it into the preheated oven. Use a cup to add hot tap water to almost fill the baking dish. Bake until the custard is just set but still jiggles when shaken and a skewer stuck in about 1 inch from the edge comes out clean, about 45 minutes. Carefully lift the mold out of the pan and set it on a wire rack to cool. (Turn off the oven and let the water in the baking dish cool a little before removing it from the oven.) Refrigerate the flan to chill completely.

To serve, set the mold over direct heat until the bottom gets hot, about 1 minute. (This is to melt the caramel so that the flan will unmold.) Run a knife around the edge to loosen the flan. Invert a serving plate on top of the mold and then turn the mold upside down onto the plate. Remove the mold. Cut into wedges and serve.

lemon curd

MAKES 3 HALF-PINT JARS

This is delicious on its own, with yogurt or ice cream, or as a spread for muffins or scones. I also use it as a filling for Lemon Pavlova (page 226) and for Blueberry-Lemon Pie (page 228).

4 large egg yolks
1 large egg white
1 cup fresh lemon juice

Zest of 2 lemons
2 cups sugar
1 cup (2 sticks) unsalted butter, cut into pieces

Combine all of the ingredients in the top of a double boiler and whisk until smooth.

Bring about 2 inches of water to a boil in the bottom of the double boiler. Put the top of the double boiler over it (the water should just barely touch the bottom of the upper pan), turn the heat down to low, and cook, whisking constantly, until the curd has thickened enough to coat the back of a wooden spoon, about 15 minutes. (The curd will thicken further as it cools.)

Remove the top of the double boiler. Pour the hot water out of the bottom pan and fill with cold water. Set the top of the double boiler back on the pan (the water should just touch the bottom of the upper pan) and set aside for about 30 minutes to cool.

Pour the curd into three sterilized half-pint jars, screw on the lids, and let cool to room temperature. Then refrigerate for up to 2 weeks.

susan aunty's orange flan

SERVES 6 TO 8

I got the original version of this recipe from my neighbor in Delhi, whom we called Susan Aunty. (In India, all intimate neighbors are addressed as uncles or aunts.) I've embellished her recipe with orange blossom water and cream cheese. I cook the caramel until it's quite dark; the slight bitterness of a darker caramel contrasts nicely with the sweet custard.

1 (14-ounce) can sweetened condensed milk

1½ cups half-and-half

4 large eggs

1 (8-ounce) package cream cheese

2 tablespoons orange marmalade

¼ cup orange liqueur

1 cup sugar

¼ cup water

Grated zest of 2 oranges

A 1-inch piece cinnamon stick

Preheat the oven to 350°F. and remove all but the bottom oven rack.

Combine the condensed milk, half-and-half, eggs, cream cheese, marmalade, and orange liqueur in the blender and blend until smooth. Set aside.

Combine the sugar, water, orange zest, and cinnamon stick in a medium, heavy-bottomed saucepan. Bring to a simmer and remove from the heat. Stir until the sugar is dissolved and the syrup is clear. Then return to the heat and boil, swirling the pan every now and then, until syrup caramelizes to deep brown, 4 to 5 more minutes. Immediately pour the caramel into a 2 ½-quart metal charlotte mold or 9 × 5-inch loaf pan, and tip the mold or pan to coat it with the caramel. Let cool a few minutes and then pour the custard mixture into it.

Line an 8-inch square baking dish (or a larger rectangular baking dish, if using a loaf pan) with a doubled kitchen towel. Put the mold in the baking dish and then put the dish into the preheated oven. Use a cup to add hot tap water to almost fill the baking dish. Bake until the custard is just set but still jiggles when shaken and a skewer stuck in about 1 inch from the edge comes out clean, about 1 hour, 25 minutes. Carefully lift the mold out of the pan. Turn off the oven and let the water in the baking dish cool a little before moving it. Refrigerate the flan to chill completely.

To serve, set the mold over direct heat until the bottom gets hot, about 1 minute. (This is to melt the caramel so that the flan will unmold.) Run a knife around the edge to loosen the flan. Overturn a serving plate on top of the mold and then turn the mold upside down onto the plate. Remove the mold. Cut the flan into wedges and serve.

lemon pavlova with fresh berries

SERVES 8

This dessert reminds me of trips to the tropics, where a light dessert like this is a perfect end to a meal, and of the little café in Bombay where I used to eat it while I was in school. It's beautiful—it looks like a garland of fruit with a meringue at the center—and it has a trio of delightful textures from the crunch of the meringue, to its gooey center and the silky cream of the lemon curd.

The dessert should be assembled just before serving so that the meringue doesn't get soggy. You can make the meringue the night before; store it in an airtight container so that it doesn't lose its crunch. You can also make eight small rounds of meringue from this recipe to make individual pavlovas; cook them exactly the same way, but use two baking sheets. If it's more convenient, macerate the berries overnight; they'll get much sweeter and softer.

This is my mother's recipe for meringue that is a little unusual in that it is made with cornstarch; the cornstarch helps to dry out the meringue.

MERINGUE

4 large egg whites

1 cup superfine sugar

2 teaspoons white vinegar or lemon juice

1 tablespoon sifted cornstarch

1 quart strawberries, washed, hulled, dried, and sliced

1 pint blueberries, washed and dried

1/2 pint raspberries, washed and dried

1 cup granulated sugar

1 cup heavy cream

2 tablespoons confectioners' sugar

1 tablespoon orange liqueur, such as Grand Marnier

1 cup Lemon Curd (page 223) or store-bought lemon curd

Preheat the oven to 275°F. Line a baking sheet with parchment paper and set aside.

For the meringue, combine the egg whites, superfine sugar, and vinegar in the bowl of an electric mixer and beat until soft peaks form. Turn out into a bowl. Sift the cornstarch over the whites and carefully fold in with a rubber spatula.

Spoon the meringue mixture onto the parchment-lined baking sheet and spread it out to a circle about 8 inches in diameter. Bake on the center rack of the preheated oven for 2 hours. Turn the oven off and let the meringue continue cooking in the residual heat of the oven for another hour. Remove from the oven and let cool on a rack to room temperature. If serving that day, set on a cake tray or serving plate and wrap in plastic until ready to serve. If serving the next day, put it in an airtight container.

An hour or so before you plan to serve, put the strawberries, blueberries, and raspberries in a bowl with the granulated sugar and toss. Cover the bowl with plastic wrap and put in the refrigerator to macerate for 1 hour.

When ready to serve, combine the cream, confectioners' sugar, and orange liqueur in a mixing bowl and beat until stiff peaks form; set aside.

To assemble the pavlova, set the meringue in the center of a large serving plate. Use a spatula to spread it with the lemon curd. Layer the whipped cream on top. Arrange all but about 1 cup of the fruit around the meringue and pour the juices over it. Arrange the macerated fruit on top of the cream. Cut the pavlova into wedges and serve.

vanilla pudding

SERVES 4 TO 6

This is a classic American vanilla pudding, but made fresh. Served with fruit or cake, it makes a lovely, simple ending to a rich Indian meal, when the palate is surfeited with the taste and fragrance of spices.

½ cup sugar

3 tablespoons cornstarch

2 cups whole milk

½ vanilla bean, or 1 teaspoon pure vanilla extract

1 tablespoon unsalted butter

1 large egg

Sift the sugar and cornstarch together into a medium, heavy-bottomed saucepan. Whisk in the milk, a few tablespoons at a time at first and then ¼ cup at a time, whisking thoroughly to make sure there are no lumps. Add the vanilla bean, if using.

Bring the milk almost to a boil over medium-high heat and cook, whisking, until thickened, 3 to 4 minutes. Remove from the heat and whisk in the butter and set aside.

Whisk the egg in a medium bowl. Add about ¼ cup of the pudding and whisk until smooth. Whisk in another ¼ cup of the pudding. Then pour this mixture back into the saucepan. Bring almost to a boil over medium-high heat. Remove from the heat and stir in the vanilla extract, if using. Place the pan in a larger pan of cold water and let stand, whisking occasionally, until cool, about 30 minutes

Transfer to a serving bowl and chill completely before serving.

blueberry-lemon pie

SERVES 8

This easily assembled pie is a bit fragile—it tends to fall apart when cut—so I just serve it in bowls so that my guests can eat it with a spoon. If you have lemon curd on hand (you can buy it ready-made in specialty stores and some supermarkets), this is a practically instant dessert. I like to serve it at the end of an Indian meal in the summer, when blueberries are sweet. The fruit flavors, so simple, clean, and refreshing, are a delightful contrast to the complexity of Indian spicing.

COOKIE CRUST
1/2 cup (1 stick) chilled unsalted butter, cut into
**   8 pieces, plus more for the pie dish**
2 cups crushed vanilla wafers

1 1/2 cups heavy cream
1 1/2 cups Lemon Curd (page 223) or store-bought
**   lemon curd**
3/4 cup fresh blueberries
1/4 cup granulated sugar
Juice of 1 lemon
Confectioners' sugar, for sprinkling

Butter a 9-inch pie dish. For the cookie crust, combine the butter and cookie crumbs in a food processor and process until the mixture is the texture of cornmeal. Press it into the pie dish, wrap in plastic, and freeze 45 minutes.

When the crust has chilled, beat the cream to stiff peaks. Fold in the lemon curd. Spoon into the prepared crust and chill overnight.

One to 2 hours before serving, toss the blueberries with the granulated sugar and lemon juice, and put in the refrigerator to macerate.

When ready to serve, top the pie with the macerated berries and some of the juices, and dust with confectioners' sugar, if you like. Cut into wedges and serve.

banana pudding

SERVES 6 TO 8

A child's favorite, this sweet vanilla-scented dessert, luscious with soft, ripe banana, is comfort food at its best. Make sure to use bananas that are almost too ripe so that they melt in your mouth. You can also substitute nectarines for bananas. If you like, top the pudding with another layer of wafers just before serving. This gives it a nice crunch.

1 recipe Vanilla Pudding (page 227)

2 cups heavy cream

6 tablespoons confectioners' sugar

2 tablespoons rum (optional)

1 large box (12 ounces) vanilla wafers

4 very ripe bananas, sliced crosswise as thin as possible

Make the vanilla pudding; set aside.

While the pudding is still warm, combine the heavy cream, sugar, and rum, if using, in a bowl and beat until stiff peaks form.

To assemble the pudding, spoon about one-quarter of the warm pudding into the bottom of a 6-, 8-, or 10-cup serving bowl. Cover with a layer of wafers; make sure you are generous with the cookies and place them close to one another. (You should use about one-quarter of the box for each layer.) Layer half of the banana slices on top. Spoon another quarter of the pudding over the bananas and cover with another layer of wafers. Spread with about half of the whipped cream.

Now spoon another quarter of the pudding over the whipped cream. Cover with more wafers. Spoon the rest of the pudding over the wafers and layer the rest of the bananas on top.

Spread the rest of the cream over the bananas and chill until very cold, 3 to 5 hours.

nani's quick and easy kulfi

SERVES 6 TO 8

During the summers in the north of India, there is no dessert more popular than *kulfi*. This Indian version of ice cream is made just like the puddings in the preceding recipes, by reducing cream until it thickens naturally, then flavoring and freezing it. *Kulfi* is traditionally molded and frozen in special conical molds. You can buy these in Indian grocery stores or freeze the mixture in a loaf pan to be sliced, or in Popsicle molds.

My maternal grandmother, who has lived in San Francisco for about twenty years, has, in that time, developed or borrowed many a "convenient trick and shortcut," as she says, in her cooking. This *kulfi* recipe is one of these shortcuts. It requires no cooking and gives you such a near-perfect rendering of an authentic *kulfi* that I'm including it instead of an authentic recipe in this book.

You can add your own favorite mix of nuts and dried fruits to the recipe or flavor it with rose water or screwpine essence *(kewra)*. For a richer *kulfi,* use full-fat evaporated milk and condensed milk.

¼ teaspoon saffron strands

10 green cardamom pods, peeled, seeded, and ground to a fine powder

1 (12-ounce) can fat-free evaporated milk

1 (14-ounce) can low-fat condensed milk

1 cup heavy cream

1 cup assorted nuts and fruits (I like a mixture of almonds, pistachios, and raisins)

Warm the saffron strands in a small frying pan over very low heat until they turn deep maroon, 30 seconds to a minute. Grind to a fine powder in a mortar and pestle, or crush in a bowl with the back of a spoon.

Place the saffron in a blender with the remaining ingredients. Process to mix well, 3 to 4 minutes. (The nuts will get coarsely chopped.) Pour into *kulfi* molds, a loaf pan, or Popsicle molds and freeze until solid.

rice pudding

CHAAWAL KEE KHEER

SERVES 8 TO 10

Rice pudding is the quintessential Indian dessert, and this recipe of Panditji's is the rice pudding to beat all others. With his priestly training he understood puddings as a means to inspire the senses in a way that was otherwise impossible for mortals to experience: eating this was the closest we could come to tasting the divine in this earthly life. And so he made a practice of stirring and "entertaining" the pudding for as long as it took to make it absolutely exquisite.

Rice pudding like this is a creamy substance lightly thickened with rice, traditionally made by reducing cream very slowly, stirring constantly, until it thickens naturally to a pudding consistency. Although you do need to be at home for several hours to stir the pudding, you need only give it a stir every half hour or so. Some people try to rush the cooking time by adding more rice, sugar, condensed milk, or even blotting paper. But the truest way to make it is to let the cream cook unhurriedly, at its own pace. I have streamlined the process a bit by using part half-and-half, which seems to speed things up some without compromising the sublimely creamy texture. And I find that if I set a timer for 30 minutes to remind myself to stir, I can be at home taking care of my life, on the phone or paying bills, and the rice pudding almost makes itself. If you like, you can also cut the recipe in half.

You can pry open the cardamom pods with your nails; just pull the pod apart until you see the tiny black seeds inside.

1 gallon half-and-half	1 cup chopped blanched almonds
2 tablespoons water	1/2 cup golden raisins
4 tablespoons ghee or unsalted butter	1/2 cup basmati rice
8 to 10 green cardamom pods, pods crushed, tiny black seeds removed and ground to a fine powder in a spice grinder (about 1/2 teaspoon), plus more for garnish	2 cups heavy cream
	1 cup sugar, or to taste
	1/4 teaspoon saffron strands

Combine the half-and-half and water in a heavy-bottomed, 6-quart saucepan and bring to a boil over high heat. Then turn the heat down to very low and simmer very gently for 2 hours. Stir often and scrape the bottom of the pan with a flat metal spatula or wooden spoon every 30 to 35 minutes to keep the half-and-half from burning. Scrape down the sides of the pan at the same time.

Meanwhile, heat the ghee or butter in a small frying pan over low heat until liquid. Add the ground cardamom seeds, almonds, and raisins and cook, stirring, until the almonds turn golden brown, about 5 minutes. If the mixture begins to stick to the bottom of the pan, drizzle in some of the hot half-and-half and stir.

Add the rice to the pan with the almond-raisin mixture and cook, stirring, until the rice turns opaque and you smell its fragrance, 2 to 3 minutes. Spoon a few tablespoons of the simmering half-and-half into the pan to cool it and remove from the heat; set aside.

When the half-and-half has cooked 2 hours, add the almond-raisin mixture along with all but 2 tablespoons of the heavy cream and stir to blend. Continue cooking, stirring and scraping the bottom (so that

the rice doesn't stick and burn) and sides of the pan every 30 to 35 minutes, until the rice begins to float up to the top of the mixture and the mixture thickens enough to coat the back of a spoon, about 2½ more hours. (The mixture will have reduced by about one-half.)

Put a small bowl in the freezer to chill.

When the pudding is cooked, spoon about 2 tablespoons into the chilled bowl, stir in a scant teaspoon of sugar, and return the bowl to the freezer for 5 minutes. Test for thickness: the pudding should be the consistency of a cooked custard and still jiggle when you shake it. Keep testing and reducing until you're happy with the consistency. Then remove the pudding from the heat and stir in the sugar. Taste; you may want the custard sweeter. (Remember that the custard will seem *less* sweet once it has been chilled.) Add sugar if you like. Let cool to room temperature.

Warm the saffron strands in a small frying pan over very low heat, stirring, until they turn deep maroon, about 30 seconds. (Be careful: saffron burns very quickly.) Grind to a fine powder in a mortar and pestle, or crush in a bowl with the back of a spoon. Add the reserved 2 tablespoons of heavy cream and stir.

Spoon the pudding into serving bowls (or one large serving bowl) and drizzle the saffron cream over the top. Garnish with a pinch of ground cardamom. Cover with plastic and chill until very cold.

variation

PISTACHIO PUDDING *(Piste Kee Kheer):* Follow the instructions for the Rice Pudding, but add 1½ cups coarsely chopped blanched pistachios when sautéing the spices in the 4 tablespoons of ghee or butter. Then add 1 cup finely ground pistachios and ½ cup raisins when you add the rice to the almond mixture.

holy vermicelli pudding

ID KEE SENWANYEE/SHEER KHURMA

SERVES 4 TO 6

This dessert is made just like the rice pudding that precedes it, and with many of the same ingredients, but instead of resulting in a light, creamy pudding, this traditional Muslim pudding is thick and firm. The vermicelli causes it to set up quickly and so it is quite a bit faster to make as well. This dessert is always served at Meethi-Id, the Muslim festival that marks the end of the fast of Ramadan.

Charoli nuts, also known as *chironji,* are tiny nuts that look like small beans. They have a sweet, almost musky taste; they don't really taste like nuts. You can buy them at your local Indian store or order them online.

½ gallon half-and-half

2 tablespoons water

¼ cup ghee or unsalted butter

8 to 10 green cardamom pods, pods crushed, tiny black seeds removed and ground to a fine powder

1 (200-gram) package Indian vermicelli *(senwayee),* or very thin supermarket-variety vermicelli, broken in half

½ cup chopped blanched almonds

½ cup blanched pistachios, finely chopped

½ cup golden raisins

½ cup seeded and pitted dates, chopped very fine

3 tablespoons *chironji/charoli* nuts (optional)

2 cups heavy cream

1 cup sugar, or to taste

¼ teaspoon saffron strands

Combine the half-and-half and water in a heavy-bottomed, 6-quart saucepan pan and bring to a boil over high heat. Turn the heat down to very low and simmer very gently for 30 minutes. Stir and scrape the bottom of the pan with a flat metal spatula or wooden spoon a few times during cooking to keep the half-and-half from burning. Scrape down the sides of the pan at the same time.

Meanwhile, heat the ghee or butter in a small frying pan over low heat until liquid. Add the ground cardamom seeds and the vermicelli and cook, stirring, until the vermicelli turns golden brown, about 5 minutes. If the mixture begins to stick, drizzle in a teaspoon or so of the hot half-and-half, and stir to keep the vermicelli from burning; set aside.

Add the almonds, pistachios, raisins, dates, and *chironji* nuts, if using, and cook, stirring, until the almonds are golden brown, about 5 more minutes. If the mixture sticks, drizzle in more half-and-half.

When the half-and-half has cooked 30 minutes, add the vermicelli mixture and continue cooking, stirring and scraping, until the half-and-half has reduced by half, about 10 more minutes.

Add all but 2 tablespoons of the heavy cream and stir well. Continue cooking, stirring and scraping to make sure the vermicelli doesn't stick and burn, 5 more minutes.

Meanwhile, put a small bowl in the freezer to chill.

When the pudding mixture has cooked about 45 minutes total and has thickened enough to coat the back of a spoon, spoon about 2 tablespoons into the chilled bowl, stir in a scant teaspoon of sugar, and return the bowl to the freezer for 5 minutes to test for thickness. The pudding should be the consistency of a cooked custard and still jiggle when you shake it. Keep testing and reducing until you are happy with the consistency.

Then take the pudding off the heat and stir in 1 cup sugar. Taste; you may want the custard sweeter.

(Remember that the custard will seem *less* sweet once it has been chilled.) Let cool to room temperature.

Toast the saffron strands in a small frying pan over very low heat until they turn a deep maroon color, about 30 seconds. (Be careful: saffron burns very easily.) Grind to a fine powder in a mortar and pestle, or crush in a bowl with the back of a spoon. Add the reserved 2 tablespoons of heavy cream and stir.

Pour the pudding into a serving bowl or individual bowls you will serve in and garnish with the saffron cream. You can also sprinkle on more ground cardamom seed powder if you like. Serve chilled.

christmas banana bread

MAKES 1 LOAF

Every holiday season, our neighbors Susan and Joe leave a beautifully packed bag of banana bread on our door. This is Susan's mother's recipe. I love this because the cake is exceptionally moist, not cakey, and it is lightly spiced with Indian spices—cinnamon, mace, and ground ginger. Serve warm with vanilla ice cream and candied walnuts.

¹/₂ cup (1 stick) unsalted butter, softened	¹/₄ teaspoon ground cinnamon
1 cup sugar	¹/₈ teaspoon ground mace
2 large eggs, well beaten	¹/₈ teaspoon ground ginger
3 ripe bananas, broken into pieces	¹/₂ teaspoon salt
1¹/₄ cups all-purpose flour	1 teaspoon baking soda

Preheat the oven to 350°F. Butter and flour one 8¹/₂ × 4¹/₂-inch loaf pan.

Cream the butter with the sugar until light and fluffy. Add the eggs and beat until combined. Beat in the bananas.

Combine the flour, spices, salt, and baking soda in another bowl, then fold the dry ingredients into the creamed mixture just until combined; do not overmix. Pour into the pan and bake until a tester stuck in the middle of the banana bread comes out clean, 50 to 60 minutes. Let cool on a rack before removing from the pan.

SWEET LASSI

MANGO LASSI

SAFFRON-CARDAMOM LASSI

PISTACHIO LASSI

*drinks

HONEY-BASIL TEA

STRAWBERRY LEMONADE

INDIAN LEMONADE

INDIAN FRUIT PUNCH

CHAI

TANGERINE TEA

INDIAN ROSE MILK

Wonderfully refreshing fruit drinks such as Strawberry Lemonade and Indian Fruit Punch, fruited or spiced yogurt drinks called lassis, and teas are especially effective thirst quenchers because the acid in the citrus juice and yogurt both cools and cleanses the palate. (Beer, wine, and soft drinks taste good with Indian food, too; my friends and I are particularly partial to Limca, which tastes like an Indian 7-Up, or Vimto, an Indian berry soda.)

Nimbu pani (Indian lemonade) is the perfect drink for the summer months. Lemon is a refreshing antidote to the hot winds that blow across most of the Indian plains during that season. I find lemonade to be a great way to introduce spices to the uninitiated: I offer my guests ginger lemonade with no explanation, and let them discover that it is the unfamiliar taste of fresh ginger that makes it taste so good.

With the exception of Tangerine Tea, which I chill and serve with lunch or dinner, I don't serve teas with meals. Teas are enjoyed not only for their caffeine but also to heal the mind and body. Honey, spices, and citrus are added to calm the nerves, purify the blood, and soothe the mind. Teas are served both as a social drink and also as a restorative tonic first thing in the morning or just before going to bed.

Sweet lassis—sweet yogurt drinks such as Mango Lassi, Pistachio Lassi, and Saffron-Cardamom Lassi—are desserts in a glass. They also help soothe our palates when they have been flooded with spices and herbs. Lassis are also served salty (see page 238), as digestives.

sweet lassi

Lassis are chilled yogurt-based drinks, something like a smoothie, often flavored with fruit and/or spices. They are the preferred drink in northern Indian homes, especially in the Punjab. They are usually served in the summer, but most Punjabis are more than happy to drink these sweet yogurt concoctions year-round. Lassis may also be served salty; see the variation below.

3 cups plain yogurt
½ cup milk
12 ice cubes

2 tablespoons sugar, or to taste
2 teaspoons rose water

Combine the ingredients in a blender and process until the yogurt is frothy and the ice is crushed into small pieces. Pour into tall glasses and serve immediately.

variation

For a salty lassi, combine the yogurt, milk, and ice cubes with ¾ teaspoon salt, ¼ teaspoon ground toasted cumin (see sidebar, page 39), and 2 tablespoons chopped fresh mint in a blender and proceed as in the recipe above. Garnish each glass with a pinch of ground toasted cumin.

mango lassi

Mango lassi, a sweet mango-yogurt shake, is a well-loved fixture on most Indian restaurant menus. When I was a kid, we drank something similar called "Mango Shake" that was made of whole milk, vanilla ice cream, and mango pulp blended with some ice cubes. Now I rely on this very refreshing recipe during the hot New York summers. You can also make it with cream instead of water and serve it as a rich tropical dessert. Fresh mango pulp won't work for this; the pulp has fibers that are impossible to strain out. Canned mango pulp is sold in Indian grocery stores.

3 cups plain yogurt
Juice of ½ lemon
1 cup canned mango pulp (preferably
**   Ratna Alfonso brand)**

½ cup cold water
20 ice cubes
¼ cup sugar, or to taste

Combine all the ingredients in a blender and process until the yogurt is frothy and the ice is crushed into small pieces. Taste for sugar. Serve in tall glasses.

saffron-cardamom lassi

PATIALA WAALI LASSI

SERVES 4 TO 6

This is another lassi variation, one of my favorites—it is a gentle, delicate drink in which the flavor of the yogurt is exquisitely balanced by the cardamom and saffron.

1/4 teaspoon saffron strands

1 tablespoon warm milk

3 cups plain yogurt

2 tablespoons sugar, or to taste

1/2 teaspoon ground cardamom

1/8 teaspoon pure vanilla extract

10 to 12 ice cubes

Toast the saffron strands in a small frying pan over very low heat, stirring, until they turn a deep maroon color, about 30 seconds. (Be careful: saffron burns easily.) Grind to a fine powder in a mortar and pestle, or crush in a small bowl with the back of a spoon.

Add the warm milk to the saffron and stir. Put in a blender with all the remaining ingredients and process until the yogurt is frothy and the ice is crushed into small pieces. Taste for sugar.

Pour into tall glasses and serve immediately.

pistachio lassi

SERVES 4 TO 6

When I was very young, an aunt of mine used to make this lassi with pistachio essence and food coloring. It had a fake pistachio flavor and an unreal green tint—delicious and beautiful to my young eyes and palate. This recipe is made with real pistachios so it doesn't have that wondrous color, but the flavor's a lot better!

3 cups plain yogurt

2 tablespoons sugar, or to taste

1/2 teaspoon ground cardamom

1/4 teaspoon ground black pepper

3/4 cup pistachios, ground in spice grinder to a powder

1/2 cup milk

1/8 teaspoon pistachio extract (optional)

10 to 12 ice cubes

Combine all the ingredients in a blender and process until the yogurt is frothy and the ice is crushed into small pieces. Taste for sugar. Serve immediately in tall glasses.

honey-basil tea

SHAHAD AUR TULSI KE CHAI

SERVES 4 TO 6

My mother used to drink this ginger-scented tea every day, first thing in the morning. Indians believe it helps purify the blood and also keeps one strong and fit. It's also supposed to be very good for the skin. In India, we use holy basil, which has a slightly different flavor from common basil. Holy basil is available in Asian and Indian grocery stores, but if you cannot find it easily, regular basil will work just fine.

1 cup fresh basil leaves, preferably holy basil
4¼ cups water
4 teaspoons loose Orange Pekoe tea

A 1-inch piece fresh ginger, peeled and cut in half
2 to 3 tablespoons honey, or to taste
6 black peppercorns

Combine the basil leaves and water in a saucepan. Bring to a boil, cover, and simmer very gently for 5 minutes.

Add the tea, ginger, honey, and peppercorns and bring back to a boil. Remove from the heat and steep, covered, 5 more minutes.

Just before serving, return to a boil and strain into tea cups.

strawberry lemonade

MAKES ABOUT 2 1/2 QUARTS

I serve this throughout the summer, when the strawberries are particularly sweet. This is a good beverage for a summer Indian meal or snack. The key is to use just enough lemon juice to balance the sweetness of the berries. Serve in tall glasses with sundae spoons to fish out the sliced berries.

2 pints ripe summer strawberries, finely sliced
1 cup sugar, or to taste

Juice of 4 lemons
8 cups water

Combine the strawberry slices, sugar, and lemon juice in a bowl and macerate in the refrigerator for at least 2 hours. Spoon all but 1 cup of the strawberries, and all of the juices, into a food processor or blender and process until smooth.

Combine the strawberry puree and the sliced strawberries in a large pitcher. Add the water and stir. Taste for sugar. Serve in tall glasses filled with ice.

indian lemonade

NIMBU PAANI

MAKES ABOUT 1 1/2 QUARTS

In India, we make this with a variety of lime that has a paper-thin skin, called *kaagzi nimbu*. If you can find them, Key limes are the closest in taste, but you can use any lime or even lemons, if you like. Without exaggeration, it is safe to say that each of us kids drank close to half a gallon of this lemonade every day during the summer. This is excellent with any Indian meal. If you like, spike it with some rum for cocktails.

A 3-inch piece fresh ginger, peeled and coarsely
   chopped
4 1/3 cups water

2 cups sugar
1 cup lemon, lime, or Key lime juice,
   or any combination

Combine the ginger and 1/3 cup of the water in a blender and process to a paste. Strain through a very fine strainer or a strainer lined with cheesecloth, and set this ginger essence aside.

Bring the remaining 4 cups of water and the sugar to a boil in a medium saucepan. Remove from the heat and let cool. Add the lemon or lime juice and the ginger juice. Pour into a container, cover, and chill.

Serve in tall glasses filled with ice.

indian fruit punch

MAKES ABOUT 2 QUARTS

A cup of cream smoothes and enriches the sweet-tart taste of fruit juices and turns the juice into an ethereal drink. I make this with a number of commercial fresh fruit juices that I buy at my supermarket. If you can't find these exact juices, feel free to substitute any that you like. You can make this with half-and-half, too, for a leaner punch.

2 cups fresh raspberry juice

2 cups fresh strawberry juice

2 cups fresh mango juice

2 cups fresh banana-mango or other banana fruit juice

1 cup fresh orange juice

2 tablespoons grenadine syrup

1 cup heavy cream

Combine all of the ingredients in a 2-quart or larger plastic pitcher with a lid and shake to combine. Chill and serve cold.

variation

For a lighter, more refreshing punch, substitute an equal amount of plain yogurt for the heavy cream. Put the yogurt into a blender and blend until smooth (it's important to get out the lumps now). Add about half of all the juices and blend again until smooth. Combine with the remaining juices in a 2-quart or larger plastic pitcher with lid and shake to combine as usual.

chai

If you are used to store-bought chai, you'll find this one somewhat less sweet and more vibrant tasting. I use just enough sugar to bring out the taste of the spices. Add more sugar, if you like.

2 cups milk

1 cup water

1 1/2 tablespoons loose Darjeeling or Earl Grey tea

A 1 1/2-inch piece cinnamon stick, broken in half

9 green cardamom pods, crushed slightly in a mortar
   and pestle to open

7 whole cloves

A 1 1/2-inch piece fresh ginger, peeled and
   cut into chunks

6 black peppercorns

1 tablespoon sugar

Combine the ingredients in a medium saucepan and bring to a boil. Remove from the heat, cover, and let steep 15 minutes. Then return to a boil, strain, and serve hot.

tangerine tea

NARANGI KI CHAI

SERVES 4 TO 6

Drinking this tea in the evening is the perfect way to unwind. In the summer, I serve it chilled, just like American iced teas. For the best flavor, use organic citrus and quality tea from a real tea shop.

4 cups water
Peel of 3 tangerines or oranges, thinly sliced
A 3-inch piece fresh ginger, peeled and sliced
½ lemon

4 whole cloves
5 teaspoons loose Darjeeling tea
3 tablespoons honey

Combine the water, sliced citrus peel, ginger, lemon half, and cloves in a medium saucepan. Bring to a boil, cover, and simmer very gently for 3 minutes.

Add the tea and honey and return to a boil. Remove from the heat and let steep, covered, 5 more minutes.

Strain into cups and serve hot.

indian rose milk

DESI GULAB KAA SHARBAT

SERVES 6 TO 8

When I was in my early teens, we kids spent several summers with my aunt who lived in Jaipur, in the desert state of Rajasthan. Several times a week, she took us shopping in the Johari Bazaar, the diamond district of Jaipur. While my aunt was conducting her business, the driver would take us to get some fragrant rose milk, the perfect antidote to the scorching heat of Rajasthan. The Indian rose used to make this drink is the *desi gulab,* a rose that has a particularly intense scent. Years later, I'm still smitten by this drink. You can buy rose petals in any Indian or Middle Eastern grocery store, or online.

1 pound unsprayed or pesticide-free fragrant, dried
   rose petals, washed and drained

4 cups water

2 cups sugar, or to taste

$^1/_2$ cup rose water

4 cups chilled whole milk

Combine the rose petals and the water in a large pot. Bring to a boil and cook until the water is reduced by about one-half.

Strain the infused water and return it to the pot. Add the sugar and return to a boil, stirring every now and then. Reduce the heat and simmer for 2 minutes. Remove from heat and let cool.

Add the rose water and milk to the cooled liquid. Serve chilled.

*glossary

Most of the ingredients in this book are probably already familiar to you, and are available in any well-stocked grocery store: whole and ground cumin and coriander seeds, cayenne pepper, whole cinnamon stick and cloves, and fresh cilantro. Eventually, you may want to stock your pantry with a few of the more exotic items, usually available at Indian or Asian grocery stores or online from spice purveyors such as *namaste.com* or *ethnicgrocer.com*.

ASAFETIDA (HEENG): A sand-colored powder made from the root of a fennel-like plant. When cooked, asafetida has a pungent flavor and smell, reminiscent of the flavor of onion and garlic. It is used in the cuisines of Hindu Brahmans and Jains, whose religions prohibit eating onion and garlic, because the asafetida adds a savory taste to the food.

If you don't have asafetida, you can simply omit it from recipes that call for it, or substitute a bit of garlic and onion.

CARDAMOM (ELAICHI): A seed pod from the cardamom plant, in the ginger family. Whole green cardamom is a small, pale green pod that contains many tiny brown seeds. The taste is sharp, and both sweet and bitter, but mellows to a lovely warm taste as it cooks; raw, it has a resinous smell that clears the head, like camphor. Green cardamom is also sometimes bleached white; green and white cardamom are interchangeable and, for simplicity, I use only green. The taste of cardamom complements both sweet and savory dishes—it is an important spice in Rice Pudding (page 232)—and it is used in desserts and savory foods throughout India. It is one of the spices that make up the North Indian spice mix garam masala.

Green cardamom is sold whole or ground. Store-bought ground cardamom is made from both pod and seed, all ground up together; you'll like the taste better if you grind your own just from the seeds. To do so, open the cardamom pods with your nails, brush the brown seeds out, and grind.

CAROM SEEDS (AJAWAIN): This tiny oval seed, also known as lovage, is the seed of the thymol plant, closely related to dill and caraway. Carom has the green-brown color of cumin. When crushed, it has a strong, bitter, thymelike fragrance and taste. Carom seeds are used whole or crushed, in pickling mixtures, in vegetable dishes, in breads, and to flavor the crisp crackers called *mathri* (page 199).

CAYENNE PEPPER, OR GROUND RED CHILE: A reddish-orange powder made from grinding the dried fruit of the *Capsicum* family. Cayenne pepper is very hot, but doesn't have much flavor. Indian red chile powder, which looks the same as cayenne and is available in Indian grocery stores, is milder than cayenne and adds more chile taste.

CHILES, FRESH GREEN (HARI MIRCH): The young, green pods of the *Capsicum* family. There are many types of green chiles, varying in size and heat. Green chiles are used often in vegetable dishes, dals, soups, and pickles (see Green Chile Pickle on page 204). You can use any hot, green chile you find in your supermarket when hot green chiles are called for in these recipes—jalapeños or the smaller serranos are easy to find. Pick jalapeños if you don't like too much heat—serranos are hotter. I also like to use the tiny, fiery-hot Thai bird chiles, sold in Indian and Asian grocery stores.

CHILES, WHOLE, DRIED RED: The small, slender, reddish-brown, dried pods of the *Capsicum* family. Whole red chiles are used in dals, soups, stews, rice dishes, and often in *tarkas,* when only mild heat and the flavor of the chile are desired. Sautéed, whole red chiles add a wonderfully warm, smoky taste to the food. Dried red chiles are used in the North Indian spice mix garam masala, as well as in South Indian *rasam* and *sambhaar* powders.

CILANTRO (HARA DHANIYA): The fresh leaves of the coriander plant, a member of the parsley family. The light green leaves are shaped something like flat-leaf parsley leaves, but are more rounded, with a more delicate, prettier shape. Cilantro has a strong fragrance and pungent taste.

Chopped, raw cilantro is added to curries, dals, soups, and rice dishes at the end of cooking to give the food a bright, clean note. Or, it may be cooked whole into sauces, as a green, in which case it has a more muted, bitter taste. Both the leaves and the young, fleshy parts of the cilantro stems, chopped together, add a unique spark to Indian dishes.

CINNAMON (DAL CHEENEE): The dried, inner bark of a tree in the laurel family, cinnamon has a sweet, woody taste and fragrance. It is used only in savory dishes in India, to flavor vegetable and meat dishes, dals, biriyanis, and rice pilafs. It is also one of the ingredients in the North Indian spice mix garam masala. Cinnamon is sold whole, in slender, rolled sticks, or ground; I use only whole cinnamon in my recipes, although I often grind it into spice mixtures.

CLOVES (LAUNG): The dried, unopened flower of the clove tree. Whole, this small, dark brown spice is shaped like a tiny torch. Sharp, hot, sweet, and bitter, the taste of clove lingers in the mouth. Cloves are used whole and ground in curries, dals, biriyanis, and rice pilafs, and clove is one of the ingredients in the North Indian spice mix garam masala.

COCONUT (NARIYAL): The fruit of the coconut palm, coconut adds a tropical, almost floral note to dishes. The white flesh is extracted from the brown husk, shredded (see sidebar, page 153), and used in many South Indian dishes, often as a thickener for sauces. I usually use unsweetened powdered or shredded coconut (available at Indian grocery stores or online) in place of fresh. Sweetened shredded coconut is not a

substitute, except in desserts, but ground cashews, blanched almonds, or peanuts may be substituted as a thickening agent.

Some recipes in this book call for coconut milk. You can use either the canned coconut milk that you find at your supermarket or dried coconut, moistened with a little milk instead: use ¼ cup milk to 1 cup unsweetened, shredded, or powdered coconut.

CORIANDER (DHANIYA): The small, light green-brown seed of the coriander plant, a member of the parsley family. The seed is about the size of a peppercorn, but with a slightly oval shape. Coriander seed has a mildly sweet, nutty flavor, and tastes slightly of citrus.

Coriander is used in minced meat dishes, soups, curries, and pickles. It is an essential part of South Indian curry powder, as well as the North Indian spice mix garam masala.

CUMIN (ZEERA): The dried seed of the cumin plant, in the parsley family. Cumin is a small, light green-to-brown seed that looks like a caraway seed. It has a wonderful, warm, earthy taste.

Whole and ground cumin are used lavishly and ubiquitously in India. Cumin is one of the spices in the North Indian spice mix garam masala.

CURRY LEAVES (KARI PATTA): Small, shiny, dark green leaves from the kari plant, a small, pretty tree native to South India. Curry leaves have a uniquely citrusy, nutty taste and a fragrance that has no substitute. They are used in South Indian cooking, in spice pastes, and sautéed whole, in oil.

Curry leaves are sold fresh or dried at Indian grocery stores, or online. Buy them in quantity and freeze what you don't use. (Use about one and a half times the quantity of frozen curry leaves as you would use fresh.)

DALS: The Indian name for legumes, as well as a cooked dish of legumes. Indian cooking uses lots of varieties of legumes— lentils, peas, and beans. Lentils and peas may be cooked with the hull, or hulled and split. Besides being a side dish or main meal, dals are also used whole or ground as a spice in South Indian cuisine, and in *rasam* and *sambhaar* powders. My grandmother always soaked dal for about 10 minutes in water, to soften them before cooking, when she was using whole dal as a spice. I don't because I like the crunch, but you may want to.

You can use any supermarket variety of lentils and yellow split peas (use yellow rather than green) in recipes that call for any type of lentils or peas. And in any event, all of the legumes available in your supermarket can be used interchangeably in any dal recipe.

FENNEL SEEDS (SAUNF): These pale green, ridged seeds of the fennel plant have a sweet licorice flavor. Fennel is used in vegetable and meat dishes, particularly in South Indian cooking, and as an ingredient in pickling spice mixes. It is also an ingredient in the Bengali spice mix *panchphoran*. Fennel and anise, smaller licorice-tasting seeds that resemble fennel in taste, can be used interchangeably.

FENUGREEK SEEDS AND LEAVES (METHI DANA, TAAZI METHI, KASOORI METHI): The seeds and leaves of the fenugreek plant. The seeds are small, squarish, and amber-colored. The greens are sold fresh in season, or dried. Fenugreek seeds have a strong, bitter taste. They are used, whole and ground, in curry powders and pickling spice mixtures. Dried fenugreek leaves, sold as *kasoori methi,* add a wonderfully complex, slightly bitter taste to foods. Fresh, whole cilantro leaves have a different flavor, but may be substituted for fresh or dried fenugreek leaves. The dried leaves, which freeze very well, are sold at Indian grocery stores, along with all other types of fenugreek.

GARAM MASALA: The most important spice mixture used in northern Indian cuisine. It goes particularly well with onion-based sauces for meats and poultry but it is used to flavor many other dishes, including vegetables, *chaats* (snacks), *dals* (legumes), and raitas. Sometimes the spices are used whole and simply cooked into the dish. Or the spices are toasted and then ground together into a blend (as in the recipe below) and the mixture is stirred in at the end of cooking. Although garam masala is not as fiery hot as some Indian spice blends, black pepper, cloves, and cinnamon give it a different kind of heat that comes on slowly and lasts awhile. Since many of the recipes in this book use garam masala, it's worthwhile to make a good quantity to have on hand. You can keep it for up to 3 or 4 months in an airtight container. This is my favorite blend:

1 cinnamon stick, broken into pieces
2 bay leaves
1/4 cup cumin seeds
1/3 cup coriander seeds
1 rounded tablespoon green cardamom pods
1 rounded tablespoon black peppercorns
2 teaspoons whole cloves
1 whole, dried red chile
1/8 teaspoon ground mace

Combine the cinnamon, bay leaves, cumin, coriander, cardamom, peppercorns, cloves, and red chile in a frying pan and toast over medium heat, stirring constantly, until the cumin turns uniformly brown, 4 to 5 minutes. Put into a spice grinder and grind to a powder. Stir in the mace and store in an airtight container.

INDIAN CLARIFED BUTTER (GHEE): Ghee is butter that has been clarified and comes in jars that needn't be refrigerated. Ghee is more expensive than oil in India, so it is often used as a flavoring agent rather than a fat. (So, for instance, a dal will be made with oil, but the final tempering oil will be made with ghee, that tablespoon of ghee added at the end providing enough buttery flavor.) Traditionally, ghee is replaced with clarified butter, but you may also use whole butter, or half butter and half oil, when something is to be cooked for a long time over high heat.

MACE (JAVITRI): The dark red, lacy membrane that covers the nutmeg kernel, the fruit of the nutmeg tree. Mace has a spicy aroma and bitter taste, like a stronger version of nutmeg. Mace is sold in "blades"—the dried membrane itself—or, more commonly, ground. It is used in northern Indian cooking and is an ingredient in the spice mix from that region, garam masala.

MANGO POWDER, DRIED (AMCHUR): This beige-colored, sour-tasting powder is made from dried, ground, unripe mango. It is used as a souring agent, primarily in dals and vegetable dishes. You can substitute lemon or lime juice.

MUSTARD SEEDS (RAI DANNA): The tiny, round, blackish-brown seeds of the mustard plant. They are used extensively in South Indian dishes, in *rasam* and *sambhaar* powders, and as an ingredient in pickling spice mixtures. Sold whole, they may be used whole or ground.

Mustard seeds have a pungent, bitter, hot taste that becomes mild and nutty when cooked. Unlike many spices, the seeds have no smell until crushed or cooked. The larger, more common yellow mustard seeds are not a substitute; if you don't have black mustard seeds, omit them from the recipe.

NIGELLA (KALAUNJI): Also called onion seeds, which they resemble, these tiny black seeds have a sharp, oniony, and slightly nutty taste. Nigella is used in pickling spice mixes, and in South Indian cooking, particularly as a flavoring for vegetables. It is an ingredient in the Bengali spice mix *panchphoran*.

POMEGRANATE SEEDS, DRIED (ANARDAANA):
The small, dried brownish-red seeds of the pomegranate. Like dried mango powder, pomegranate seeds are used as a souring agent in Indian cooking. They are usually ground and then toasted or sautéed in oil to bring out their flavor. Lemon or lime juice may be substituted for the seeds.

POPPY SEEDS, INDIAN (KHUS-KHUS): These light-colored seeds are traditionally used in Mogul cooking as a thickening agent, in stews, and in vegetable dishes. Black poppy seeds cannot be substituted. If you don't have Indian poppy seeds, leave them out or substitute ground cashews, peanuts, or blanched almonds.

RASAM POWDER: Rasam powders are spice mixtures used to flavor rasams—the fiery hot, brothy soups of South Indian cuisine. Here is my favorite recipe:

> 1 tablespoon coriander seeds
> 1 teaspoon black mustard seeds
> 1/2 teaspoon cumin seeds
> 2 whole dried red chiles, or 1/2 teaspoon dried red
>   pepper flakes
> 4 fresh or 6 frozen curry leaves
> 1/8 teaspoon asafetida

Combine in a spice grinder and grind to a powder. Store in an airtight container for up to 3 or 4 months.

SAFFRON (KESAR): The reddish-brown stamens of the flowers of the Crocus sativus plant. Saffron has a sweetish taste and an unforgettable fragrance, and turns the food it flavors a lovely deep yellow color. Saffron is sold powdered or as threads; I suggest buying the threads because they have more vibrant flavor. Saffron is used to flavor savory dishes (most famously, Mogul meat dishes and biriyanis), desserts, and the yogurt drink *lassi* (see page 239). It is usually crushed and then infused in hot water or milk before being added.

TAMARIND (IMLEE): Tamarind is the pulpy fruit of the tamarind tree, contained in the long brown pods that hang from it. The pods are peeled and seeded, and the blackish pulp is dried and processed into a cake, or into a softer concentrate, sold as Tamco. Tamarind is very sour and adds a sour, fruity taste to food. It is used as a souring agent throughout India in *rasams,* dals, and vegetable and meat dishes, as well as in relishes and chutneys such as Tamarind Chutney (page 210). Lemon or lime juice can be substituted for tamarind; unlike tamarind, citrus juices lose acidity as they cook, so add them at the end of cooking.

Tamarind concentrate is easier to use than the cakes of tamarind. It's available at Indian grocery stores or online, and lasts practically forever in the refrigerator. To use the concentrate, add a measured quantity to about 1/2 cup warm water in a small bowl or measuring cup. Stir to dissolve the sticky tamarind in the water. Rinse the measuring spoon and your fingers in the water to dissolve all of the tamarind.

TURMERIC (HALDI): The ground dried root of a tropical herb. Turmeric is a bright orange color and turns food a yellow color. It has a mildly bitter, woody, slightly musty taste, but is used mostly to add an appetizing golden color to dals, curries, meat and vegetable dishes, and marinades.

acknowledgments

Many people helped us write this book. In particular, we're indebted to our agent, Angela Miller, for introducing us, believing in us before we did, and helping to grow and sell this project. On the publishing end, our editors, Pam Krauss and Adina Steiman, did a fabulous job of helping us translate our cross-cultural cooking partnership to the page; Adina was tireless in her meticulous attention to the text. Ben Fink, Marysarah Quinn, and Maggie Hinders made this a beautiful book. Thanks also to Jean Lynch, Joan Denman, and Katherine Dietrich. On the home front, Chuck Edwards put up with and entertained us. Thanks to Joey, who tested recipes with us and is still willing to try un-American food. And we'd be nowhere without the support of Lauren Shakely, publisher of Clarkson Potter, and Jenny Frost, President of Crown Publishing Group.

—Suvir Saran and Stephanie Lyness

I am grateful to so many family members and friends for contributing to this first book towards which I have been working for years. I would not be enjoying life and food today if it were not for my extended family. My mother, Sunita Saran, is a great cook; she gave me the priceless gift of self-confidence. My father, Guru Saran, always encouraged me to do what I loved, despite cultural opinion, and to do it with pride and sincerity. Panditji, the family's Brahmin chef and my greatest cooking teacher, filled my family's lives with the joy of his food. To Charlie Burd, for his support and for taking care of my family at a crucial moment, and so very willingly. Other family members supported me and shared Indian culture and their passion for life and food: Bare Papaji, my paternal grandfather; Nana, my maternal grandfather; my sister and brother, Seema and Samir; my brother-in-law, Ajit Sagar; my nephew, Karun Deep Sagar; my aunts and uncles, both in India and the United States; my grand-aunts and uncles; my parents' friends (all of the Aunties and Uncles).

In New York, I thank Carol Guber, my first employer; Ed Schoenfeld, my brother, father, son, and friend, who introduced me to Angela Miller; Hemant Mathur, my left and right hand in the kitchen, and his lovely wife Surbhi Sahni; my champions, Arianne and Michael Batterberry at *Food Arts* magazine, who first took the risk of publishing me (Beverly Stevens and Jim Poris as well); to Gael Greene, Steven Richter, and Mary Ann Joulwan who each in their own special way opened the city to me; Marion Nestle, who gave me a platform to teach Indian cooking at NYU (and Gypsy Lovett, who loaned able hands); my first two students, Ann Rawlings and Kirsty Hume; Julian and Lisa Niccolini of the Four Seasons restaurant, who made me feel welcome; Cara De Silva and Alice Fixx—dear friends and sage advisors; my teacher, Marina Ahmed Alam; Marina and Shaukat Fareed, their mother, Khalida Rachid, and their late chef Majeed, who opened home and kitchen to me.

And then there are my many friends, who daily share their passions and inspire me, and who are always there for me: Sushil and Rita Bhardwaj; Sunil and Sangeeta Bhardwaj; Aruna and Anil Lakhwara; Niti Srivastava; Lekha, Rajan, Anjali, and Seema Shankar; Gauri and Girdhar Modi and their daughters Mitali and Ritika; Bim and Monsoon Bissell; my New York sister, Nisha Sabharwal; Nalin Tomar and Kaka Singh; Mann Singh Wazir (who chopped so much okra!); Mamta and Nitin Madan; Jyoti, Sebastian and Simran Ruta; Lekha Poddar; Viraj Mehta (Chotu), from Geneva; Kumkum Bhasin; Art Smith and Jesus Falgueiro; Naushab Ahmed; Sally Holkar; Krishna & Kavita Chaudhary; Padma Deogun; Steven Wiesman; Elizabeth Bumiller; Shamsher Wadud; Nathalie Dupree; Elisa Herr; Sue Ann and Chris Hughes;

Melanie Edwards; Tina Ulajki; Trideep Bose; Damian and Ann Didden; Fern Berman and Faith Middleton; Lynne Rossetto Kasper; Karim Ladakh; Ashok Rao Kavi; Sohail Abbasi; Melanie Joseph; John Kluge; Neerja Shah; Sunanda Kashyap; Jyothi Subbarao; Judy Kilachand; Karen Karp; Hesh Sarmalkar; Vishakha Desai; Czaee Shah; Madhur Jaffrey; Mahesh and Christina Naithani; Ralf Beuschlein; Chakor Doshi; Amita Chatterjee; B.V. Durga; Rachna Iyer; Vibhuti Patel; Rohit Bal; Peter Beck; Bachhan Rawat; Manish Malhotra; Arunesh Mayyar; Robert Parker; Florence Fabricant; Prasad Charnmoula; Joy Lewis; Zeyba Rahman; Lily Brett and David Rankin; Grandma Elaine Hayes; Beth Burd; Eric Asimov; Ruth and Paul Leserman; David Karp; Peggy and Myron Pollenberg; Monica Bhide; Meenu and Kusum Gaind; Paula Wolfert; Mark Bittman; Julie Sahni; Camelia Punjabi; Vicki Haupt; Robin Gupta; William Grimes; Gillian Duffy; Maya Kaimal; Dana Jacobi; Charlie Pinsky; Scott Campbell; Kalyan Dandala; Farzana Contractor; Alicia Haldenwang; Bibhu Mohapatra and Bobby Beard; Leone Ohnoutka; Mark Ginsburg; Hamid Dubashi; Cornel West; Vikram Sheel Kumar and his family; Sir Ian Holm; Rose Levy Beranbaum; Rita Thamman; Devagi Sanmugam; Raquel Pelzel; Matt Grady; Samina Imam; Avinash Pathak; Rohit Chawla; Nakul Munim; Rozanne Gold and Michael Whiteman; Arthur Schwartz and Bob Harned; Jerry Kleiner; Marissa Molinaro; Mark Block; Steven Shaw; Steve Klc; Martha Jo Katz; Jason and Rachel Perlow; Aloo Gomes Pereira; Anju and Dev Sharma. And thanks to Stephanie Lyness, for believing in my recipes, her meticulous writing and superior editing skills, and for walking beside me as we realized this book.

—Suvir Saran

Particular thanks to Chris Kimball and the staff at *Cook's* magazine, who published my first article on Indian food; to Usha Cunningham and Samia Ahad, who gave me my first training in Indian cuisine, and to Jane Freiman and Katherine Alford, who introduced these women to me. Thanks to my rich tribe of friends and colleagues who have participated in and inspired my conversations over the years about cooking and cultural diversity. Thanks to Dick Nodell for his editorial help and love. And thanks to Suvir Saran, who has not only been my muse and a truly excellent Indian cook, but who weathered the vicissitudes of partnership with me and was constant in his passion for our work and this book.

—Stephanie Lyness

index

credits

Many thanks to all the companies listed below for their generous kitchenware contributions to this book.

All-Clad Metalcrafters
www.allclad.com
800-ALL-CLAD

Bridge Kitchenware
www.bridgekitchenware.com
212-684-4220

Calphalon Corporation
www.calphalon.com
800-809-7267

Chantal
Cookware, Ceramics and Kitchen
  Tools
www.chantal.com
800-365-4354

Chicago Cutlery
www.chicagocutlery.com
800-999-3436

Cuisinart
www.cuisinart.com
800-726-0190

DeLonghi
www.delonghiusa.com
800-322-3848

Emile Henry
Oven-to-tableware
www.emilehenry.com
302-326-4800

Falk Culinair Copper Cookware
www.copperpans.com
888-575-3255

Foods of India
121 Lexington Avenue
NYC, NY 10016
Tel: 212-683-4419
Fax: 212-251-0946

Furi Professional Knives
www.furiknife.com

**The Homer Laughlin China
Company**
www.hlchina.com
800-HLCHINA

J.K. Adams Company
P.O. Box 248
Dorset, Vermont 05251
www.jkadams.com
866-362-4433

Kitchen Aid
www.kitchenaid.com
800-541-6390

Kuhn Rikon
Pressure Cookers and Kitchen Tools
www.kuhnrikon.com
800-662-5882

Le Creuset
www.lecreuset.com
877-CREUSET

Lodge Cast Iron
www.lodgemfg.com
423-837-7181

Messermeister
Cutlery and Kitchen Tools
www.messermeister.com
800-426-5134

OXO Good Grips
www.oxo.com
800-545-4411

Sabatier Knives
www.sabatier.com

Scanpan USA Inc.
www.scanpan.com
201-818-2280

Waring
www.waringproducts.com
800-492-7464

Weber Stephen Product Co.
www.weberbbq.com
800-446-1071

William Bounds
Pepper and Spice Mills and Gourmet
Ingredients
www.wmboundsltd.com
800-473-0504

Zwilling J.A. Henckels, Inc.
www.jahenckels.com
800-777-4308

conversion chart

EQUIVALENT IMPERIAL AND METRIC MEASUREMENTS

American cooks use standard containers, the 8-ounce cup and a tablespoon that takes exactly 16 level fillings to fill that cup level. Measuring by cup makes it very difficult to give weight equivalents, as a cup of densely packed butter will weigh considerably more than a cup of flour. The easiest way therefore to deal with cup measurements in recipes is to take the amount by volume rather than by weight. Thus the equation reads:

1 cup = 240 ml = 8 fl. oz. 1/2 cup = 120 ml = 4 fl. oz.

It is possible to buy a set of American cup measures in major stores around the world.

In the States, butter is often measured in sticks. One stick is the equivalent of 8 tablespoons. One tablespoon of butter is therefore the equivalent to 1/2 ounce/15 grams.

LIQUID MEASURES

Fluid Ounces	U.S.	Imperial	Milliliters
	1 teaspoon	1 teaspoon	5
1/4	2 teaspoons	1 dessertspoon	10
1/2	1 tablespoon	1 tablespoon	14
1	2 tablespoons	2 tablespoons	28
2	1/4 cup	4 tablespoons	56
4	1/2 cup		120
5		1/4 pint or 1 gill	140
6	3/4 cup		170
8	1 cup		240
9			250, 1/4 liter
10	1 1/4 cups	1/2 pint	280
12	1 1/2 cups		340
15		3/4 pint	420
16	2 cups		450
18	2 1/4 cups		500, 1/2 liter
20	2 1/2 cups	1 pint	560
24	3 cups		675
25		1 1/4 pints	700
27	3 1/2 cups		750
30	3 3/4 cups	1 1/2 pints	840
32	4 cups or 1 quart		900
35		1 3/4 pints	980
36	4 1/2 cups		1000, 1 liter
40	5 cups	2 pints or 1 quart	1120

SOLID MEASURES

U.S. and Imperial Measures		Metric	
Ounces	Pounds	Grams	Kilos
1		28	
2		56	
3 1/2		100	
4	1/4	112	
5		140	
6		168	
8	1/2	225	
9		250	1/4
12	3/4	340	
16	1	450	
18		500	1/2
20	1 1/4	560	
24	1 1/2	675	
27		750	3/4
28	1 3/4	780	
32	2	900	
36	2 1/4	1000	1
40	2 1/2	1100	
48	3	1350	
54		1500	1 1/2

OVEN TEMPERATURE EQUIVALENTS

Fahrenheit	Celsius	Gas Mark	Description
225	110	1/4	Cool
250	130	1/2	
275	140	1	Very Slow
300	150	2	
325	170	3	Slow
350	180	4	Moderate
375	190	5	
400	200	6	Moderately Hot
425	220	7	Fairly Hot
450	230	8	Hot
475	240	9	Very Hot
500	250	10	Extremely Hot

Any broiling recipes can be used with the grill of the oven, but beware of high-temperature grills.

EQUIVALENTS FOR INGREDIENTS

all-purpose flour—plain flour
baking sheet—oven tray
buttermilk—ordinary milk
cheesecloth—muslin
coarse salt—kitchen salt
cornstarch—cornflour

eggplant—aubergine
granulated sugar—caster sugar
half and half—12% fat milk
heavy cream—double cream
light cream—single cream
parchment paper—greaseproof paper

plastic wrap—cling film
scallion—spring onion
shortening—white fat
unbleached flour—strong, white flour
zest—rind
zucchini—courgettes or marrow